The Call of the Mountains

Other books by Max Landsberg:

The Tao of Coaching

The Tao of Motivation

The Tools of Leadership

The Call of the Mountains

Sights and inspirations from
a journey of a thousand miles across
Scotland's Munros

MAX LANDSBERG

Luath Press Limited
EDINBURGH
www.luath.co.uk

Dedicated to the memory of my father,
Peter T. Landsberg
... whose advice was to be always
at least a little bit adventurous...

First published 2013

ISBN: 978-1-908373-70-0

The paper used in this book is recyclable. It is made from
low chlorine pulps produced in a low energy, low emissions manner
from renewable forests.

The publishers acknowledge the support of

ALBA | CHRUTHACHAIL

towards the publication of this volume.

Printed and bound by
ScandBook, Sweden

Typeset in 11 point Sabon

Contents

Further photographs, videos and fly-throughs are available at
www.thecallofthemountains.com/graphics.hml

The principal Munro ranges
with selected lochs and cities

Contents in Detail

Everybody needs beauty as well as bread,
places to play in and pray in,
where nature may heal and give strength
to body and soul alike.

JOHN MUIR, *The Yosemite*

The Calling

Every day is a journey,
and the journey itself is home.

MATSUO BASHO *Narrow Road to the Interior*

THE MOUNTAINS OF Scotland: towering in grandeur above ancient foundations, born two billion years before the first plant saw life; rifted and faulted by earthquake and then gouged and pock-marked by ice; once home to the Gaels and their kings – and now haunted by their spirits and the stag.

You can walk into these mountains, but you never come all the way back. For though Scotland's mountains may not be the highest in the world, they are certainly amongst the most awe-inspiring and enchanting. From the towering pinnacles of Skye, to the high rolling plateau of the Cairngorms; from the bonnie braes of Ben Lomond to the weeping cliffs of Glencoe; from the rocky battlements that encircle Loch Arkaig, to the gentle folds of Ben Lawers as it spills down to Loch Tay: on offer here are scenes of unrivalled splendour, landscapes of unparalleled variety, and a magic ground for personal connection, inspiration and transformation.

These are places of accessible adventure – we leave behind the safety of the lush glen to cross the swooping moor, clamber up through craggy corridors, and with tinkling burn then spatey cascade as our sometime guide, we reach at last the grand summits of these lands.

It is through these realms that I hope you will accompany me on a journey for body, for mind and perhaps for something more.

* * *

My own journey started by way of the accident described in the next chapter. Then, having fallen into the wonderland of Scotland's mountains, I was quickly captivated and drawn into an ardent adventure that called me northwards from my home in London, to the land I had left when I was just three years old. My mission eventually became a series of expeditions to climb all 282 'Munros' – Scotland's mountains of 3,000 feet or more in height. Working my way through the list of mountains that Sir Hugh Munro had originally published in 1891 became my vast and roving obsession. More importantly, it brought me to the highest vantage points from which to embrace the best of Scotland's landscapes.

Just as I had not originally intended to climb all those peaks, neither had I intended to write about them. But several years ago, my neighbours' children clamoured so loudly to hear of my recent trek to Everest Base Camp that I agreed to give a short presentation at their school. I could not resist mentioning Scotland too, and so wide-eyed with excitement were the kids as my own passion for those nearer hills became evident that I resolved to share these life-affirming experiences.

So with field notes, sketches, photos and maps spread out before me, with memory as a guide and with pen and paper as company, I recalled my circuit of the hills set out in this account.

The Call of the Mountains is intended as an impressionistic companion for your forthcoming Munro journey, whether you are about to embark on it in earnest or in your armchair – or perhaps it will be a reminder, as you recall the outings you have already completed.

This account offers you: 1) short stories that conjure a sense of place in these magical lands; 2) anecdotes that give you a comprehensive sense of the drama and adventure involved in climbing all the Munros; 3) some digestible 'sandwiches' along the way, for as I take you through each walk-scape I also aim to give you a hint of history here, a gist of geology there, and a bit of flora, fauna and culture in between, and 4) a reflection on the stages by which any interest can swell into a passion and escalate into an obsession.

To share the sense of expedition, of discovery and of growth, I have sequenced the chapters around the actual journeys and side-trips I made in compleating the round of Munros.[1] You can of course climb the Munros in any sequence, and though they may be visited piecemeal by those who live in Scotland, those who live abroad will require longer visits. This account is therefore typical rather than prescriptive.

Primarily, though, I want to take you where the scenic ingots are buried: a few are overgrown, some overlooked, all under-visited.

* * *

But what can you expect from such an adventure, beyond the delights and inspirations I have already mentioned? If you walk these routes in full or in part, you will certainly witness the soaring eagle, and perhaps the birth

---

1 Traditionally, a round of all the Munros is 'compleated', and I have used that spelling throughout this book.

of a fawn; you will share the camaraderie of canny ghillies; you will gain benefits to health and heart, and you will have unexpected adventure.

Whether you want it or not, there will be adventure. Though Scotland's mountains are not as high as those in some other countries, they *are* among the highest in Britain: of the 1,000 highest peaks in Britain, all bar 58 are in Scotland. As you walk for more than 1,000 miles horizontally, and over 100 miles vertically; as you expend half a million calories; as the weather changes within a few minutes from brilliant sunshine to storm-force wind, rain and hail and back again: there is bound to be adventure, and something will go wrong! So take a detailed guidebook, maps and compass, and take the precautions indicated in the section on Safety, so you will not have to call on the Mountain Rescue Service, whose excellence and professionalism probably saved my life, as you will soon see.

You can reach all bar one of the summits on foot; only the 'Inaccessible Pinnacle' requires roped climbing. In just 120 days of hillwalking, this entire journey is within the grasp of most reasonably fit people, and uniquely in Scotland with its generous Access Code, you can walk almost anywhere. The opportunities are unbounded, and the benefits immense.

* * *

Ultimately, this book aims to offer signposts to 120 days of rapture. For that is surely the true power of Scotland's mountains: their ability to hold us in awe – day after day, visit after visit, in rain or in shine. This account is perhaps the last cry of an obsession determined to find a new host before its old host lays it to rest. It is offered as a conspiratorial escort: one to help you escape in mind or body from the yang of town to the yin of country.

But mountains change us more than we change them. That is why we must visit them, cherish them and preserve their purity. They allow us to revive our connection with the natural world. They hold the potential to be our art galleries, our gymnasiums and our sacred sanctuaries all in one.

'These are *my* hills,' I think, irrationally, as I reach the top of my last Munro. 'I have been up them, and on them, and across them, and down them. I know their ways, their idiosyncrasies and their secrets. And they will live within me while my memory still functions.'

These may be my hills, but they can be your hills too.

Phase 1 – Hooked

EVERY JOURNEY OF a thousand miles starts with a first step, said Lao Tzu. But of course not every first step is destined to grow into a journey of a thousand miles!

So how does a fancy become a fascination, a pastime become a passion, a step become a journey?

My own enthusiasm for hillwalking and the Munros started from a modest base: though I was reasonably fit, I had never run a marathon or even a quarter of one; I enjoyed a jog in Richmond Park, but was neither health fanatic nor eco-warrior.

My interest in the Munros was ignited by a lucky spark and was undoubtedly fanned by provident weather and fortunate choices of early outings. Gradually I became beguiled by the spectacular scenes, sounds, and smells, by starting to progress through Sir Hugh Munro's List, and by the bewitching culture of Celtic and Gaelic Scotland.

Over the course of the next three chapters, I chart how I came to be in turn attracted, intrigued, fascinated and then hooked by hillwalking in general and the Munros in particular. *First Steps* recounts the inspiring circuit of a glaciated valley, an outing that, with hindsight, I realise was a fortunate first expedition. Scenic beauty is surely one of the main attractions for any walker, so this chapter also examines our notions of beauty, intrigue and awe, drawing from some unusual sources.

Gentle Foothills recounts two journeys across the southern Highlands, with auspicious blue skies and no sign yet of the gales and storms that would eventually beset me. I discover the attraction of bite-sized adventures – and start to take a greater interest in The List, which this chapter explains in more detail.

Inaccessible Pinnacles brings me close to danger and indeed to death, with perils emerging from the least likely places. Although I am no junkie for adrenaline, this danger does add simultaneously excitement and sobriety to what might otherwise have become a more frivolous pastime. On Skye and the mainland, a magic brew of rich history and Gaelic murmurings secure my commitment to continue.

It is often by accident that we embark on those personal missions that we will ultimately value most highly. We are intrigued when we are open to novel experiences or callings. Early on, our progress is driven more by motivation and enthusiasm than by the acquisition of skill or technique.

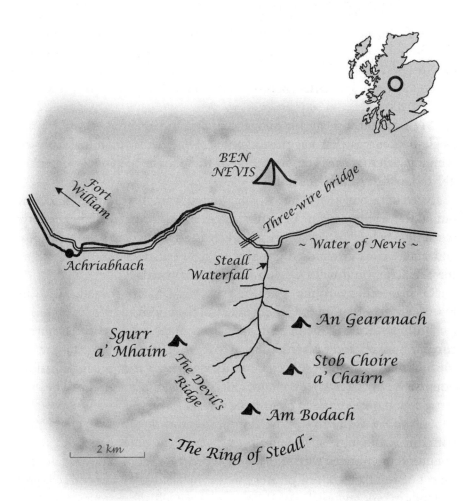

The Ring of Steall, South of Ben Nevis

CHAPTER I

First Steps, Perfect Vistas

Mountains are the beginning and the end of all natural scenery.
JOHN RUSKIN *Modern Painters*

THE FIRST STEP on my journey of a thousand miles is down off the single-decker bus that has brought me from Fort William, through the winding glen that skirts the base of Ben Nevis, to the tiny hamlet of Achriabhach, which means 'speckled field'.

Stretching out before me, the route starts off through a gorge often dubbed 'the Himalaya of Britain', then emerges into Arcadian meadows spreading below the shimmering feet of the country's second highest waterfall, before crossing a three-wire bridge that straddles an oft-gushing torrent. Later on it will range onwards and upwards to one of Scotland's finest ridge walks, around a perfectly glaciated hanging valley, via 'The Devil's Ridge' – and all of this under the brooding watch of Ben Nevis...

With this Ring of Steall as my first Munro adventure, I am bound to become hooked, for it combines within one longish circular walk some of the best hillwalking in Britain, if not the world. But it does carry a risk of fatality, as I am to discover.

A few months earlier, I had decided to test my mettle. Was I still fit enough to complete the Three Peaks Challenge – climbing the highest peaks in Scotland, England and Wales within 24 hours? I had Googled the event and noticed the momentous words: 'the challenge includes the ascent of Ben Nevis... one of Scotland's 283 Munros'. 'What's a Munro?' I wondered. A few clicks of the mouse revealed the grandeur of these hills, and a few more clicks had me booked on my first trip to visit them.

Later, with years of hillwalking experience under my boots, I will realise how ill-prepared I am for this venture: too few warm clothes, no spare gloves, inadequate headwear, too little food, no spare compass. And despite walking solo, I have not left details of my route with anyone who could raise the alarm if I fail to return. I am an accident waiting to happen. In my defence, I can only claim that I am following the route from a guidebook published by the Ramblers Association. I have mistakenly conjured up images of their members being matronly aunts in well-polished brogues successfully rambling through this challenge. They have lured me into a false sense of security!

The Ring of Steall

Although the hamlet of this speckled field is set in meadowy surroundings, the violent smash and splutter of water under its bridge warns of large corries and churning cascades higher up.

The easy gradient of the preliminary tarmac road therefore comes as a surprise, though after the upper car park the road soon narrows into a walkers' path, which itself slims to a ledge barely a foot wide in places. On stones that are just a bit too sloping and nearly always too polished, I tread carefully through the delightful gorge alongside the energetic river – The Water of Nevis.

This stretch of the trek has an otherworldly feel to it, with the Water now churning many feet below me, cascading down the rift it has incised, having sped over its ten-kilometre journey from the corners of its huge catchment basin which straddles the southern slopes of Ben Nevis and other more secret places.

I am shaded by towering canopies of trees that somehow cling to crack and fissure of the steep rock walls above me. And it is then that I find one of the greatest delights of British hillwalking: to emerge suddenly into a vast, meadowy expanse of grassy sward that stretches across gravelly flats.

Flat as a billiard table, this glacially deposited plain is a stage on which all the required elements of hill-theatre have been set: the gently meandering river, the lone rowan tree, the hummocky foothills offering a step up to higher peaks beyond. And ahead, centre-stage, spouting from a hanging valley that emerges high up on the hillside, is the lead actor – the Steall waterfall itself. One hundred and twenty metres of churning, tumbling spume first spews then sprays and spatters in near-vertical fall. This waterfall has one of the longest cascades in Britain – more than twice the drop of Niagara Falls.

The flat Steall Meadows mark the turning point into the next stage of the expedition. This area is also a crossroads for other paths through the adjacent glens and over neighbouring hills, and so the small cluster of tents is perhaps to be expected. I approach, but there is no sign of life: if a walker is not walking, he or she is probably sleeping...

The precise point of transition from the easy first section of the day to the harder next section must surely be the famous three-wire bridge that straddles the Water of Nevis, stretching from its tentative hold on the eastern side of the meadows. The bridge looks rickety, but my desire to avoid wetting my boots in the river eventually overcomes my fear of the required high-wire act. I edge out and as I sidle my feet along the single lower tightrope, I slide my hands cautiously along the higher wires which stretch out taut at shoulder level.

On the farther bank, I soon see that the hope of keeping my boots dry is naïve in the extreme. They will surely be sodden, and thus much heavier, after the immediate next challenge: the crossing of the Steall Waterfall after its 120-metre cataract. In fact, I remain dry-shod as I cross the tumbling Waterfall, but the boggy stretch on its far side eventually gets me, consuming me up to the ankles.

It is now a hard pull up to the ridge, even though a stalkers' path lofts me helpfully. When I had first read of such paths, I had assumed that stalkers' paths were *poachers'* paths. This was of course a mistake, because while it is perfectly feasible to shoot a deer without the knowledge of the estate owner, it would be hard work to drag its carcass off a 3,000-foot high mountain. Poaching does take place, especially at night and at lower levels, but these higher-level paths are used by the estates for required culls or commercial shoots.

This first experience was supposed to be an easy introduction, but is now becoming quite testing. It demands that I continue uphill at a gradient of 45 degrees for over an hour, while scanning for the correct route all the way. I would find that no treadmill training can prepare you for this. Yet my motivation is strong as my first Munro beckons, and from behind me Ben Nevis is watching, perhaps waiting to see whether I will make it.

Easing gradients bring life to weary legs, and soon I escape the solitary, heather-edged tramline of the stalker's path and am now high up on the shoulder of the hill. I would learn that every walk has a false summit or two: the bound-to-be-broken promise that the true summit beckons. This hill has more than its fair share of false summits and the suspense grows.

Finally, finally, over the next brow, a tiny pimple appears and it grows as I approach. The path flattens further and the cairn gradually comes into full view. It is in a sorry state – more a pile of stones than an edifice. But it *is* the top. At last I am face-to-face – or rather, boot-to-bald-pate – with my first Munro, *An Gearanach* (the complainer).[2]

Of even greater reward, however, is the stunning spectacle spread out before me – the huge hanging valley that is the catchment bowl for the Steall waterfall extends out far below, laced with its meandering river that suddenly dives off over a lip and out of sight, down to the place where it tried to drench me earlier. You are not alone up here, though, for joining

---

2 Italics mark the first mention of ascending a Munro; see Appendix 1 for pronunciations, heights, and precise locations.

you in peering into this valley from all angles are both an exaltation of rocky arêtes and a herd of mountains, their broad shoulders muscular, as if permanently flexed.

After a five-minute stop, a sandwich and an airing of the socks, I press onwards. The path soon narrows severely to just a few feet in width, with sharp drops on both sides. This experience is not yet scary, though it does provide several kilometres of brisk introduction to true Scottish hillwalking: that is, a rope would not go amiss, a helping hand would be appreciated, and fingers are crossed against a gust of wind...

The ridge slopes down steeply, then demands a stiff hike up before reaching the top of the next Munro: *Stob Coire a' Chairn* (peak of the corrie of the cairn). It is well-named, for the frost-shattered quartzite top has clearly offered the cairn builders more material than did the previous top, and I too contribute a stone to the structure.

The next ridge twists away into the mists, but halfway along it – with four hours of walking behind me, and with another four still to go – I start tiring rapidly, yet to understand what 'hill fit' really means. And the clouds are descending fast.

With great reluctance I play it safe, and decide to miss out the third Munro of the day, Am Bodach (the old man), and this has two consequences. Firstly, it will be another six years before I reach the top of the Old Man, with a great deal of extra re-climbing required to do so. Secondly, it means I shall have to take the not-to-be-recommended bypass route, which contours around the inside surface of the bowl-shaped corrie.

You will recall from school geography that a 'corrie, cirque or cwm' is a scooped out hollow, gouged from the mountain by the head of a glacier. Across the extremely steep rock-face of such a scoop, I try to follow what the Ordnance Survey map promises is a path. Later, Google Earth will prove there is indeed a path, but underfoot I can find only huge jumbles of large slippery rocks temporarily lodged at inconvenient angles. It would have been less effort to have climbed the Old Man after all, but it is too late to return and, with reassuring glimpses of the onward route visible through occasionally lifting cloud, I re-join the ridge beyond the Old Man's feet.

The path snakes on along the rim of the corrie and over Sgor an Iubhair – a peak that had been a Munro for 16 years until it was demoted in 1997 (these things do happen!). I now believe there is only one obstacle ahead: The Devil's Ridge. I had spent several weeks worrying about this crest, with the need either to tiptoe over its pinnacles, or to take the alternative bypass path with its 'bad step'. For the uninitiated, negotiating a 'bad step' feels a bit like driving a car with bald tyres around a bend that suddenly becomes tighter, icier and increasingly cambered off in the wrong direction – with the accelerator jammed on. The adrenaline carries me over the step; it would be a more serious proposition in winter.

But there is a further obstacle: *Sgurr a' Mhaim* (peak of the large rounded hill). It is an obstacle not because this Munro is so high, but because of the unrelenting challenge of losing 1,000 metres of altitude down the steep slopes on its far side – slopes strewn with large stones and rubble for most of the way. From my earliest days on the Munros, and in common with many a walker, I have kept brief notes of the highlights and the lows. My entry for this day includes: 'Lo: final knee-crunching descent in one long haul back to Polldubh. 15 / 1,900 / 8:30' (the numbers indicate kilometres travelled / metres of ascent / and time passed, excluding stops).

The safety of the valley eventually attained, however, I turn around to survey the mountains of the day. But they are gone, obscured by the vastness of that mountain called 'the peak of the large rounded hill'. Other mountains crowd around me though. They radiate a timeless quality that somehow exudes familiarity. The vast rounded knobbles of hillside and mountain profile seem to be the brows of immense elephants, and the herd is gathering around me to bid goodbye. I wonder for how long they will remember me.

* * *

The Caledonian Sleeper takes me back to London overnight, and once in the office I strike up conversation with a burly Scot – a colleague I have not met before. It transpires he was a Royal Marine, and when I tell him of my weekend's outing, he turns white.

'You have to be so vigilant on that ridge,' he says. Two years earlier a friend of his, a fit Marine in his 20s on manoeuvres with 30 other Marines, was blown off the eastern side of the high-level horseshoe walk, to his death.

Seared into my memory for all time, however, is the way this first experience of the Munros combined Beauty, Intrigue, and the Awe-inspiring sublime. And from the first day on these fair hills I start an unbroken habit: to replay each route in my mind several times a year. I know the fragility of memory, for my father's Alzheimer's has just deprived him of any memory that the seminal textbooks on theoretical physics that sit on his bookshelves had been written by him. The sound of my own voice, recorded in my camera on snippets of video, provides me with a more tangible insurance policy against ever forgetting the hills; and there would be more fabulous hills to come.

▲▲▲

Beauty, Intrigue, Awe: what makes for an enthralling landscape vista?

Once seen, the Steall Meadows are never forgotten, and at least once in every Munro outing, we are treated to a vista so utterly captivating that it makes us gasp. A full tour of the Munros presents in spectacular manner all of the elemental themes, including 'the forest primeval, the river of life, and the sacred mount', as Simon Schama dramatises them in *Landscape and Memory*. Indeed, walkers typically cite such visual treats as the primary reason that they go out hiking.

So it is worth pausing a moment to examine what it is that grips us: what are the most archetypal landscape scenes, and why do they resonate with us so strongly?

Beauty

Firstly, there is the scene of sheer prettiness that evokes an instant feeling of wellbeing and relaxation. A vision of distant hazy mountains, symmetrically arranged and viewed across a placid loch, perhaps with a jetty in the foreground, and a light mist rising. You breathe in deeply and exhale gently; you are literally inspired; any tension you are holding dissipates instantly; you drink in your surroundings; your mind is eased.

This picture comes from the world of the Neo-classical and the Old Master painters. Symmetry and the Golden Ratio prevail. There is order, and in order lies stability. From stability derives security. And from security seeps a feeling of relaxation and wellbeing. Not surprisingly, a vista like this has become the best-selling image for Britain's largest poster company.

Our subconscious – or at least a part of it – seeks this smooth, rhythmic, predictable, safe elegance of the Beautiful scene.

Intrigue

There is a different type of scene; one that draws us in and makes us wonder what lies beyond it: there is perhaps a path or river in the foreground, winding past a clump of trees and ruined building in the middle distance and disappearing off into the foothills to the mountains beyond. It calls on us to explore it, to get involved.

Research from around the world shows that most cultures prize such a scene highly. It has features that offer a greater likelihood of survival in an evolutionary sense.

For example, in *With People In Mind: Design And Management Of Everyday Nature*, researchers from the University of Michigan found respondents assigned low preference to views that are hard to read: ones that have either large expanses of undifferentiated landcover, or have dense vegetation and obstructed lines of sight.

In contrast, favoured scenes are easy to read and explore. They are *coherent* (orderly, with distinguished areas and a few repeating images showing simply contrasting textures), and *legible* (a few distinctive features or memorable landmarks that ease orientation and navigation). The favoured scenes also foster exploration when they are *complex* (rich in variety and replete with opportunity) and *mysterious* (holding the promise that one can find out more if one keeps on going: curved pathways and partially exposed glimpses and prospects).

The Intriguing scene asks us to engage with it. It may be less pretty than the Beautiful scene, but instead it provides a canvas on which we can project our journey.

Awe

But we have a darker side too; the one that craves the scene that *almost* overwhelms us. We stand right next to a towering cliff and stare upwards, it is so high that – even standing on the ground – we are overcome with vertigo; or we are perched at the extreme edge of a crumbling precipice, gaze down at the scene below and know we are on the very brink of calamity, millimetres from death.

Our appetite for these Awe-inspiring views has more recent and complex origins. Before the 18th century, there is virtually no record on canvas or paper of delight in this feeling. But the Industrial Revolution and the Age of Enlightenment – from roughly 1650 onwards – changed all that. Perhaps because basic human needs were becoming better met (at least those of the upper and emerging middle classes), our forebears could afford to adventure and, perhaps, were driven to it by increasing levels of comfort.

And across what vast territories they adventured: from politics (American Independence in 1776, the French Revolution in 1789); to theology and geology (James Hutton's ground-breaking *Theory of the Earth* in 1785); through the Arts (Romanticism making the whole person the observer, not just his brain; Shelley, Byron, Coleridge, Wordsworth); mountaineering (Horace-Bénédict de Saussure and the Benedictine monk

Placidus a Spescha systematically exploring every Alp prior to 1800); and tourism (with the continental Grand Tour *de rigueur* from the 1750s onwards).

This was the age that saw the Awe-inspiring distinguished from the merely Beautiful or the Intriguing. It introduced horror, terror and brute Nature as experiences to be sought out and relished.

The English critic and dramatist John Dennis recounts crossing the Alps in 1963, where the attraction of the experience is in part that it is *'mingled with Horrours, and sometimes almost with despair.'*

Thomas Gray, poet of *Elegy* fame, wrote in 1765 of his trip to the Scottish Highlands that

> the mountains are ecstatic, and ought to be visited in pilgrimage once
> a year. None but those monstrous creatures of God know how to join
> so much beauty with so much horror.

In *A Philosophical Enquiry into the Origin of Our Ideas of the Sublime and the Beautiful* (1757), Edmund Burke writes that

> whatever... operates in a manner analogous to terror is a source of
> the sublime; that is, it is productive of the strongest emotion which
> the mind is capable of feeling.

In *Mountains of the Mind*, Robert Macfarlane isolates a succinct statement from David Hartley (1749):

> If there be a precipice, a cataract, a mountain of snow etc. in one part
> of the scene, the nacent ideas of fear and horror magnify and enliven
> all the other ideas, and by degrees pass into pleasures, by suggesting
> the security from pain.

The Awe-inspiring prospect shows us our modest station within the grandeur of Nature; it threatens us and provokes our adrenaline, and in doing so, it enlivens us too.

▲▲▲

While over-analysis can ruin any vista, mindful reflection on the scene can deepen the experience and sear it more deeply into the memory. I carry these thoughts with me into the second year of my Munro journey, which is to present a few unexpected challenges...

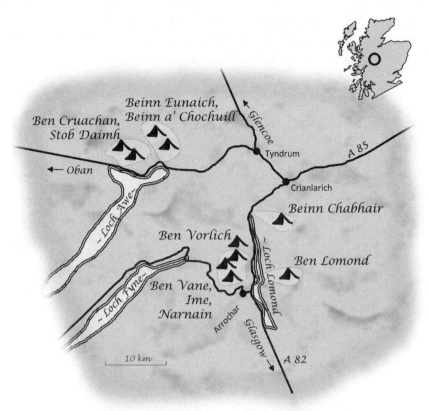

Light grey loops indicate outings described in the chapter that include more than one Munro

Around Loch Lomond

CHAPTER 2

Gentle Foothills

Hills peep o'er Hills,
and Alps on Alps arise!

ALEXANDER POPE *Essay on Criticism*

SCOTLAND HAS ITS very own Alps: the Arrochar Alps. Though the four dramatic Munros that rise to the west of Loch Lomond revel in the epithet of Alp, they are the most southerly Munros and at first glance do not look very alpine. In fact, they provide a perfect introduction for the up-and-coming hillwalker, as their position less than 50 kilometres north of Glasgow makes them easy to reach, and though no Munro is to be underestimated, these summits are fairly accessible.

In this year after my trip to the Ring of Steall, I acquired Cameron McNeish's excellent book *The Munros*. Part coffee table volume and part guidebook, every mountain it portrays seems a gem, every glen breathtaking, and every route achievable. I have also invested in mapping software so I can prepare more thoroughly than for my first trip.

Anyone for grass-holds?

Today's *Ben Vorlich* (mountain of the bay) overlooks a bay on Loch Lomond. Some Munros share the same name, and today's hill is not to be confused with another Ben Vorlich that overlooks a bay in Loch Earn, 40 kilometres away.

As I set out from my overnight base at Arrochar, the June weather is warm and sunny and I head up the mountain on this start of my three-day expedition. I count my blessings, since this is a rainy part of the world. Indeed, the huge reservoir ahead of me is sited here for a reason: the area gets over three full metres of rain a year, which is more than twice the rainfall of Glasgow and five times that of parts of southern England.

Visible from the road are four gargantuan pipes – each two metres wide and nearly 300 metres in drop – which feed the monster that is the largest conventional hydro-electric power station in the UK, set on the east-facing slopes of the ben. The vast reservoir that feeds these pipes has a catchment area of nearly 100 square kilometres, from which the water cascades right through the heart of Ben Vorlich via a tunnel that is over three kilometres long.

My route to the summit starts easily enough along a Land Rover track that winds through low scrub and shrub, then around a bluff to face the towering dam, which is half a kilometre wide and 50 metres high.

Several paths lead to the top of today's hill and the experienced hill-walker will want to take a few moments to find one of them. In these early days, however, I am more impatient than I am considered, and opt for a direct assault up the west-facing side. Not apparent from below, the slopes gradually become steeper and steeper – starting from 45 degrees and becoming almost vertical in places. These provide some of my earliest feelings of nervous hillwalking. But with ample use of grass-holds (hanging on to tufts of grass rather than rocks; of which more later), I make it to the top and gaze down over the many square kilometres of reservoir.

As I share lunch with a surprisingly friendly raven, there is a feast for the eyes too: over the reservoir that is Loch Sloy, then southwards to Ben Lomond, and far beyond to the wonderfully named Kyles (narrow or straights) of Bute. In superb weather, the azure blues of the waters blend up into the purple hues of the hills then dissolve further up into the cerulean blue of the skies.

My route of descent from the summit remains high for as long as possible, for a kilometre or so along the mountain's main ridge, and then dives down via a little zigzag path, back to the Land Rover track. Here are the first inklings of the origins of the name 'Arrochar Alps', for the gradient, width and condition of the path really does remind me of childhood walks near Alpine Grindelwald.

Ironic, I reflect as I bid farewell to the dam, that this reservoir built back in the early 1950s should provide a safety net (through storing water pumped uphill) for the new-fangled but less consistent technology of wind farming!

The Cobbler askance

The giant watchtowers of *Ben Vane* (middle mountain), *Beinn Ime* (butter mountain), and *Beinn Narnain* (notched mountain) are linked by craggy battlements, and offer three coigns of vantage over the huge corrie and viridian plantation below.

With the weather apparently set fair for the next day, the conditions are perfect for the 20-kilometre hike, which will also include nearly two kilometres of ascent. For although the Arrochar Alps may not be as high as the Swiss ones, in Scotland you normally start your expedition from near sea level.

The chill morning air has a sharp crystal edge to it as I set off under skies of absolute blue. I start along yesterday's Land Rover track, but take an early left turn over a bridge and then right, up the side of Ben Vane. Again, this path has an Alpine feel, though the climb is hotter than that of yesterday (tip: on sunny mornings, try to avoid slopes that face a hot south-east).

The summit is shrouded in light cloud, which obscures both the views and the path to the next Munro across the bealach (a bealach is a pass or col, though the terms 'pass' and 'col' rarely appear on Highland maps). Thus arises a challenge familiar to every hillwalker: how to avoid unnecessary loss of altitude when descending to the bealach between two hills, by keeping to the high-line. I have neither line of sight, nor GPS, nor intuition of how to feel the brow of the path, so veer slightly off-track, though not disastrously so.

Down near the bealach, the cloud has lifted now, and I wolf down a cheese and raspberry jam sandwich while reclining in sunshine, as I gaze down a perfectly U-shaped valley, glaciated 10,000 years ago, and now home to butterflies and a gently-flowing river with textbook meanders.

The speed with which a morsel of food can restore power and energy to tiring legs never ceases to amaze me, and duly empowered I set off for the top of Beinn Ime, which is reached without issue. Passing through the slightly craggy summit a lone walker appears, treading the same route as me but in the opposite direction, and I say hello.

To my surprise, he walks straight past me, muttering only the briefest of responses. This is only the third day of my hillwalking career, and I shall later learn that some people just want to be by themselves on a hill – all the time, and even after hours of walking solo.

The path towards Ben Narnain is clearly visible from the summit, as it skirts the top rim of the corrie that a powerful glacier had scooped out. To the left there is a gradual slope down to river and forest, but I keep to the rim, eventually reaching the summit, albeit tugged sideways by the aspect of The Cobbler. Though not a Munro, this hill is beloved of climbers and walkers, as its peak is a rock formation which resembles a cobbler bent over his last and which requires the daring move of 'threading the needle' – i.e. squeezing through a tiny, lofty gap – to reach its summit.

There are various descents off Ben Narnain and I aim for the one that heads along the ridge and then angles down left into the valley. I find a promising path, and start my descent. But gradually an unexpected and strangely-shaped bay comes into view, and I am about to make the most basic of mistakes. It is a lesson I am glad to learn in benign conditions rather than in challenging ones.

Like most difficulties experienced in the mountains, this one is caused by a chain of events rather than by a single wrong action. The syndrome goes something like this: on top of mountain. Can't find path down. Search about a bit. At last find the path. Start losing altitude as expected. Something does not look right. *Must be ok 'cos I am on a very clear path… Shall I go back to the top to check? No – too much effort. I'm on a good path after all. Carry on.*

At this point, there are two possible outcomes. The outcome you don't want is one that I have overheard unfortunate walkers recount on several different occasions: the visibility is poor, you carry on, and after about three hours you reach the glen and the road – only to find that you have descended into the *wrong glen*. You were indeed on a path but it was the wrong one (no one ever said there would be two paths here…). With luck, you might hitch a lift back to your car; otherwise, you walk. Of course, this sometimes happens far from a road, and it could take you many hours of tramping off-path across wilderness to exit your 'wrong glen'.

The other outcome is that you recognise your error and try to get back on track. Next year I would not be so lucky, but here on Ben Narnain I realise just in time that my route is heading too far east – a mere two degrees off bearing, but enough to point me down the wrong side of the hill.

After a dodgy traverse around extensive crags, I at last find the correct path down and home. But this has been a big day, and I have not yet perfected the choice of boot and sock, so after ten hours of walking, blisters are starting to protrude and to threaten the final day of the trip.

High road or low road

Ben Lomond (beacon mountain) stands in commanding accompaniment to its namesake loch below. It is the most southerly Munro, and climbed by many a Glaswegian and Sassenach alike.

Having treated my feet to some TLC the previous night, I decide they can surely cope with a relatively easy hill today. A small puttering ferry takes me across Loch Lomond from one bonnie bank to the other, and in brilliant sunshine, I take the bluest photograph of loch and sky in my entire album.

The Tourist Route up the hill is a clear and polished path. Yet no Munro can be taken for granted, and despite the fantastic June weather at loch level (and decidedly sweltering through the low-lying forest), the air turns first cooler and damper, then colder and wetter, then freezing and deluged, before the top is reached. So poor is the visibility near the top that it takes another walker armed with a GPS to confirm to the bedraggled and randomly assembled group that the summit is actually a further 50 metres on.

With the weather worsening, I resist the charms of the more picturesque route down Ptarmigan Ridge and instead return by the route of my ascent.

Arriving at the bottom I find – Sod's Law – that the ferry has just departed, so I have to wait several hours for my return to the car and the now-delayed seven-hour journey back to London. There are, however, worse places to be stranded.

▲▲▲

Sir Hugh Munro and his List

It is 1890. The Swiss Alps have all been climbed. Mont Blanc was conquered a century ago. The height of Mount Everest has been known for 50 years. The Suez Canal has been open for two decades. The North and South Poles will be reached within 20 years.

Despite all this geographing, the maps of Scotland are still woefully imprecise, and the measured heights of its mountains wildly inaccurate. As the 20th century dawns, estimates of the number of Scottish mountains exceeding 3,000 feet in height range from 31 in the distinguished *Baddeley's Guide*, to 236 in *The Highland Sportsman and Tourist*.

Step forth Sir Hugh Munro, fourth Baronet of Linderits, aged 34, Alpine climber and founder member of the Scottish Mountaineering Club (SMC), possessed of a Victorian rigor that some say bordered on pedantry. It would be hard to invent a man more suited to one of the earliest tasks envisaged by the SMC: to catalogue all the Scottish mountains exceeding 3,000 feet in height.

Munro starts with desk research, using the best available Ordnance Survey maps and augmenting these with the knowledge of locals. He works quickly and the SMC first publishes his Tables in 1891, just one year after he has started. The list of 538 peaks causes astonishment, but is accepted as definitive.

Munro, however, knows that the accuracy of the data from which he has constructed his Tables falls far short of his own high standards. There is only one solution: he himself will have to climb all the peaks, and use an accurate barometer to establish their heights more precisely. And Munro makes the job harder for himself by climbing many of the peaks at night, and by candle-light! Himself a member of the landed gentry, he is loath to upset local landowners as his surveying mission trespasses on their properties.

The degree of Munro's determination to be the very first person to climb all the peaks is unclear, and with over 500 to ascend, that mission would be a challenging one. But a Reverend AE Robertson defines a shortcut – or rather 'redefines the rules of a game that has not yet been invented', to quote Dave Hewitt, founder of *The Angry Corrie*. While Munro's list and climbing mission include *all* the peaks on *all* the outlying shoulders of the mountains, Robertson decides to gain only the very highest summits of each discrete mountain. That goal requires climbing far fewer peaks.

In 1901, Robertson compleats the list of Munro summits as it then stands, and in doing so establishes a more feasible goal for the rest of us. (There are now doubts about whether he actually reached the tops of either Ben Wyvis or Stuc a' Chroin.) But he also created a problem for himself – by famously kissing his last cairn before he kissed his wife...

Munro himself missed compleation by just three Munros and he died in 1919, aged 63.

As surveying methods become more accurate, the SMC periodically adds hills to The List or subtracts them. At the time of writing there are 283 Munros, Beinn a' Chlaidheimh having been measured as just too low but not yet officially demoted, and Sgurr nan Ceannaichean having been demoted in 2009 (having been promoted in 1981).

After Robertson, it is 20 years before another climber compleats The List, and compleations then run at two to three per year. Recent decades, however, have seen these figures rise to 150–200 per year, and to date over 5,000 people have self-certified themselves as having compleated the full round of Munros. Compleating the round means you are a Munroist and are thus eligible to become a member of The Munro Society; it is all based on trust, for there are no marshals waiting to log you in at the summits...

Later in this book you will meet Steven Fallon, who holds the record for climbing the complete set of Munros the largest number of times. Other records have been set by, amongst others, the youngest compleater (Ben Fleetwood, at just over ten years old), the fastest self-propelled compleater (Stephen Pyke in 39 days, nine hours, including cycling between Munros and kayaking to and from Mull and Skye), and the first compleater of a continuous round in winter (Martin Moran in 1984/5).

▲▲▲

My own tally of Munros now totals a meagre eight: three last year and five this year, including Ben Lomond. But with a long weekend available in July and a ridge of high pressure (the hillwalker's harbinger of delight) due to settle over Britain, I ease on my boots.

The notion of climbing all the Munros seems a goal far too big to countenance, but with the benefit of hindsight I later see that I may have been fooling my friends and myself. Perhaps there was already a subconscious inkling that I might compleat the round – for I choose as my next destination not a set of hills with the best vistas, but rather a set of mountains in a compact locale, close to where I have already been. In other words, there are already niggling thoughts of, 'I don't want to have too many odd hills scattered all across Scotland when I get near to finishing them all…'

Can walkers talk?

I rise with the dawn on a sunny July morning in London, and eight hours later have arrived at Ben Glas farm near the top of the now familiar Loch Lomond. There is still plenty of time for my first Munro of this, my second trip of the year.

The route up *Beinn Chabhair* (mountain of the sparrowhawk) starts along a well-kept but steep path from the farm, then via a long flat march over peaty moorland to a relatively large lochan. The path unfortunately peters out before the ridge, which forces me to ascend the hard way – directly up heathery and grassy slopes.

The summit area is tiny and offers few rocks flat enough to sit upon in comfort. I take an awkward seat and chomp on a sandwich as I survey the scene. One of the joys of climbing the higher hills in a specific area is that you soon get to see the same hills from different angles. Though still a novice hillwalker, I already feel buoyed by a sense of progress, as Ben Vorlich and Ben Lomond out to the west present a familiar look, recalling my trips earlier in the year.

Swivelling to look east, my line of sight swoops down the side of my mountain for 300 metres, then up 300 metres to the top of neighbouring An Caisteal (which really does resemble the castle that its name implies). I consider myself reasonably fit, but am amazed that some guidebooks suggest a single day to link my Beinn Chabhair with An Caisteal over there and a further neighbouring Munro. Stubbing out a cigarette, I do not suspect that within a few years my hill-fitness will have improved sufficiently to call that route a walk in the park.

Suddenly and without a word of greeting, another walker joins me on the summit. He will not be drawn into anything more than rudimentary conversation, and based on the limited evidence of this chap and the walker on my previous trip, I start to wonder whether all walkers are so reserved.

I soon depart the summit, and the return is easier, with the path along the knobbly ridge evident right from the summit. I keep my eyes focused on the track to avoid stumbles, and guess that the smooth lumpiness of the stones is a sign that the rock-scape has been heavily cooked in ancient times. Strange that it seems so different underfoot from the more gravelly paths of my previous outings on mountains not ten kilometres away... I make a mental note to brush up on geology when I get back home.

My descent is marred only by being overtaken by the chap from the summit who mutters by way of explanation that he is 'practising going downhill more quickly'. There seems to be an edge of competitiveness – of which I would see more in coming years.

Having covered ten kilometres laterally and 1,000 metres of ascent, I reach the car after four and a half hours of walking, and go in search of the accommodation I had booked nearby, to prepare for the bigger trip tomorrow.

Magic horseshoe

The longest freshwater loch in Britain is Loch Awe – all 37 kilometres of it – and *Ben Cruachan* (stacked mountain) rises sharply from its northern shoreline. In fact, the Cruachan range rises so sharply that the railway line that separates loch from ben even has special signals that trigger automatically if there is a rock-fall.

A kilometre beneath Ben Cruachan lies a vast, magic kingdom in which alchemy is wrought. Housed in a cavern higher than the Tower of London, whirring and humming is a huge hydro-electric power plant, fed by the reservoir that nestles within the high-level Cruachan Horseshoe.

Whenever you see a reservoir and hydro scheme, expect an immediate upward hike. Today, my steep upward pull begins from road level and passes through native woodland to reach the impressive dam. The length of the slog up reflects the head of water pressure needed to power the turbines at Cruachan below. While there is a path, which I find on my descent, I am still too immature a hillwalker to know the value of spending a few extra minutes finding it for the ascent!

It is 25°C and in those days I carry all the water required for the entire walk: anticipating eight hours at half a litre per hour means I am carrying four kilograms of dead weight. So merely having struggled through the straggling undergrowth of the initial woodland, my brow shows more than a drop of perspiration. But the sight of the huge corrie that rises beyond the dam reinvigorates me.

Most of Scotland's corries are dark. This is because they tend to face north or north-east, as the gnawing glaciers were better shaded from the warming effects of direct sunshine and better sheltered from the south-westerly winds that redistributed snow. The Cruachan corrie, however, faces south along some ancient line of fault that proved more powerful than the climatic pull to face north. Its southerly aspect makes for brilliant illumination on a sunlit day.

Clearly visible as I clamber up the steps to the top of the dam is the immense semicircle of mountain wall, well over two kilometres from one side to the other. Wherever I look, the curves of descent plunge gracefully down: from near vertical just beneath the summits, to a 45-degree incline halfway down, to a gentle slope where they meet the shores of the sparkling reservoir. This is certainly one of the most impressive corries in the southern Highlands, topped by a crisp ridgeline that demands to be traversed.

Even with perfect visibility and thus easy route-finding, the slog to reach the summit is long and tiring, and later investigation reveals why. For although Ben Cruachan is 'only' the 31st highest Munro, it is the 14th most prominent mountain in Britain. As a brief aside: the list of Munros is based on the height of the hill or mountain above sea level. Apostates claim this is an irrelevant measure of a mountain, arguing instead for 'prominence' – i.e. how high the mountain rises above the surrounding land. True Munro-lovers do not bother to embroil themselves in this debate.

Ben Cruachan's summit attained, I consume half of my cheese and raspberry jam sandwich and take in the superb panorama. To the west I search out the Firth of Lorn, the Sound of Mull, and volcanic Ben More, and the closer stretches of Loch Awe's sparkle below and Loch Etive's glint behind me.

There is the faintest of movements over the folds of mountain that lead down to Glen Etive, and as I tune in to the motion, discern an eagle wheeling in huge circles. This is the first time I have seen an eagle in flight, and I am amazed that it can stay airborne while apparently coasting so slowly and without a single wing-beat. The old Zen koan about posture in meditation springs to mind:

the gull soars on nothing
but slight corrections
to the tilt of its nose.

As I complete a second 360-degree scan, I now notice on the ridge ahead a concerning slab of rock: large, shiny, inclined steeply downward towards the corrie some 400 metres below, and unavoidable if the Horseshoe is to be completed. It looks like one of those nightmarish places where, if you start slipping, the pull of gravity will accelerate you gradually but inexorably over the edge…

Mobilising after my mini lunch, I reach this spot, and the slab does turn out to be awkward, lacking obvious footholds. Fortunately, the coefficient of friction between boot and rock is just sufficient to support the traverse.

And so I press on to *Stob Diamh* (peak of the stag), the second Munro of the day. This requires the upping and downing typical of most ridge walks – in this case 100 metres up and down – before I reach Stob Diamh's cairn. Some joker has arranged the cairn so that in profile it looks like a face with jutting nose and jaw, and with a hart on top. I would later wish I had photographed the extensive exhibition of such unusual cairns. My favourites include a Mexican hat arrangement on Ben Chonzie, and two meerkats on Lochnagar!

The path off Stob Diamh eventually becomes quite steep, and since it passes through heather, it allows me to try an invention that I think will save time and knee cartilage. This consists simply of a rubble sack on which to glissade down the hillside. It works well, and I continue to use it for several years. It works especially well when there are no hidden rocks; when on grass rather than on heather or bracken; when the angle of the hillside is at least 45 degrees; and ideally when there has been a light sprinkling of rain to reduce friction. Even if it is the perfect lightweight sledge, I later deem the use of this rubble sack as 'cheating' and resist the temptation to take it with me on the hills.

Having returned to the dam, and with path and stile to aid my descent, I can now appreciate the native forest in full. For perhaps the first time in my travels through the Munros, I am struck by the aromas coaxed out by the near-sweltering afternoon heat: base notes of fetid earth, midnotes of nostril-flaring pine, and topnotes of heather.

Picture-perfect

Across the top of a tin of Marks & Spencer biscuits that I once gave an aunt is a wonderful picture of Kilchurn Castle – Clan Campbell's 15th century home – standing proud at the top end of Loch Awe before two striking Munros.

The picture is impossibly stunning, with a vivid blue sky, richly hued mountains covered in heathery braes of deepest purple and slightly browning bracken, all reflected in mirror-flat water. Impossibly stunning – except that it really does look like that on the wonderful July day of my visit.

Although the route up behind the castle to *Beinn a' Chochuill* (mountain of the shell) and *Beinn Eunaich* (fowling mountain) has interest, it is a relatively uneventful jaunt. My notebook records merely that these hills really are better viewed from loch level, and ideally from across the waters of Loch Awe, per the biscuit tin.

Returning home from my third visit to the Munros, I reflect on the 13 I have climbed so far, and the seven days spent on the hills – 'quality mountain days' as the Mountain Leader Training course would designate them.

I can start to envisage the Munros becoming a powerful force in my life: a force that would indeed nourish body, mind and spirit. The effects on body are already becoming evident; it is clear that a few days on the hills are more toning than a few weeks in the gym – though the Munros have not yet rescued me from the cigarettes.

The effects so far on mind are more diverse; on the one hand, the need to avoid tripping or stumbling requires continuous and total concentration and so requires empty mind. Yet on the other hand, there are so many questions for mind to answer. Geology: how were these mountains made? History: just who was Bonnie Prince Charlie; what were the economics of the Highland Clearances? Mathematics: what is the shape of nature's idealised rockslide? Ecology: how are flora and fauna interrelated on these hills? Linguistics: what does all this Gaelic mean? On the one hand, there is perfect Zen emptiness. On the other hand, there is anti-Zen complexity. Perhaps more hills will resolve this, I reflect. The effects on spirit are probably developing, but they are hidden in a cloud of unknowing and are yet to be revealed.

I now feel ready for a route more demanding than the ones I have so far followed in the southern Highlands. I feel ready for Skye – and perhaps I should go for that hardest Munro of all, while I still have relative youth to help me: The Inaccessible Pinnacle, or 'In Pinn' to aficionados. I will need a guide, because it will take ropes and proper climbing to get to the top and abseiling to come down.

But it is not the In Pinn that will bring about my introduction to the exceptional services of the heroic Mountain Rescue Service...

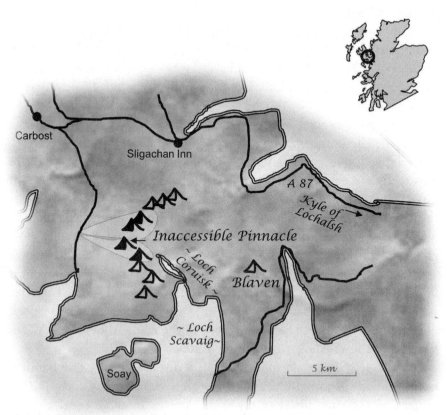

Only inked-in Munros are described in the chapter

The Cuillin of Skye

CHAPTER 3

Inaccessible Pinnacles

I keep a mountain anchored off eastward a little way,
which I ascend in my dreams both awake and asleep.

HENRY DAVID THOREAU *Letter to Harrison Blake*

'IMAGINE WAGNER'S *Ride of the Valkyries* frozen in stone and hung up like a colossal screen against the sky,' HV Morton wrote of Skye.

> It seems as if Nature when she hurled the Coolins up into the light of the sun said: 'I will make mountains which shall be the essence of all that can be terrible in mountains. I will pack into them all the fearful shapes. Their scarred ravines, on which nothing shall grow, shall lead up to towering spires of rock, sharp splinters shall strike the sky along their mighty summits, and they shall be formed of rock unlike any other rock so that they will never look the same for very long, now blue, now grey, now silver, sometimes seeming to retreat or to advance, but always drenched in mystery and terrors.'

And on top of the Cuillin sits the In Pinn. I figure that no one gets any younger, and if I am ever going to climb the In Pinn I had better get on with it. So I call one Tony Hanly – ex-Paratrooper and now mountain guide and resident of Skye. I am impressed that, when his wife answers the phone and says Tony is out, she adds, 'it's his day off, so he's out on the hills'. There's a man who loves his work.

Once again, I arrive in Scotland by car since I can throw more into the back of it than I can lug up on the train. But to break the lengthy journey to Skye, and to re-build a semblance of hill-fitness, I take in a few other supposedly easy Munros en route.

A wee timorous hill

Lying north-west of Perth, *Ben Chonzie* (mossy mountain) is variously described as one of the dullest, or most boring, or least interesting, of the Munros.

I agree with the guidebooks, although the large clan of mountain

hares that I encounter near the summit, appropriately taxonomised as
Lepus timidus scotus (yes, it's true!), provides light relief.

The path is clear and easy, but I dawdle and take longer than originally
planned on the way down. As a result, I do not get around to booking
accommodation for the night and so decide to stop near Fort William,
preparing for the first time to camp in the car.

From my first Munro venture, I know that Glen Nevis will provide a
great camping spot on the way to Skye. Arriving around 11pm, I am soon
sound asleep.

My in-car camping technique works extremely well. By chance, I discovered that my car, although only a coupé, is just long enough for a
perfect night's sleep. With the back seat down, I can extend a fully inflated
Lilo across the back seat and into the boot, with just enough clearance to
allow a sleeping bag and me on top. This approach to camping is much
easier than using a tent – especially since it avoids the need to wrestle with
a wet tent after a night's rain. It provides the perfect safety net for use on
occasions such as on this trip, when other accommodation may not be
available, and creates great flexibility for when weather and uncertain
speed of progress make it risky to book accommodation in advance.

999

Having awoken in Glen Nevis and performed basic ablutions, I set off on
the three-hour journey to Skye via Glen Shiel and the Kyle of Lochalsh.

Just south of Loch Alsh lies a remote mountain called *Beinn Sgritheall*
(scree mountain). From Glen Shiel it takes about an hour on twisting
and largely single-track road to reach the start of the route to its summit,
though interest is provided by passing the former home of Gavin
Maxwell, author of *Ring of Bright Water* and other otterly books.

Although I have not planned to climb this ben, it seems a pity just to
drive past it, and the weather is all glorious spring sunshine. So I decide
on a quick foray. It will end up becoming a long and arduous one.

In principle, the route is simple: straight up the flank of the mountain,
turn right once on the ridge, then straight on to the summit, reversing the
route to descend.

Before starting, I take a few minutes to drink in the sight of Loch
Hourn as it extends for 22 kilometres into the Sound of Sleat. Inky black,
it looks as if it could swallow a warship. Above it, Ladhar Bheinn: a huge
mountain, practically a *massif* in its own right. Above, a cloudless sky
and warm, still conditions promise a fine day's outing.

As I climb the flank of Ben Sgritheall I look periodically over my shoulder to keep an eye on the weather, for a slight breeze has sprung up. Twenty minutes later, a few clouds are visible, and after a further 20 minutes, light rain starts to fall.

Rain wets boots and wet boots are heavy, so my progress to the ridge slows slightly in deteriorating conditions and then slows significantly as the wind and rain suddenly whip and flurry up into a frenzy – just as Turner had painted them.

I reach the ridge, and conditions are now so bad that I should be turning back. But I have come all this way... all the way to Scotland, all the way driving around the headland, all the way up this mountainside... so I tie on my glasses to prevent them blowing away, such is the force of the wind, and bent double I press on, ready to hit the ground if the wind strengthens further.

Visibility is now between five and 15 metres, so it is with intense relief that I finally glimpse the summit cairn ahead. Yet as I reach the ragged pile of rocks, the visibility improves fractionally and I spy another cairn just 20 metres further on – surely at a slightly higher elevation?

No one will check whether I actually make it to the top. No one else will even care. But it seems a pity to go all that way and not do it properly. So I continue, several times seeing cairns set at higher levels. Eventually I make it to the true top, though still in the stormiest of conditions.

I do not dally on this top: I touch the cairn then turn around almost immediately to leave. This is my first such touch-and-go manoeuvre (except for once at Chicago's O'Hare airport when, in a Boeing 747, the pilot landed for just two seconds then had to thrust off again, to avoid an Alitalia jet that was idly loitering across the end of the runway), though there would be many more. Now the descent is simple: quickly along the ridge and then turn left down the flank of the ben.

Yet now, after ten minutes of stormy assault and battery on the ridge, I seem to be entering entirely new terrain: rock on which I have not previously trod, a bowl I have not previously traversed. I soldier on for a few more minutes and then fish out the trusty compass.

Or is it so trusty? To my surprise, concern, worry, then horror, it tells me I am going north-east, when I should be going west. There is no way could I be so wrong in my path finding. There must be something wrong with the compass. *Of course! Volcanic Skye is well known to have rocks that are magnetic, and I am only a few miles away; probably the rocks here are magnetic too.* With relief, I rationalise my error and in doing so, make things a whole lot worse.

I march on, and so does time. 3.30... 4.00... 4.30. I am frozen and sodden. My ex-Marine friend from the office once said, 'there's no such thing as bad weather – just inappropriate clothing,' but it doesn't apply here and now. The only thing that is completely waterproof is a rubber tarpaulin, and I am not wearing one of those.

I start to shiver. My fingers are numb sausages. I can feel my energy running low – too low. I am lost. Every exploratory venture up a slope drains my dwindling reserves of energy. I am increasingly reluctant to take the uphill steps that might help me out of this mess.

My map – carefully printed from my computer, but onto poor quality paper – has now completely disintegrated. Not that it matters, because by now there is no visibility anyway, no consistency to the direction in which the ground is sloping and no landmarks. The map would not help me much.

As well as an absence of landmarks, there is neither a single large stone behind which to shelter for minute, hour, or night, nor ditch in which to bury myself temporarily or permanently. And I have foolishly not told anyone where I was going – after all, this is just a quick, convenient side-trip.

A week or so earlier in London, my car had been broken into and my in-car phone charger was one of several items that disappeared. Now, after a few days on the road with no charging, I know my phone battery is low, but I take it out anyway. One bar of battery shows, and miraculously, one bar of reception too. For the first time in my life, I dial 999.

Through to the controller, I speak quickly in case the battery runs out and am immediately put through to Mountain Rescue. The gritty, composed, controlled, confident Scottish voice makes me feel I am already saved.

But then the enormity of the situation really hits me: visibility is so low that even if a team comes out to look for me it is unlikely they would find me. And if I really am going north-east, as the compass indicates, then I could be just a tiny needle in the vast haystack that is Beinn Sgritheall's hinterland of road-free wilderness.

'Can you tell me where you are?' asks the voice.

I attempt an answer.

'Where is your car parked?'

I tell him where.

'What is its registration number?'

I try and try and try, but just cannot remember the licence plate of the car I have owned for eight years! Hypothermia setting in.

'Orientate your map.'

'My map is pulp.'

'Ok. Go due south. If you hit a deer fence, go over it. Then continue southwards. But if you get to steep ground, come back, because there's a precipice and you'd need ropes. Switch off your phone. Then call me back in 30 minutes. We'll get you down. Don't worry.'

I follow the instructions. South... losing altitude... hope I don't have to climb back up this ... ten-foot deer fence... over the fence... down-hill... getting steep... very steep... too steep. Grudgingly, back up the hill... back over the fence. Switch on phone.

'It was too steep.'

'Ok. Follow the fence.'

'Which way?'

'I don't know. You'll just have to pick a direction. Then switch off the phone and call me back in 30 minutes.'

'I'll follow it west.'

For two hours I trudge on, periodically calling back to my lifeline. I see a stile ahead, bridging over the high deer fence. I call the voice again. 'There's a stile. What shall I do?'

The voice could tell me not to be so stupid since the route must now be obvious, but its owner realises I am not thinking straight. Instead comes, 'yer safe laddie – where there's a stile there's a path. Just cross the stile and follow the path down. Call me when you get to the road.'

I eventually make it back to the car, and know I would not have made it without the man from Mountain Rescue. I call him back, and ask how I can ever reward or repay the life-saving assistance (make a donation to the Mountain Rescue Team of your choice). After that trip, I always carry a GPS with maps loaded – but even that would not always guarantee safety, as I would find out.

Like an impish child smiling sweetly just after stealing sweets from her sister, the weather clears and the sun is shining by the time I set off from the car park, heading for Skye.

Blade running – the thin In Pinn fin

One of the great institutions of Scottish mountaineering is Skye's Sligachan Inn (pronounced 'slier-ghun'), and it is to there that I thankfully repair that evening. Once there, I take the clothes that I have tried to dry using the full blast of the car's heating system and sling them over a hastily improvised washing line, erected in my room.

I dine on haggis, neaps and tatties, then head over to the bar to meet the aforementioned Tony Hanly. He turns up punctually, a spry and sinewy figure with alert darting eyes and a stance that seems permanently primed for action. After a few beers and more than a few shared stories of hills and climbs, I hit the sack, grateful to be alive after the earlier events of the day.

Next morning, the non-Munro hill called Glamaig peers in over my porridge. A magnificent shapely hill, it is the midpoint of the annual race from the Sligachan Inn and back – with a record once held by a Nepalese Sherpa, who famously completed the race barefoot. And as I cast an eye Heavenward, I notice the ominous gathering of clouds.

As we head off for Glen Brittle, Tony describes the plan for our expedition. With the prospect of poorer weather for coming days, he has kindly selected the In Pinn for an immediate assault. The weather starts well as we gain height from our starting point in Glen Brittle and pass the huge waterfall a kilometre from the road.

To approach and enter Coire Lagan is a geological delight. Along the skyline are ridges more notched than anywhere else in Scotland – the igneous intrusions standing to attention, determined to fight on and show their metal in the unending elemental game of erosion-and-uplift. Lower down, beneath the notches and slopes, you'd swear the layered rocks must have been laid down as sediments in some long-gone sea – but in fact the layers are igneous, deposited instead from slow cooling of vast and ancient chambers of magma, beneath towering volcanoes, with different minerals crystallising out in sequence. Underfoot is the gravelly till deposited later, as the glaciers came and went; the boulders turned by scouring ice to mutton-shaped rocks that geologists call *roches moutonées*.

In deteriorating conditions, we start the hard work of the day and haul ourselves up Sgurr Dearg and over a crest that has so far kept the fearsome *Inaccessible Pinnacle* conveniently hidden. But gradually, from peak downwards, the pinnacle materialises into view, leering over the intervening ridge.

And it really is a pinnacle. This jagged spike of rock thrusts upwards for 50 metres from near the top of Sgurr Dearg. From the side, it is a sharp serrated fin with a steep climb up its back and a vertical drop to abseil down its front. From the front, it is a perilously thin pin with a curiously warty head. Although rock climbers grade the climb as Moderate, which in practice means 'pretty easy', anyone unused to climbing finds it extremely daunting. For many aspiring Munroists, this is the obstacle that prevents them compleating a full round of the hills.

And it gets worse, for Sgurr Dearg itself sits right at the heart of the Cuillin ridge, which serves as Skye's backbone. The central situation of the fin means that it is surrounded by corries on all sides. So in practice, the drop is 1,000 metres all around. WH Murray, an early and accomplished climber, described the fin as 'a knife-edged ridge, with an overhanging and infinite drop on one side, and a drop on the other side even steeper and longer'.

So it is with extreme trepidation that I don helmet and harness, let Tony rope me up and watch as he glides effortlessly up the Pinnacle.

My movements are less smooth than his, and accompanied by more expletives per minute than I knew I had, but with help and guidance, I slither slowly to the top.

'Glad we can't see the drop,' I mutter, for once glad of extremely poor visibility.

'With winds like this, you can definitely say you've done it in style,' replies Tony.

I certainly do not want to down-climb the In Pinn by the route of ascent, and indeed the normal route down is by abseil off the opposite side. Tony ties me to the safety rope, coils the main rope I will descend down and starts to swing the looped bundle back and forth. He takes a surprisingly large number of exploratory swings, and the reason becomes clear once I have lowered myself irretrievably over the edge.

For after dropping ten metres, I look down to see that the rope on which I am abseiling does not reach the ground. Instead, the end has snagged in a crack of rock six metres to my left, clearly blown there by that gusting wind, despite Tony's ample precautions.

I call to Tony but he can't hear me above the howl of the wind, and there is no way I can grapple myself back up over the outcrop above. There is no alternative – I have to bounce leftwards, in a pathetic imitation of an SAS manoeuvre. Fortunately it works; I free the rope and lower myself to terra firma. Tony follows and we exchange a spontaneous handshake.

With conditions deteriorating, we now press on to *Sgurr Mhic Choinnich* (MacKenzie's peak), which also involves a scrambly ascent. We decide to leave the neighbouring Sgurr Alasdair for another day, and by way of the Great Stone Chute return to base for a celebratory drink.

Ride of the Valkyries

In the reception area of the Sligachan Inn stands a painstakingly-constructed, two metre square model of the Black Cuillin of Skye, and after breakfast I study it, my respect for the hills having been enhanced by yesterday's experience of the In Pinn.

Better than any 3D computer graphics programme, the model allows you to grasp in an instant the stretch of the volcanic ranges, and the sprawl of the ridges and rims across 70 square kilometres of the island. With yesterday's weather having obscured all high-level visibility, this was my first real orientation to the hills.

I set off again with Tony from Glen Brittle and we eventually reach a scree chute, up which we claw our way, to reach a huge notch in the ridge called An Dorus (the door). With a technique called 'Grade Three Scrambling' (i.e. rock climbing without a rope) we get up and out of the An Dorus gap before reaching easier slopes and a simple scramble to the summit of *Sgurr a' Mhadaidh* (peak of the fox). Many of the ridges and peaks of the Black Cuillin are such thin tendrils that the summits are pinheads on which few angels could dance, and on which the cairns are tiny. Sgurr a' Mhadaidh is no exception.

We return to An Dorus, scramble farther up the opposite ridge, and pass an imperious turret of rock called The Wart before reaching the summit of *Sgurr a' Ghreadaidh* (peak of torment).

Ridges that have so far seemed perilously narrow now appear as broad motorways in comparison to the ridge that stretches ahead to *Sgurr na Banachdich* (peak of the milkmaid). This is no exaggeration, and indeed, for much of the way there is no actual top to the ridge, only edges of rock that have splintered at a slant to create a knife-edge, interrupted periodically by turrets and parapets that appear to be unstable piles of jagged rock.

Diligently, I am following Tony's early advice: 'only do one thing at a time; if you want to look at the view then stop walking!' Reaching the final summit of the day, and stopping to take in the enormity of the range, I recall fragments of HV Morton's depiction of Skye, with his 'essence of all that can be terrible in mountains... drenched in mystery and terrors'.

Suddenly the pen seems mightier than the plaster model in the Sligachan Inn, but of course, Nature is mightier than either...

* * *

My original plan is to spend five days on Skye, to complete the full round of 12 Munros there. But as I arise the next day, the weather has deteriorated further and my back is hurting badly. I guess I have compressed a few vertebral discs by descending steep slopes on hard rock without fastening the rucksack's belt (tip: always fasten the rucksack's belt!).

I have had four eventful days, but the weather shows little sign of improvement, so I pack my bags ready for the ten-hour drive back to London.

'At least you've done the In Pinn,' observes Tony. 'Of course, there's still Sgurr nan Gillean to do and in bad weather some of the routes up that are twice as hard as this one.'

I look up; he is smiling, but evidently not joking.

On the way home I reflect: the Munros are becoming a project (to experience more of them), but not yet a mission (to climb them all). I have learned something of hillwalking from books, and have learned more from the mistakes I have made. In retrospect, I can see I was about to enter a new phase of my pastime: one in which I would test my limits, not recklessly, but in terms of fitness, stamina and planning more complex routes. This would be a phase mainly about body, partly about mind, and unapologetically more superficial than the world of spirit.

▲▲▲

Of place-names, Gaelic and how many words for 'mountain'?

The more you pore over maps of the Highlands, the more you are confronted by strange-sounding names. The more you gaze across mountainous horizons, the more you search for labelled anchor-points to help make sense of the confusing jumble.

A name confers an identity; as Paul Theroux says in *Fresh Air Fiend*, 'a landscape looks different when you know the names of things'. And Gaelic names confer a soul too. The language of the Highlands, like its complex geology, has been sedimented, intruded and metamorphed over aeons. Gaelic is crystallised myth.

On a more practical note, when micro-navigating through opaque cloud and suddenly glimpsing an accumulation of white stones, it can be very helpful to know that the name Clach Geala on the map actually means White Stones; this can help you orientate yourself. Understanding how Gaelic and other languages have influenced Highland place-names has certainly helped me appreciate the mountains more fully, and has even helped me read the map.

Whenever I have looked across Loch Ossian from Corrour railway station towards Culra, for example, I have been surprised to see that the Bealach Dubh really is a *bealach* (col) that always does seem *dubh* (black), regardless of sunniness or time of day. I am equally surprised that when I have remarked on this to the staff of the station hotel, they have looked at me blankly, not knowing the meaning of the name of a place that stares at them through the window every day.

Names like Ben Lomond and Ben Vane might sound simple and straightforward, but things look a bit harder with 'Mullach Coire Mhic Fhearchair', and my favourite: 'Braigh Coire Chruinn-bhalgain'. So where do the Highland place-names come from, and are there more words for 'mountain' in Gaelic than the Eskimos have for snow?

Although Irish Gaelic has been the primary influence on the Highland language, Pictish, Norse, French and English have all left their marks too.

The Picts were the principal inhabitants of the Highlands when Hadrian started building his Wall in 122AD. Little has been found of their language and debate rages over whether it was even Indo-European in origin. The suffix *Pit-* as in Pitlochry probably means 'part' or 'piece of land', and has the strongest claim to being a Pictish word. Another possible example is 'Urquhart', probably deriving from the Pictish *Air-cardden* (at the thicket).

Other early Pictish roots – also found in Wales – include *aub* denoted 'life-sustaining water' surviving in *abhainn* or *avon* (river).

The Gaels, their myths and their language arrived sometime between the third and sixth centuries. Groups of Irish (whom the Romans named Scotii), started to migrate from Ireland to what is now Scotland, Wales and Cornwall. It was in western Scotland that their Gaelic influence was most enduring, as the nexus that was the Kingdom of Dal Riata took shape (and gave its name to the geological term 'Dalradian'). This web of trade relationships, feuding clans, bloody deeds and inter-marriage thrived from the sixth century, driving northwards and eastwards, for example to Loch Earn (Earn deriving from an ancient word for 'Irish').

In parallel, St Columba's sixth century mission from Ireland to Iona, not to mention the spread of Christianity more broadly across Scotland, helped carry Gaelic deeper inland. The widespread name 'Malcolm', for example, derives from the epithet of the Gaelic monks: *maol Colum* meaning bald followers of Columba.

For hundreds of years from the ninth century onwards, **the Vikings** controlled large tracts of Scotland – especially the western coast and isles. Thither they brought words that morphed with Gaelic, especially terms relating to trade and sea-faring such as *akkeri* which became Gaelic *acair* (anchor) and *batr* becoming Gaelic *bata* (boat).

This influence is most evident where the Vikings became ensconced – for example, approximately 40 per cent of place names in Skye have Norse origin or influence, such as *–ness* for cape, *-vik* and *–aig* for bay *-ay* for island, etc.

The Lordship of the Isles flourished during and after the Viking invasions. Through this trade empire, which spanned western Scotland and eastern Ulster until as late as the 16th century, Gaelic continued to extend its role in Scotland, taking root as the strongest influence on the Highland place-name. These names often relate to nature – including colours such as *dearg* (red), animals such as *daimh* (deer), plants such as *chaorainn* (rowan), as well as anthropomorphic features such as *socach* (snout-like hill).

The Normans' arrival after 1066 and the assumption by French barons of Scottish lands brought a French influence to the Gaelic-Norse amalgam that had thrived for centuries.

Place-names often honoured French family names – *St Clair* (becoming Sinclair), *Brus* (Bruceton), *Fraser* (Fraserburgh) – though sometimes translations were literal descriptions of an area: *Beau lieu,* beautiful place (Beauly).

The English were too close for comfort and eventually, between 1800 and 1900, Gaelic became almost extinct as a daily language. The persecution which followed the Battle of Culloden in 1746, coupled with the Highland Clearances, meant that the number of people speaking (only) Gaelic fell from 300,000 in 1800 to just 30,000 a century later. English names such as Fort Augustus had arrived, but could not eradicate the names of the Gaels.

'Mountain': so, how just many words are there for 'mountain' in Scots Gaelic? There seem to be at least 25 different words in the names of the Munros alone (and more if variants such as Bheinn and Ben are counted separately). The naming of any specific hill often reflects its length (*aonach* and *druim* are long and extended) and how pointed it is (*Sgurr* are sharp, while *meall* are rounded).

Names For 'Mountain' In Scotland			
Number of Munros	Name	Meaning	Example
76	Ben	Mountain	Beinn Narnain – Hill of notches
49	Sgurr	Peak	Sgurr Eilde Mor – Big peak of the hind
38	Cairn	Cairn	Stob Coire a' Chairn – Peak of the corrie of the cairn
23	Meall	Rounded hill	Meall Garbh – Rough rounded hill
19	Stob	Peak	Stob Binnein – Peak of the pinnacle
7	Creag	Peak	Creag Pitridh – Peak of the little loch
6	Aonach	Ridge	Aonach Beag – Little ridge
6	Mullach	Summit	Mullach nan Coirean – Summit of the corries
4	Clach	Stone	Mullach Clach a' Bhlair – Summit of the stone of the plain
3	Bhraigh	High place	Seana Bhraigh – Old high place
3	Binnein	Pinnacle	Binnein Mor – Big pinnacle
3	Socach	Snout	An Socach – The snout
3	Spidean	Peak	Spidean Mialach – Peak of the louse
3	Stuc	Peak	Stuc a' Chroin – Peak of harm or danger
3	Tom	Pointed hill	Tom Buidhe – Pointed yellow hill
2	Bidein	Peak	Bidein a' Choire Sheasgaich – Peak of the barren corrie
2	Stac	Stack	Ruadh Stac Mhor – Big red stack
1	Chno	Nut	Chno Dearg – Red nut
1	Cruach	Heap	Cruach Ardrain – The high heap
1	Druim	Ridge	Druim Shionnach – (broad) Ridge of the fox
1	Mam	Hill (breast)	Mam Sodhail – Hill of the barns
1	Monadh	Hill, cairn	Monadh Mor – Big hill
1	Mount	Mount	Tolmount – Hill of hollows
1	Mounth	Mount	White Mounth – White mount
1	Tulaichean	Hillock	Beinn Tulaichean – Hill of hillocks

An Appendix provides further examples of useful terms including water features, colours, other descriptors, parts of the body, types of people, etc.

Loaned to English from Gaelic are several interesting words. Though not strictly necessary for reading map or landscape, the following may be of interest and could even help you win a pub quiz or two:

English	Gaelic origin
Bard	The word's earliest appearance in English is in 15th century Scotland with the meaning 'vagabond minstrel'.
Bog	From *bog*, soft (related to *boglach* swamp)
Claymore	A large broadsword, from *claidheamh mór*, great sword.
Galore	From *gu leor*, enough.
Gob	From *gob*, beak or bill.
Mackintosh	After Charles Macintosh, who invented it. From *Mac an Tòisich*, son of the chieftain.
Mod	A Gaelic festival, from *mòd*, assembly, court.
Pet	From *peata*, tame animal.
Pillion	From *pillean*, pack-saddle, cushion.
Plaid	From *plaide*, blanket.
Slogan	From *sluagh-ghairm*, battle-cry
Sporran	Via *sporan* from Old Irish *sboran* and ultimately Latin *bursa*, purse.
Strontium	from *Sròn an t-Sìthein* meaning 'the point at the fairy hill', name of a mountain, near which the element was discovered.
Trousers	From *triubhas,* via 'trews'.
Whisky	Short form of whiskybae, from *uisge-beatha*, water of life.

▲▲▲

Phase 2 – Bagging

DURING MY FIRST few years of hiking the Munros, I want merely to 'get out walking', to see whether it is for me. I test myself with a few situations that are extreme, though primarily I just want to 'get out walking'. This phase has primarily been about 'body', rather than about 'mind' or 'spirit'.

Having climbed only 20 Munros, I am keen to notch up more, to claim a few more scalps, to see more sights, to experience landscapes representative of more of Scotland's terrain.

My focus starts to shift, avidly and unashamedly, to blatant peak-bagging – increasing my tally to satisfy the hunger for visible progress on map, land and Sir Hugh's List, as well as to test my physical limits. While writing of how my passion for the Munros developed, I search for some way to make sense of the stages through which I passed. Fortunately, the work of Professors Robert Jackson and Robert Norton of the University of Wisconsin-La Crosse was relevant.

From 1975 to 1980, they studied more than 1,000 game hunters, trying to understand how they developed their skill and their obsession. The professors' Stage One was called the Shooter Stage. The hunter's satisfaction is tied closely to being able to 'get out shooting'. The beginner deer hunter will talk about the number of shooting opportunities. Missing the target means little to hunters in this phase. A beginning hunter wants to pull the trigger and test the capability of his firearm.

That parallels my first phase of Munroing, and I see that I am now entering what the Professors call the Limiting Out Stage. In this stage, a hunter still talks about satisfaction gained from shooting. But what seems more important is measuring success by the number of animals 'bagged'. Progress towards reaching some sort of limit or milestone is the prime measure of success.

For me this translates into 'the more hills bagged, the better.' Though I find the term distasteful, I become a voracious Munro-bagger. I do continue to seek the bewitching vistas and rapturous panoramas of my earlier hiking, but the bottom line becomes quantity, not quality: the number of peaks bagged, mountain days expended, kilometres hiked, vertical metres climbed.

My journey is still about body, but I notice that mind is becoming more engaged, too. For as I range across Scotland I decide to revive my knowledge of geology; there are few places in the world better than Scotland in which to view a complete geological showcase.

My next two trips involve *Tracing the Fault* (the Highland Boundary Fault that runs diagonally from Glasgow to Aberdeen) and along the way I come to understand both how Britain became the sum of two disparate parts, and also how the Earth was weighed in 1778.

The next venture is *North by North-West* to the far fringes of Britain, which are among the oldest landscapes on the planet, before visiting *Lochnagar and Beyond* and *The Utter North*.

Perhaps inevitably, as the obsession takes hold, I eventually reach *The Point of No Return* near Glencoe.

* * *

As a mission continues, we become more serious, more focused and more conscious of how we will progress: using metrics (such as Munro's List) and making sense of the variety of our experiences (for example, by understanding the geology of the mountains). We get into the learning cycle: Try, Observe, Reflect, Adjust... Try Again.

Around Loch Tay

CHAPTER 4

Tracing the Fault Line

'Behold the Tiber!' the vain Roman cried,
Viewing the ample Tay from Baiglie's side;
But where's the Scot that would vaunt repay,
And hail the puny Tiber for the Tay?

SIR WALTER SCOTT *The Fair Maid of Perth*

DIAGONALLY ACROSS SCOTLAND run three deep fault lines. The south-ern-most of these is the Highland Boundary Fault, which runs through Loch Lomond and ends up in the North Sea just south of Aberdeen. North of this is Munro country: the hills are high and the mountains steep. South of the Fault the land is flatter.

By early May of this next year, spring is already turning into summer, and for no particular reason other than ease of access from southern England and an opportunity to brush up my geology, I dedicate two trips to climbing as many as possible of the Munros that border the Fault.

Due to the pressures of work, relationships and family, it has been a year since my last expedition to the Highlands of Scotland. It is hard to believe I have left the mountains alone for so long.

South of the Irish loch

Loch Earn – the Irish loch, named from the Irishness of the Gaels who expanded their territories east and north into Pictland – lies 40 kilometres west of Perth.

From the southern shores of this loch, a well-built path bears me upwards, peters out and then reappears nearer to the steep, stony, conical and windy top of *Ben Vorlich* (mountain of the bay).

Perched on the edge of the Highland Boundary Fault, the southward views inevitably show flatter plains, while those to the North reveal the beginnings of more intriguing terrain. Of immediate surprise, however, is the size of the drop needed to the bealach I have now to cross: it looks like at least 200 metres of drop and 200 of re-ascent. I double-check my bear-ings and wonder if I am on the right hill, since this is my first trip of the year, and I had awoken very early that morning to drive up from London.

Alas, this is indeed the bealach I need to cross, so I take a deep breath and set off. Lingering snow and ice is plastered on the face of *Stuc a'*

Chroin (peak of danger), and from its base the climb looks daunting. By good fortune, a couple descend from the summit and assure me there is a path 'round there to the left', and I am soon on a steep semi-path aided only by grass-holds.

Until recently, I have been hesitant to rely on 'grass-holds' – hanging onto tufts of protruding grass to ease a climb – and had grabbed onto only tried and tested rock. But a publisher friend of mine had recommended the excellent writings of WH Murray, in which the occasional use of grass-holds is recommended. Murray was an inspiration to many during the Second World War, famously writing his *Mountaineering in Scotland* from memory while imprisoned in Colditz. The guards having found and destroyed his original manuscript, which had been drafted on toilet paper, Murray joined the small band of writers who have had to write the same book twice. [For example, if you allow me a tangent off a tangent: TE Lawrence lost his original 250,000 word manuscript of the *Seven Pillars of Wisdom* in Reading railway station. Thomas Carlyle had to re-write his entire 300,000 word manuscript of the first volume of *The French Revolution: A History* when it was mistakenly burned by the maid of his friend, John Stuart Mill.] Anyway, grass-holds were good enough for WHM, so they are good enough for me – though I do find heather-holds to be stronger.

I finally reach the cairn atop the path. It is easy to be fooled by misplaced cairns; fortunately I have read that the true summit of this hill lies half a kilometre further on and reach it easily.

There I pause for lunch and for a chat with members of a nearby walking club, who have swarmed up the other side of the hill. The club's members are in chatty form, and their camaraderie reminds me of the one problem I have yet to solve in my new favourite pastime of hillwalking: the lack of company. Neither brother, sister, nor girlfriend can be persuaded to accompany me. My fittest 'mates' are currently scattered across New York, Hong Kong and Sydney. Walking groups in Scotland and England typically cater for weekend, not week-long, walks. I can survive with solo, but reaffirm my intention to find company.

Descending the opposite side of the summit's nose, I find a route simpler than that of my ascent. Then, rather than retrace the inbound route, I speed down into the corrie, over the lip of what seems to be another corrie and through much heathery bogginess to the car.

En route, I treat myself to one secret indulgence: rampaging at a full-speed run down heathery slopes. I am not yet fit enough to keep it up for long, and there is always a risk of twisted ankles. But the next best thing to 'free as a bird' must be 'free as a deer'. This abandon is hard to replicate when going uphill, but I now feel well limbered up for the peak-bagging work of the next three days.

A big hill

Ben More (big mountain) near Crianlarich is huge. Three-quarters of a mile high, it is the tallest of the many Ben Mores in Scotland, the sixteenth highest mountain in Britain and the sixth most prominent, so it can be seen for many miles around.

Unfortunately, this hill offers no preamble to its ascent. It is all heavy venison main course, with no *hors d'oeuvre*. An early track does offer the odd zig and a few redundant zags, but then I am left to my own devices, lugging myself straight up the grassy slopes at an angle of 40 degrees for just over one and a half kilometres. It would make demanding training for the army, and perhaps does.

The panorama from the top presents distinct segments: to the south and east a few ridges run down to mark the transition from the Highlands to the flatter plains beyond; to the north the land appears to perk upwards wherever ancient glaciers and more recent rivers have cleaved and scored the land; and to the west, the two parallel ridges that I would be climbing next are laid out in more orderly fashion.

I dig out my lunch: again the cheese and raspberry jam sandwiches that are becoming my staple diet in the hills. I guess the jam's sugar gives immediate energy, the bread's carbohydrate provides medium-term fuel and the cheese's protein yields longer-term power. But a big day on the hills can require 5,000 calories or more – hence my large additional bag of peanuts and raisins for continual grazing.

After a quick bite, it is onwards to *Stob Binnein* (anvil peak), where the drop down to the bealach and ascent to the summit are steep and uncannily similar to the swoop and soar of yesterday's slopes.

The wind springs up and it is at this point that I have an idea for how to make a low-tech anemometer, to measure the wind speeds. I did build a prototype one day, and it works quite well: make a spindle by cutting an inch off a wire clothes hanger; make a pendulum arm from the same wire and make a loop at the top for the spindle to pass through; fasten a cup (e.g. a plastic coffee cup) to the bottom of the arm to catch the wind; stick some card to the arm to mark the wind scale on; add a plumb-line to the spindle, e.g. a heavy bolt, to mark vertical. When you hold this apparatus up, any wind deflects the cup-arm by a certain angle. So far, so good: the challenge is how to mark the scale, calibrating it to the wind speed. So, with the help of a friend, drive a car at say ten miles per hour with the anemometer held out of the window, and mark the deflection of the arm from vertical; repeat for other speeds, and voila!

The paths for the return from anvil peak are well-trodden and easy to follow – fortunately contouring around the side of the big hill rather than back over it. There will be Munros I shall have to climb twice, but fortunately, not Ben More.

Scarred remains

Neighbouring *Cruach Ardrain* (stack of the high peaks) is a lumpen mass of ancient Dalradian rock, the geology of which I shall explain shortly. But it is the action of relatively recent glaciation that gives it its characteristic knobbly shape, visible from afar.

From my starting point just west of Crianlarich, I cross under the railway line, ascend a track that shadows the River Falloch, skirt a plantation, and am soon treading that unyielding Dalradian bedrock. Along the way, the names of intermediate bumps reflect the austere and uncompromising nature of this hill, including The Grey Height, and Hillock of the Ox.

The hill's upper reaches are ice-scarred and ice-smoothed, and have been the subject of much geological research. Of all the Munros, I remember Cruach Ardrain as having been one of the hardest underfoot – in many places there is not even gravel, just hard-polished, unforgiving bedrock laid down a billion years ago, cooked and compressed many times since then and then glacially sandpapered for good measure.

Along the ridge I make a sharp left turn – easily missed – to the hill's summit; the continuation to *Beinn Tulaichean* (mountain of the hillocks) is a straightforward affair, with crystal-clear visibility.

Knowing I shall be retracing my steps on this linear (as opposed to circular) route, I dump my pack to ease the walking. Others are less trusting than I and would always retain oversight of their pack – but I have a secret weapon: a curse in ancient Gaelic sewn into the rucksack, but visible to any pilferer. It promises mishap and catastrophe on the remotest hill for anyone who helps themselves to the rucksack or its contents. So far it has worked…

Enchanted castle

The ice-carved knobbles of *An Caisteal* (the castle) are somehow arranged into a far more attractive topography than that of its jumbled next-door neighbour, Cruach Ardrain. Viewed from most angles, the massive ramparts lend authority and gravitas to this edifice, yet the fortress also demands that you pay it a visit.

I duly set off to pay homage from the same start point as yesterday, then climb up the western slopes of the River Falloch, rather than up its eastern side.

After a few rising stints I reach the virtual motte and bailey of the castle and am rewarded by vistas similar to those from Ben More, but with the added interest of broadside views of the scarred Cruach Ardrain.

From the south-west, however, a long grey line is forming on the horizon and a threatened weather front is approaching at speed. The air before the front is heavy with moisture, and over the ridge that I hope to cross, a thick bank of leaden cloud is beating me to it: rolling in, with long fingers and descending tendrils of mist, stretching out and reaching down into the corrie beneath. There is a brief break in this phenomenon, and aiming to take advantage of it, I press on towards the ridge.

As the name implies, the route to *Beinn a' Chroin* (hill of danger) does have a slightly dangerous stretch – a brief scramble offering exposure to a large drop. But the perils do not terrify, and soon I reach the ridge to the summit. Past wind-sculpted figures resembling large heads and human figures, I pass two minor tops – each of which has at some point claimed to be higher than the other one.

The bank of cloud in time evaporates, but not without dropping a few gratuitous raindrops on me. As the cloud marks its territory, I scan the contours for the dividing line between east and west: for on this hill eastern raindrops become the River Falloch, then Loch Lomond, then the Atlantic Ocean by way of the Firth of Clyde and the Irish Sea, while western drops become the North Sea on the other side of the country, by way of the Firth of Forth.

My return is down the protruding nose of the ridge, to the wide open valley, accompanying the River Falloch from its tinkling infancy to its roaring and petulant adolescence. But just as I reach the point where the glen opens up, above the jog and gurgle of the water I hear an eerie strain that has the hairs of my spine on end. It appears to come from the hills, but I cannot see its source. I turn and look up the glen.

The hills are cooling now in the dusk, and the wind is turning down-hill towards me. Gradually the notes are more distinct; someone is playing the pipes. I still cannot see the piper, but am convinced he is approaching. This is an enchanting piper, and I take a seat on a large rock to await his arrival with his strident skirling chords. I am transported by the melodies and lose track of time, and still he does not come. Perhaps this is the changeling piper, or the fairy piper with its crystal chanter and the lost pibroch melody now found?

▲▲▲

The Highland Crumple Zone

Standing on An Caisteal, you are at the centre of one of the best geological treats on the whole planet. It is no coincidence that many of the founders of geology hailed from Scotland, for into this tiny area of the planet every type of global tectonic jostling impinged and the resulting artefacts were then left exposed by later glaciers.

More specifically, Scotland was formed in six main phases, as ancient continental plates migrated, collided and ruptured.

1. In Pre-Cambrian times (from two and a half billion years ago to half a billion years ago), one of the Earth's ancient continents was a block we now call Laurentia, which now underlies North America. On its south-eastern margin, wind and river deposited rock, which was eventually re-cycled into continental crust. This crust came to form some of the deep basement areas north of what is now Scotland's Highland Boundary Fault (the fault line that runs from Arran through Loch Lomond and Loch Tay to just south of Aberdeen).

2. Laurentia had been wedged next to two other continents, but from about 800 million years ago these started to pull apart, creating a widening ocean. Into this gigantic sink, more sediments were deposited for 300 million years (the Dalradian period). They would later be squashed up to form the mountainous regions from the Highland Boundary Fault up to Loch Ness.

3. The world's tectonic plates lumbered along in a giant game of slow-motion dodgems, and during the brief but cataclysmic Caledonian period (480–400 million years ago) three continents had the geological equivalent of a three-car pile-up: Laurentia, Avalonia and Baltica. With Scotland on the southern margin of Laurentia, and England on the northern margin of Avalonia, this collision was the initial act of union in which Great Britain was formed from two completely separate continents (some argue that a fourth plate – French / Spanish / Portuguese Armorica – was also involved; others argue that it piled into the scrum later).

This pile-up compressed the Dalradian sediments to the north of the

Highland Boundary Fault, changed their sands to quartzite and their muds to slate, and within the crumple zone pushed up mountain ranges as high as the Himalaya (the height has been estimated primarily from the known pressures required to form certain observed minerals).

The pile-up also caused partial melting of the Earth's crust, creating volcanoes such as the ones that underlie Ben Nevis and Glencoe (though not the volcanoes of Skye, which were created later).

This crumple zone, where England joined Scotland, is still visible as a raised line of hills. It now supports the Wall that Hadrian understandably chose to site atop a high crumpled ridge.

4. **The next 300 million years saw further erosion of hills and mountains**; sediment from their eroded tops and slopes was spread across lowland areas. Bouts of igneous activity burst out regionally too.

5. **Then, starting around 50 million years ago, Laurentia started to break up** and the Atlantic was established as Britain and North America went their separating ways. This led to the volcanic creation of the Skye Cuillin and other tectonic features of Scotland's West Coast.

6. **Finally, the Big Freeze arrived.** The most recent sequence of Ice Ages started about two and a half million years ago, scouring Scotland as recently as 8–10,000 years ago. The glaciers gouged high corries: ice-cold lollies sticking to the corrie mouths and plucking bits away. Industriously they smoothed rocks, carved valleys, and then dumped rocks, soil and till far and wide.

Throughout these phases, which later chapters cover in more detail, Scotland's latitude, weather, altitude, and marine coverage fluctuated markedly, and had substantial effects on rock, land, plant and animal.

So, if you go back to the Ring of Steall, the mountains you stand on would be made from rocks originally deposited as sediments on the edge of an ancient continent nearly a billion years ago, which were then cooked, bent, and chemically changed (metamorphosed) as a three-way collision of continents, crunching what is now England into Scotland to form the British Isles. Throw in a couple of Ice Ages to erode out the valleys and corries, and you are left with today's amazing spectacle.

▲▲▲

Later in May, I return to continue tracing the Fault in the region around Loch Tay. As I have started 'bagging' in earnest, I plan a trip that will deliver not merely eight Munros (my previous maximum on a trip) but instead, 15 over five days.

Even back in the Stone Age, the area around Ben Lawers and Loch Tay was inhabited. Standing witness to habitation as long ago as 3,500 BC are many hundreds of standing stones, stone circles and rocks bearing cup-marked rings.

This continuous habitation is due in part to the soil's fertility. The Dalradian schists were originally mineral-rich clays and muds, deposited into the giant sink-hole between tectonic plates and then compressed and squeezed. Being schists, they crumble easily once weathered (the term comes from the Greek *skison* meaning 'to split' as in scissors and schism). The soil thus provides accessible nutrients for plants – and *homo modernus* has designated the area a National Nature Reserve, now home to thousands of species of plant and animal.

It is to visit this fertile area that I now journey, barely two weeks after my last visit to the hills, as I have fortuitously managed to part a week-long gap between meetings at work.

The Loch of the Stags

… And a magically beautiful loch it is too! Loch an Daimh lies in a classical glaciated valley, with a little bend in the middle for extra interest and steep sloping braes to north and south – some quite precipitous. On its south side are two north-facing corries, one with its own wee lochan.

As I view the glen from the dam, mists are clinging to the mountain tops, though the loch itself is visible for its entire length. It is May, spring, warm and still, and the soft call of woodpigeon is interrupted only by the more insistent chirp of the greenshank.

With this stunning loch as both the setting and the centrepiece for the trips up *Meall Buidhe* (yellow hill) to the north and *Stuchd an Lochain* (peak of the wee lochan) peering in from the south, I will not recount the details of the route – save to advise that the line of fence posts to be followed to the latter top has one extensive gap, at which point one must pay close attention to the path, so as not to go astray, as I did.

A round of four

Some have written of the redeeming features of the round of four Munros above Glen Lyon: *Carn Gorm* (blue hill), *Meall Garbh* (rough hill), *Carn Mairg* (hill of sorrow, or boundary hill) and *Meall nan Aighean* (hill of the hind). My own view is that those writers do claim too much.

On a day during which the misty cloud-base is barely rising above 500 metres, the relatively flat ridge has little of obvious interest. Perhaps if I ski the route on a brilliant winter's day I shall see the positives that Cameron McNeish claims.

Instead, in the few moments between concentrating on where and how I am treading, my mind is primarily occupied with the prospects of tomorrow's route, and hoping that the skies will clear as promised.

Ben Lawers

A gang of men once built an upward projection 17 feet high on top of Ben Lawers so that the mountain could enter the elite 4,000-foot list and, with luck, boost local trade! The extension was eventually demolished, but Ben Lawers is still the 10th highest mountain in Britain and holds visual sway over the entire ancient region of Breadalbane.

Fair weather arrives and I am grateful, for I readily see why trekking the round of the Ben Lawers massif is considered a classic hillwalk of the southern Highlands.

Starting from the Nature Reserve, all the expected charms of flower and tree, bird and butterfly, insect and creepy-crawly, scent and aroma parade before you in an extravaganza of sensory delight.

The senses fulfilled, however, it is then on to the hard graft of the day. I leave the fenced reserve and head quite steeply up the nose of *Beinn Ghlas* (grey-green mountain), from which the complex glen that flanks Ben Lawers' backside comes into length-wise view. Reaching the summit of *Ben Lawers* (mountain of the loud stream), I look for marks of the lost 'building extension', but without success.

The hill is vast, with broad shoulders that obscure much of the nearer valleys, unless you are willing to take a detour out onto those shoulders. My attention is therefore drawn instead to the prospect of the wide and sinuous ridge ahead that looks like the spine of a well-fed dragon.

The wonderful ridge walk takes me next to *An Stuc* (the peak). Though ascent is always hard work, I worry more about descents on routes so steep that the map shows even the *thick* contours as broken. Don't come un-stuck on An Stuc, as they say.

The downward scramble negotiated, I press on towards *Meall Garbh* (rough hill), but slow down to tag along with a family which is out together on this demanding day. We stroll over a crest and down a massive blockfield, enjoying talk of hills and glens, and sharing lunch in a warm sunny spot out of the breeze. They remain good friends and walking companions.

Then it is on for a further three kilometres of high-level walk over the broad rounded massif to *Meall Greigh* (hill of the horse studs), and finally the long walk down to the road, with frequent glances to my right to take in the corrie and the dark blue loch that Ben Lawers cradles.

The walk back to the car from the hamlet of Lawers would add almost ten kilometres to the outing – but the barman at the Ben Lawers Hotel kindly offers me a lift. I will be staying there on my next visit to the Tay!

Two Mealls for the price of one

My camping credentials are modest. As a student, I had once spent a night under the stars in the foothills of Mount Olympus in Greece, on an Inter-rail holiday with no tent at all, so that does not really count. Around the same period, I had also spent a week in a rainy Lake District with five university friends in a parent's marquee, which we had somehow lugged up there: not sure that counts either. And as a teenager, I had somehow persuaded my parents to allow me an adventurous two days on the Brecon Beacons with a large plastic bag to sleep in: hardly *real* camping; but I did once have a week of 'proper camping' in Scotland with fellow college oarsman Jim Harrison (who carried extra rocks in his rucksack for 'training').

Given my limited experience, it is with some trepidation that I set off for tomorrow's hike, during which I aim to camp on the way up to *Meall Corranaich* (notched hill). The Vango 200 ridge tent – even the Vitesse one – weighs 1.3 kilograms, and in total my pack weighs about five kilograms more than usual. I should probably pitch camp near the bottom of the route, at the head of the dammed reservoir that has become Lochan na Lairige, but the weather is fine, so I decide instead to head two kilometres up verdant slopes to a ridge just below the summit. The springy bounce of peat makes for a soft carpet. It is much more valuable in descent than in ascent, and so I hope to encounter similar ground on the far leg of the circuit tomorrow.

The single-skin tent pitches easily, and the night starts uneventfully, but even with earplugs I wake at about midnight to a rustling outside. The rustle grows rowdier, and eventually the wailing and howling starts as the wind picks up. Though I had selected a site on the protected leeward slope, that seems to be of little value, and for several hours I am reminded that this is called the hill of lamenting.

I am a bit groggy next morning as I strike camp, but I survive my first Munro night, and have a feeling that camping will help me bag Munros more efficiently on future trips.

Given my extra pack weight, I am glad that I do not have to pirouette prodigiously on high peaks to take in the day's views. And while this route is not so mystical as to transform my life, nevertheless its graceful topography secures it a place in my heart as one of my favourites. It is the perfect little bistro hidden between Michelin 3-star giants like Ben Lawers. As I continue from the first peak to *Meall a' Choire Leith* (hill of the grey corrie), the path swoops and soars over bicep-like folds until I at last reach the second top and descend its steep far side. The return to the start is straightforward, and the weather is excellent (actually *too* cloudless, as I would discover two days later).

There is just one jab of excitement along the way. The overall lie of the land across the peat hags looks level, though the mysterious gurgle of running water a few feet underground suggests otherwise. The path seems to be on relatively firm ground... but then with no warning I am suddenly thigh-deep in a peat bog. Later I would know that my potential grave was probably a small kettle-hole: the swampy infill of a depression created 10,000 years ago, as a then unmelted block of glacier was gradually surrounded by deposited detritus. But right now I just have to get out...

The problem with the surprise bog is that by the time one leg has effectively plummeted through the mud, your weight is overbalancing and a split-second later your other leg is probably immersed too. Ankle-deep is not too bad; thigh-deep is scary. With no branches nearby to help me, I slip off my rucksack and lay it down in front of me, then bend forwards over it, trying to spread my weight and arms as widely as possible. The books say I should be able to lever myself out, but I'm not making much progress.

Eventually I fish out of my rucksack a large rubble sack and scooping up the sodden peat in it, I use the bog's own weight against itself, as you do in judo, and gradually manage to leverage myself out.

Many clothes to be washed, but Bear Grylls would be proud of me.

The fairy hill

Schiehallion (the fairy hill of the Caledonians) rises as an apparently lonely cone from the lands to the south-east of Loch Rannoch, yet is visible and highly recognisable for miles to west and east. Upon approach, you find that it is not a cone at all, but rather a long whale-backed, prism-shaped ridge oriented east-west – and this lent it its crucial role in geophysics, described below. Its evocative name is related to the word banshee – female fairy – which English has adopted from Gaelic.

Schiehallion can be climbed from various sides, but I take the tourist route up the well-made path from the north-east. At the beginning of the long flat ridge of the prism's top, the path peters out as underfoot the terrain changes to blocks – huge blocks set at rakish angles between which the gaps snap at your legs, just waiting to grab an ankle.

The real boon of the day is undoubtedly the commanding view from the summit cairn, whichever way you get there. Loch Rannoch stretches impossibly far into the distance, while to the south-east, mountain flanks stand proudly above a wide, open expanse of moorland too flat to be a valley, yet too concave to be a plain. Something between the shape of a plate and that of a saucer, this intervening land has few distinguishing marks and is impossible to calibrate with the naked eye.

I start to return by the route of my ascent, but become increasingly frustrated by the lengthy blockfield that litters the hill's whale-like back. Cutting southwards I find the thin vein of a very helpful stalker's path that I wish I had noticed on the way up, and soon regain the tourist path to the start. 'Many a stalker's path, yet few deer sighted,' I muse; the wilder north will probably address that imbalance.

Tarmachan for breakfast

Having forgotten to wear eyeshades, I am awoken at ten-to-five in the morning by sun that is already streaming in through the ineffectual curtains of my base at the Killin Hotel. My only gripe with Scotland is that virtually all my overnight accommodation has had the flimsiest of curtains; perhaps Scots have thick eyelids.

Fortunately my early awakening solves a problem: I have to be back in London before midnight today, but still have one more hill to climb in the area.

That is how I come to climb my first pre-breakfast Munro. I slip into walking gear and take the well-made path that extends almost to the ridge, then double back at a col to reach the summit of *Meall nan Tarmachan* (hill of the ptarmigan). A professional photographer who has already been there for an hour greets me and provides surprise company. I can understand his early start, since the vistas on offer are so hugely varied. At this hour they are lit up to brilliant effect: south over the vast gash of Loch Tay and only a few more Munros before you reach Stirling and flatness; east over the reservoir to the lumpy, uncouth green slopes above it; north-west to Ben Nevis's now-familiar profile; and south-west to the gothic ridge from the ptarmigan hill, which most walkers include to make a circuit. It is a panorama of huge diversity.

Alas, I can loiter only briefly, and by 7.30am I am feasting on a full Scottish breakfast at the hotel before my long return home.

▲▲▲

How much does planet Earth weigh?

In August of 1773, two men on horseback were seen wandering, fet-lock-deep, across boggy glens near Perth.

They were Charles Mason and his guide. Mason was a famed astron-omer and surveyor, having made his name by mapping the path of the Mason-Dixon Line that divides Pennsylvania and Maryland (the cultural North and South of what is now the USA).

A year earlier, the Royal Society had set up the 'Committee of Attraction', and under its auspices Mason was now combing Scotland, search-ing for the perfect mountain or valley. It had to be an oblong prism, shaped like a bar of Toblerone chocolate, orientated east-west and two to three miles long. Such a ben or glen would be central to a hugely impor-tant experiment: to find the weight of the Earth.

This was a crucial goal for reasons both scientific and political. With the Age of Reason marching on, there was a strong impetus to extend man's knowledge of the Earth. Thomas Cook, for example, had returned just two years earlier from his voyage of discovery on the other side of the planet. And Mason himself had co-led a mission to observe the transit of Venus just four years earlier, establishing that the Earth was not a perfect sphere after all, but was indeed flattened at its poles.

Politically, Britain was running hard to ensure it remained a leading power. She had won the global Seven Years War just ten years earlier, but the Americans were restless – and indeed would proclaim their independ-ence in the following year. French and Italian scientists were challenging Britain for supremacy in many fields of technical endeavour. Weighing the world would be a coup, and everyone knew it.

The experiment was elegantly simple in theory, but would turn out to be monumentally difficult in practice. The idea was to find a conveniently shaped mountain (or valley) and see by how much a plumb-line deflected from the vertical. The plumb-bob would be pulled to vertical by the massive gravitational attraction of the Earth, but deflected very slightly by the gravitational attraction of the mountain. By measuring the exact angle of deflection, Mason could estimate the relative mass of the moun-tain compared to that of the Earth. Thus, he could find the weight of the Earth... provided he knew how large the mountain was. This in turn meant he needed a hill that would be easy to map – hence the requirement for that oblong prism. To avoid other gravitational pulls, it also had to be as remote as possible from other hills.

Schiehallion seemed to be a fantastic candidate, as anyone who has seen it from afar can attest, but it took Mason several weeks of arduous surveying to satisfy himself of this, lugging barometer and theodolite to vantage points spread wide over ridge and flank, in sunshine and in tempest.

The Royal Society was duly impressed with Mason's appraisal of the site, but there were two more obstacles, only one of which was yet evident. The evident challenge was the job of surveying Schiehallion in detail. Mason was offered the job of leading the survey at the rate of a guinea a day, but declined.

His lack of acceptance was unlikely to be because of the weather's inclemency, for the experienced Mason had roamed widely across the American prairies, crossed the Atlantic four times, and had explored in Africa. More likely he felt that The Reverend Dr Nevil Maskelyne, Astronomer Royal and patron of the project, would end up stealing his thunder.

So Maskelyne got his boots to where his goal had been and took on the job himself. Out in the field with his surveyors, he took readings of plumb-line angles, stellar positions, and heights of rocky outcrops. With rain, storm, screaming winds and general driechness, the portly reverend eventually spent 17 weeks up there in a bothy, and sometimes under canvas.

The unexpected second challenge was the scale of the computational Everest to be climbed. Someone had to grapple with the vast complexity of the inter-linked calculations to make sense of all the data. It fell to Charles Hutton, miner's son turned brilliant mathematician, to perform this virtuoso act. To calculate the attractive force of Schiehallion, he had to imagine the prism-shaped hill as comprising scores of thin horizontal slices – but each of different size and shape. Alas, the survey of the mountain had not provided him with data in this convenient form, but instead consisted of quite randomly-placed observations. To collate the data, Hutton hit upon the idea of making estimates between the available points, to construct shapes that were more regular, and thus he created the world's first contour lines. But there were still hundreds of sines, cosines, and tangents to calculate by hand. The whole process took him four years to complete.

Through these stalwart efforts, the mass of the Earth was calculated in 1778 to within 20 per cent of its true value of 6,000 million million

million tonnes. Crucially, these findings provided convincing evidence for the theory that the core of the Earth was not hollow after all, and instead most probably consisted of heavy metals.

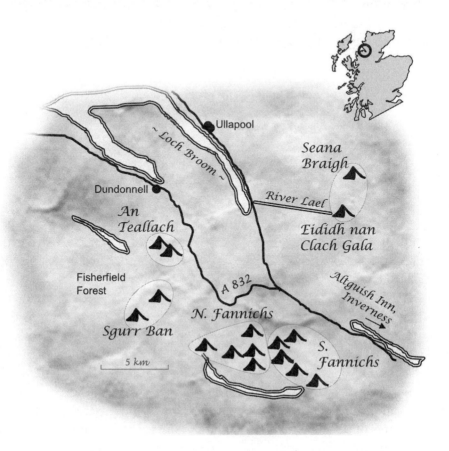

The North-West, near Ullapool

CHAPTER 5

North by North-West

*The most patient people grow weary at last with
being continually wetted with rain; except, of course,
in the Scottish Highlands, where there are not
enough fine intervals to point the difference.*

ROBERT LOUIS STEVENSON *An Inland Voyage*

A GOLDEN DAWN breaks over the high plateau of the Cairngorms massif.
The land still sleeps, yet somehow, through a few gaps in the leaden
clouds, unstopped rays of sun burst through like spears to strike the
valley-sides and bluffs. And where the rays impale the ground, the slopes
glow emerald green or smoulder peaty brown.

It is early on Midsummer's morning and I am peering out of the
window of the sleeper-train, en route to Inverness, and starting to gain
a broadside view of the Cairngorms, visible as the train tracks between
Kingussie and Aviemore.

The train does not actually travel *through* the massif of course, but
what you lose in distance and therefore detail, you gain in the sense of
vast scale and dramatic setting that the train's arcing circuit allows. The
bald pates of the gigantic ancient plutons rise from the flat surroundings,
brows furrowed and in places capped by perennial snow.

And then there's the air: stepping off the train briefly at Aviemore,
I breathe in deep lungfuls of the Highland stuff, to displace the last
vestiges of London fume. The summer warmth is already evaporating the
morning dew and spiriting up the smell of gravid earth to mix it with that
of ancient pine. If ever there were a magic carpet, the Caledonian Sleeper
is it.

For my third trip north this year, I am on a mission to sample the
stunning north-west of Scotland, and for reasons I will explain later, am
looking forward to experiencing the northernmost of Scotland's main
diagonal fault lines: the Moine Thrust. But more importantly, I am testing
the limits of my hiking and Munro-bagging prowess, culminating in an
attempt to complete the famous Fisherfield Six Munros in a single day.

Southern undulations

Snaking across the north of Scotland from Inverness to Ullapool is the
A835, and south of it lies the bulge and ripple of 100 square kilometres of

mountainous terrain. The area is called the Fannichs – a name of obscure origin, although it may relate to similar Celtic words meaning 'undulating'. Hundreds of exhausted legs can confirm that this theory is plausible.

The Munros here are distributed in a way that allows many combinations and permutations of route if you want to climb them all. For no reason other than simplicity, I decide to walk the Fannichs as a southern round followed by a northern one, and having dropped my bags at the Altguish Inn, set off on the southerly route.

My walk-in to the day's four Munros accompanies the line of a stream that sparkles with the morning sun. This year we are having a proper summer, at least so far, and today is Midsummer's Day. As an aside, Midsummer's Day is of course not quite the longest day of the year: the former is a festival celebrated across Europe and beyond, typically held on 24 June; the latter is the summer solstice, typically falling on 20 June or 21.

My first hill is to be *Beinn Liath Mhor Fannaich* (big grey hill). There are four Munros that include Liath (grey) in their name, because quartzite and schistose mountaintops are so prevalent in the Highlands. I can't help thinking, however, that today's first hill may have been named grey because it is a bit dull.

Descending to the col that joins the grey hill to *Sgurr Mor* (big peak) I become aware of a strange rumbling sound and look around, but cannot see its source. I carry on walking. The noise grows louder, I turn around, and suddenly visible in the distance is a large bird with headlights flying straight towards me at speed: a Tornado GR4 jet-fighter, with another right beside it. I watch as it approaches, then realise I am in for a treat: a victory roll immediately above the col on which I am now standing.

On the way down from Sgurr Mor I meet a man with a dog, both preparing to climb the hill. He is more talkative than other solo walkers I have met, and he mentions that he has climbed this hill a staggering 51 times. He sees my surprise and volunteers that he lives locally. After we have chatted further, I feel able to ask of his motivations for climbing this same hill so many times. He then explains that since the age of six he had climbed the hill every year with his father on the latter's birthday; that his father had died when he was only ten years old; and that he had continued this memorial rite for the last 45 years. That gave me pause to consider my own motivations.

But at the time I felt my motivations were more superficial: bag as many hills as possible, sear into memory as many spectacular scenes as possible, and an idea, not fully acknowledged at the time, that I could push this Munro-bagging to such extreme limits that I would just *have* to give up smoking 15–20 cigarettes a day...

I continue on to *Meall Gorm* (rounded blue hill) and *An Coileachan* (the little cockerel), and after 15 minutes I look back. Man and dog are somewhere on that thread-like upward path, but stare as I might, I cannot see them. For the first time I am struck by the daunting immensity and *overwhelmingness* of even a docile landscape.

Dropping down off the ridge on a line that affords little error, I track past a large, shaded lochan that nestles right up to the sheer face of the corrie, and then out through knee-high heather until I reach the final path.

It has been a long day and I am glad to return to the Inn to find I am one of the very first guests of Dario and Lesley (indeed, my booking a week earlier was with the previous owners). To celebrate their new ownership, I choose the Pasta Dario from the dinner menu – the first time I have eaten pasta with venison. It is a fantastic combination, especially when served with gravy (whisky).

Things liven up in the bar, for this is about the only place in the 50 kilometres between Dingwall and Ullapool that serves a drink. I strike up conversation with a man I will call Brodie to protect the guilty. He is a local ghillie and a man with many a story up his sly and sleekit sleeve.

He is spitting and cursing about a stalking client he has taken out today, and first gives me the background that in culling stags, the estate always tries to take out the stags with 'screwy' antlers – asymmetric ones that in a fight can take out a competing stag's eye. He took the clients up the glen, found the herd, then pointed out the stag to shoot. '... But all those * * * Germans want is a perfect trophy set of horns... they only want the perfect ones. I told him which stag to take, and I saw he even took aim on the one I pointed to. Then he just turned and shot the best stag in the herd. Dead.'

'What did you do?' I asked.

'I told Fritz to wait there, 'cos the stag wasn't dead and I'd seen men gored by a flailing stag.'

'And then?'

'I went up and shot it. It was already dead, mind. Shot it in the head; the horns all shattered.'

'I see.'

'Well, then of course I went back to Fritz and said *It's OK now, he's dead, but I think you shot him in the head – all the horns were shattered...*'

We chinked glasses and had another whisky.

Divine intervention

Today is a day of rain, just like the day when Titus Groan was Earled: monotonous, sullen, grey rain with no life in it. Melancholy and perpetual. Within the Altguish Inn, children scamper to the window, press it with noses and hands, then dash back to squash parental cheeks with frozen palms, before returning in some game with rules unspoken or unrequired, to stare out again at the splash of overwhelming rain on puddle.

I breakfast slowly, in part because it is so wet and I do not want to go outside and in part so that I can recover from the hangover. I also foolishly think that today's route will be easy, so there is no rush. In due course, I venture out and drive slowly to the start of the route up to *Am Faochagach* (the place of the shells) and wait in the car for the rain to stop, chatting through the window to the chap in the car next to me, with whom I had exchanged nods during breakfast.

Today is a day of rain, which drizzles and drones on as it patters and scatters on the metal of the car roofs. Grudgingly, we resign ourselves to it and set off together, heading uneasily towards the river that, according to most guidebooks, is 'often in spate'. It is indeed in spate, and although my walker friend of brief acquaintance tries to cross the river, I leave him to it and go around the head of the loch that feeds it. Quite a long detour, this means that I shall not be able to compare my day's speed with the quoted figures in the guidebooks, as I had started to do habitually – for reasons of safe planning rather than record breaking. I press on.

Today is a day of rain, annoyingly monotonous rain. On a clear day the summit would provide a wonderful vista including nearby Cona' Mheall's dramatic cliffs – nearly black since their east-facing aspect loses all sun after about 2pm, and over its shoulders to the Outer Hebrides of Harris and Lewis. But today is the driechest of days: the leaden clouds barely breached, by a meagre translucent glow to the south where the sun and a glen should be. I confess I am merely ticking off this hill, and am soon on my way back to the start, eventually crossing the river below the loch, despite its spatefullness.

Returning to the Inn, I find the other walker waiting (he is housed in the bunkhouse so has not been given a key to get in) and we chat idly as I drag my soaking rucksack out of the car. Reaching inside it to the safety pocket for the keys, I realise that the pocket is not zipped up.

'Nothing more worrying than a pack with an open zip,' I joke. But gradually and with increasingly frantic searching, the full horror of the situation dawns upon me: Oh My God, I am in trouble.

The plastic bag that had dropped out of my pack does not just hold the Inn's keys. It also contains my wallet and my mobile phone. I now have no money, no phone, no phone numbers, no bank account details, no passwords. The fellow walker very kindly offers to lend me £100, but that really is not going to solve the problem of the next five days' supposed holiday. And having just changed bank, I do not even remember the number of my new bank account.

Surely not worth going back, I think as I get back into the car and head back to the start of the route. The drizzle has set in again for the few remaining hours of daylight. I search the car park to no avail. *Surely not worth it*, I mutter as I start back along the day's route to the top of the mountain, following the path in reverse. *Surely not worth it*, I curse as I cross a kilometre of oozing boggy moorland and try to recall the exact point at which I had joined the main path on my return leg.

I make it back to the river. It is still rising; I search the bank, strip off, wade across, search the other bank, wade across the second strand of river, search, go up and down the river, my eyes scanning desperately. No luck. Re-cross the river, clothes on, back to the proper path. And suddenly, there, just lying on the soggy, boggy ground, is that plastic bag!

There are not many events that have made me suddenly thank God out loud, but this is one of them. To fully appreciate how lucky a man can be, check out grid reference NH 28007500, or paste 4°53'12.96'W 57°43'56.12'N into Google Earth to see the wilderness within which this treasure was found.

The northern Fannichs

I am still marvelling at yesterday's lucky find as I draw up to the start of today's walk, at a 90-degree bend in the A832 from which a short private track stretches out to Loch a' Bhraoin.

On the shores of this remote loch sits a wonderful old building that originally was a boat-house but which now appears to be inhabited. And understandably so, because from one window you could surely look down the length of the loch into the heart of the Fisherfield Forest, and from the other window gaze due south into the heart of the corrie complex, around which my route will take me.

The northern Fannichs circuit of five Munros skirts the rims of six corries, and after a steep climb I am soon inside an additional preparatory one! As on the day of my first Munro at Steall, I find I am seeking – and this time finding – a stalkers' path that clings to the inside bowl of the corrie. The risk of tipping down the slope is always present, and I wonder if I should have instead taken the more comfortable alternative ascent to

A' Chailleach (the old woman), which approaches the summit from the other side.

Dramatically changed from that of yesterday, the skies are a deep Scottish blue, and the ridge walk eastwards to *Sgurr Breac* (speckled peak) affords excellent views down into the deep dark corrie on one side, and away to the dark slug of Loch Fannich on the other. The ridge comes to quite an abrupt end, but so huge is the descent and then the ascent required to attain the next ridge that I think I must have gone astray.

Along this new ridge stretching from right to left in front of me rise the three Munros of *Sgurr nan Each* (peak of the horses), *Sgurr nan Clach Geala* (peak of the white stones) and *Meall a' Chrasgaidh* (hill of the crossing). From where I am standing, I have to drop 500 metres to a place so low that it is more valley than col, and then clamber up 300 metres without a path, at least not one I can see. By the time I reach and then traverse the next ridge, I understand why this collection of five Munros are usually tackled on two separate days.

The final stages of the return become quite a heathery affair, with bushy knee-high sprigs disguising stumbling-block and tripping-hollow alike. But good weather makes all the difference, and I have the occasional chirp of the black-throated divers to keep me company.

The Forge

Ten thousand years ago, the top of the mountain called An Teallach (The Forge) was almost certainly protruding above the surface of the glaciers of our last mini-Ice Age. The technical term for the mountaintop protrusion is *nunatak*: a word of Inuit origin that might come in useful for Scrabble if your competitors allow it.

Because An Teallach's summits stuck out like that, they were fractured by intense freezing, but not ground down by ice, and the summit range thus sports ten frost-shattered tops that exceed 3,000 feet in altitude, the highest two of which are designated Munros. You can complete the circuit of these peaks in either direction, and make it as easy or as hard as you wish: depending on your degree of bravery, you can gambol and teeter along the tops themselves, or just take the bypass paths.

I have moved to the Dundonnell Hotel for a few days, and after an early breakfast I leave through its back door and climb through the glen that leads to the ridge, on the top of which is the summit of *Bidein a' Ghlas Thuill* (peak of the green-grey hollow). The distance to the second Munro, *Sgurr Fiona* (white peak), is barely a kilometre, but the difference between their two vistas is vast.

The sun is just rising, and from the former summit I am treated to a diagonal view across the illuminated face of the An Teallach range proper. The auburn sunlight of a summer dawn strikes with a glancing blow the red and weathered rock-face, and it is clear why the Gaels named the range 'The Forge'.

And yet barely an hour later I am on the next peak looking down from a great height across the vast sweep of what is many people's favourite mountain playground: 80 square-kilometres of Fisherfield Forest, which we will visit shortly.

I hang around on Sgurr Fiona for about an hour as the newly-arrived clouds scud tantalisingly close to the tops and the horizon, but never quite clear them sufficiently for the award-winning photo.

The Magic Ground

I had viewed and re-viewed photographs of *Seana Bhraigh* (old uplands) many times during the previous months, intrigued for many reasons. First, the sound of its name, 'shenna vray', which even to a non-Gaelic speaker reeks of ancientness. Second, it sports immense cliffs that rise abruptly and assertively above a superb lochan. And third, its remoteness is challenging, with only three obvious routes of access, all of which are long and arduous.

In the end I opt for the approach that heads through Inverlael Forest, which I shall describe in a later trip. Suffice to say here that my path runs for about ten kilometres through forest and glen, and then gains height to reach an undulating plateau, still about two and a half kilometres from the summit.

There I reach a spot that is completely unlike anything I have seen before or since. It is as if the fairies had left their other home (see Schiehallion) and spent about 200 years laying out a 50-acre garden.

Oddly-shaped walls made of sloping sheets of stone, the sheets stacked one on the other, gradually lead up to ramparts of rougher and tougher cragginess. And within the hollow, a path winds around wee hummocks surely too high for a glacier to have dumped them there. All about are a thousand shades of green, some of hues so vibrant – despite the lack of sun – that they seem to have been mixed by enchantment. A Magic Ground indeed.

I wrench myself away and press on, shortly rewarded with the shelter of a stone windbreak right at the top of the ancient heights. One walker describes how from there he saw an eagle circling *beneath* his feet, and I can believe it. The drops are sheer and apparently unending, and I start to wish I had approached from the bottom of the corrie, from where I could have seen the cliffs better – although then I would have missed the Magic Ground!

Distracted by this excitement, I have failed to keep a close eye on the weather, and a cloudy front is now approaching fast. I turn and head for home, still ten kilometres away. Within ten minutes the weather worsens to storm-force winds, and it is by the slimmest of margins that I decide to keep to a last-minute added detour, to ascend *Eididh nan Clach Geala* (web of white stones).

I see the odd white stone or two underfoot but not much more. In a sense, this part of the trip is a waste of time. But as someone once quipped, 'to stand on all the Munros with a clear view requires more than one lifetime!'

The hill bagged, I make a quick descent down into the relative safety of the glen. I reflect on the fact that I am coming to terms with the wind and rain: I don't yet relish them but I can accept them, for I am getting 'cloud-free Munros' about two-thirds of the time, and consider myself lucky.

Fisherfield Forest

If from the roadside near Dundonnell you climb all six of the Munros in Fisherfield Forest (by the way, there are no remnants of a forest here, but the Gaels did apparently fish here in a field: Fisherfield), it will probably take you well over 12 hours, over 39 kilometres, and over three kilometres of *vertical* travel. Even from the bothy at Shenevall it's a very big day.

I set off from the roadside on a grey morning. It is not raining, but as the Scots say, 'there is just some water in the air'; less than drizzle but not quite dry. I am hoping to traverse the eastern ridge with its four Munros, and if possible go further to complete all six. In retrospect, it was never going to happen.

The first five kilometres are easy enough – despite the uphill slant, the origins of which I only afterwards understand (see Moine Thrust Zone). At the top of the slant is a vantage point from which to my right I can gape directly up to the pinnacles of An Teallach, and ahead can see straight up into the glen that cradles Loch an Nid. If one day you follow this route, do not linger too long here, however, for there is an even more stunning vista two kilometres ahead. From there, as you look north-west, your gaze tracks through a vast U-shaped valley that is 15 kilometres long. And although the valley is 1,000 metres deep, it is also an unbeliev-able six kilometres wide, scooped out by the granddaddy of all glaciers.

To top it off, the valley contains a perfect loch, fed by a meandering river, and on a wide meander sits the tiny white dot of Shenevall bothy. Perfect.

Though it is drizzling, the sun emerges. 'Foxes' Wedding,' I note. I cannot help a smile, since I have only recently learnt of the term, which means it is raining and sunny simultaneously. I had been searching for a small garden sculpture that a friend had wanted, showing the wedding of a fox. The internet search had as a by-product thrown up this meteorological term which, amazingly, has echoes in similar phrases across the planet from Arabic (rats' wedding) through Hindi (jackals' wedding) through Zulu (monkeys' wedding).

Below me, as expected, the river is in spate, and it is with difficulty that I cross even a subsidiary burn. On the other side, I spot a broken-off tree branch, and with lucky foresight take it with me. From a book on the outdoors I remember reading that a) river crossings are more hazardous than they look, and b) if you have a stout stick you can cross quite rapid rivers crab-style by using the stick as your third leg of a tripod. When I reach the main river, which drains Loch an Nid five kilometres farther up the glen, I execute the required technique and cross in safety, but breathe a sigh of relief that I had found that stick.

It is still morning, though it feels like evening as the leaden skies bode ill; and as I scale the smooth but steepish slopes of *Beinn a' Chlaidheimh* (hill of the sword) the wind picks up too. I grapple my way to the summit and the clouds titillate by lifting their hems, but not for long... I tough it out on the summit for a few minutes, but my Snickers bar and I soon retire quickly to a small lochan at the col that bridges to Sgurr Ban. The wind comes back vigorously.

In *The English Patient*, Michael Ondaatje famously recited the winds of the desert:

> There is a whirlwind in southern Morocco, the *aajej*, against which the fellahin defend themselves with knives. ... The alm, a fall wind out of Yugoslavia... These are permanent winds that live in the present tense... There is also the – [*sic*], the secret wind of the desert ...

I wonder grimly who has catalogued the winds of the hills. I soldier on.

The eponymous paleness of *Sgurr Ban* (pale peak) is caused by the white and grey of quartzite; that I know. That the quartzite presents itself in such extraordinarily large blocks, alas I did not know. Now, it is hard enough to see through spectacles continually re-spattered with gale-force driving winds. But to try crossing hundreds of paces over wet slippery two-metre blocks while wearing those glasses is complete folly.

Thus I arrive at my first and only termination of a trip. Fortunately I have a safety route pre-planned, and sodden but at least warmish, I lope mournfully down a minor corrie, to circle the top of Loch an Nid, thus avoiding the need to re-cross it lower down. My misery increases as my boots fill with water.

As I reach the river that I am to follow back to its meanders, I cast an eye towards the ridge I have just descended and fish out my camera to shoot a video. For the huge mountainside that fills my entire view is awash with sheets of water cascading down it – not in waterfalls, but in sheets hundreds of yards wide pouring down off sloping declines of rock many football pitches wide. I have never seen such volumes of unkettled water.

'This is Scotland just after Midsummer's Day,' I narrate. 'Do not return.'

I escape the valley late, in the end running back to the car so that I can get a phone signal and tell the proprietor of The Dundonnell Hotel not to send out a rescue party for me.

I head back home the next day – changing my train ticket at great expense, but grateful to feel the air temperature rise as I enter southern latitudes. Recalling my Fisherfield video, I vow never to return: southern climes, not northern climbs!

I forget all about the Munros… until seven months later, that is, when I find two walking buddies.

▲▲▲

How were the Caledonian mountains formed?

Walking into the Fisherfield Forest, up a gentle one-in-seven slope, you are passing a milestone in the history of geology, as well as a physical one.

For this is one of the places at which you can see the final lip of the Moine Thrust – the discovery of which in 1907 was to corroborate the theory of how Scotland's central mountains were made. The exploration of this Thrust Zone also helped confirm the broader theory of plate tectonics, first aired in 1912, and this area remains hallowed ground for geologists globally.

You will recall from a previous chapter that about half a billion years ago there was a three-plate pile-up of continents that, among other events, joined England to Scotland. This created a crumple zone – a huge mountain range that spanned North America, Scotland and Scandinavia.

That vast ancient range was named the Caledonides. But what of the more specific impact on Scotland?

After the initial pile-up, quakes continued to rumble on for about 20 million years. This activity comprised three eras, two of which determined the character of the Munros, and the first of which was the Grampian Event.

The Grampian Event

Lasting merely 15 million years, the Grampian collision was short-lived by geological standards, yet was one of cataclysmic proportions. As the Iapetus Ocean to the south of 'Scotland' finally closed, huge sheets of continental and oceanic crust were thrust underground at the Highland Boundary Fault and squeezed below the Central Highlands Terrane.

The impact was almost unimaginable. Take five sheets of warm plasticine of different colours. Then wring the package like a cloth a few times in opposite directions, then poke a stick upwards in a few places to reflect uprising magma. This will give you an idea of what was happening below Glencoe, Fort William, Braemar, and the whole Central Highlands Terrane. Stephenson and Gould in their *The Grampian Highlands* had a go at illustrating it. To see the masterpiece of visualisation please follow the link to it, in this book's Suggested Reading.

The old Dalradian sediments that had been deposited aeons ago were thus twisted and convoluted, to form fault lines that would become eroded into Glen Lyon, Loch Tay, and other valleys; and into mounds that would become hills like Schiehallion and Ben Alder.

In addition to this folding, lines of weakness allowed magma to well up, and some of our favourite mountains were formed from these intrusions: Ben Nevis and Glencoe, and broader mountainous tracts such as Glen Etive and the Cairngorms.

All this crustal folding and intrusion of magmas caused widespread metamorphism, which changed minerals to their cousins that have similar chemical composition but different physical properties. Just as diamonds and a pencil's graphite are both made from carbon atoms, albeit in differing atomic arrangements – so a whole range of other more complex chemicals can exist in different mineral forms. Garnet, for example, comes in six main types and the relative amounts of the different minerals in a location provide an important signature to local geological events and their timing.

And then there is the ophiolite. If you go to Ballantrae, you can still see the 'trapped finger' of oceanic crust, amputated as the Iapetus Ocean finally slammed shut! (Ballantrae is south of the Mull of Kintyre and across the Irish Sea from Belfast.)

The Scandian Event and the Moine Thrust Zone

In the three-plate pile up, Scandinavia collided with Scotland fractionally later than England had done. This second impact led to the event termed The Scandian, during which the north-west Highlands were shoved 100 kilometres up-and-over the north-western seaboard (the Hebridean Terrane).

Today we are sure this happened, but back in the late 1800s, there was less evidence. An acrimonious debate raged for decades. The grandee establishment figure, Roderick Impey Murchison, argued that the strange succession of rocks near the line of the Moine Thrust Zone was formed in a conventional way: newer sediments deposited upon older ones. His protégé Ben Peach, Peach's colleague John Horn, and others eventually proved this to be impossible. They went on to prove that the succession of rocks could only be explained by the thrusting of the one layer over the other. This made clear how rock beds that were physically lower down could actually be younger, rather than older, than the beds above them. Discovering and understanding the Moine Thrust were the first steps in proving the theory of plate tectonics.

The Scandian was also felt in other parts of northern Scotland, where many rocks, like their Central Terrane neighbours, were heavily metamorphosed.

The Acadian Event

The final jostling of the tectonic plates led to a third period of geological activity, though its main impact was felt mainly south of the Highlands.

As the ructions gradually subsided, the stage was now set for the Carboniferous period. The planet had already seen oceans of trilobites and corals, but soon there would be rivers full of fishes, and after the fishes, the increasingly luxuriant landscapes draped with the rest of the food chain right up to T. Rex.

▲▲▲

Monarch of the Glen

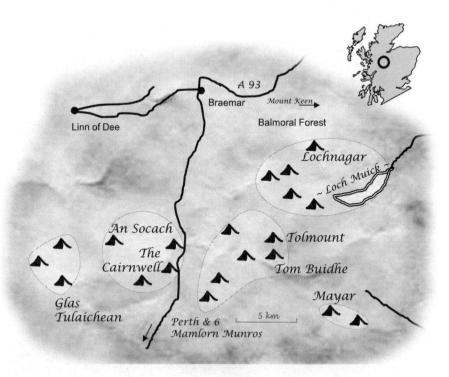

The Southern Cairngorms

CHAPTER 6

Lochnagar and Beyond

Oh! for the crags that are wild and majestic,
The steep frowning glories of dark Lochnagar.

LORD BYRON *Dark Lochnagar*

INTO THE CAIRNGORMS National Park you could simultaneously squeeze The Lake District, Dartmoor and Greater London. Or two Snowdonias and the Norfolk Broads. Or San Francisco, Cairo, Madrid, and Shanghai. The Cairngorms are vast.

In the southern half of this natural extravaganza lies the iconic Lochnagar and this next year, as I continue avidly on my mission, it makes for an excellent destination – particularly since the Cairngorms have routes that allow four, five and even six Munros to be traversed in a single day.

This first trip of the year is special for two reasons. Firstly, I have companions, and I am looking forward eagerly to the camaraderie on the hills – and in the pubs. Secondly, with a first route planned for 6 April, it is the earliest in the year that I have ventured out.

Neels will become one of my best friends, but at the time of planning the trip, he is more of an acquaintance. We had met only twice to discuss business in a low-key way, but on the first meeting I had learned he was intending to trek to Everest Base Camp, and by the next meeting he had been there and back. Hardy South African, nuclear scientist turned CEO and experienced trekker, he was up for a Munro or two.

Daniel is about seven feet tall and has explored extensively in his native Poland. Again, we had met informally through friends and stayed in touch periodically. He had been visiting me one day and asked about the maps spread out on the table. Two minutes later he had joined the team.

I am tempted to suggest we head for the famous Lochnagar, but that trip will have to wait until May, by which time the snow should largely have cleared. Instead our destination is the Mamlorn hills that lie about 70 kilometres north of Glasgow, and which fill in the line of the Highland Boundary Fault between the hills of Crianlarich and of Lawers that I climbed last year.

Irn-Bru

As a team we are united by focus and purposefulness, and on the day of our departure, we take the train to Glasgow, hire a car, dump our bags at the delightful Bridge of Lochay Hotel and are ready to walk by 1pm.

We have bonded as a team during our trip from London, and are in good cheer as we set off. We find the paths easy and easily, and make excellent progress for the first 600 metres of ascent.

Then, abruptly, it becomes apparent that early April in Glen Lyon is really winter. In the space of a mere five minutes clouds descend, winds pick up, and flakes of snow are flurrying past us. The weather deteriorates, and by the time we reach the top we rue our lack of crampons and ice-axes. I feel embarrassed that I had not anticipated the situation.

Despite the weather's atrocity we make it to the top of *Meall Ghaordaidh* (hill of the shoulder, possibly), Neels and Daniel celebrating their first Munro, I my first of that year, and my first in snow. It is vodka all round, courtesy of the secret consignment that Daniel has lugged up to the summit. But the icy wind and rime mean this is no place to loiter and we are soon off, finding a better line for the descent than on the way up.

Plastered in ice and sprinkled with snow, we cross the hotel's car park looking much more like three ghosts than three wise men. But a warm welcome hails from the hotel's bar where someone is bashing away at the piano, drinkers carouse, and a warm fire blazes. The door is stuck, and such is the depth of our thirst that we all three put our shoulders to the door at the same time. That is overkill, and with poor traction from iced-up soles, we lose our footing and spill into the bar, sprawling on top of each other on the floor.

The piano stops, the drinkers stop, the singers stop, even the dog stops slurping from its bowl. Everything just stops and stares at us in silence. This would be a tumble-weed moment, were there not snow outside. Then Neels rescues our pride, 'make that three pints of Tennents please, and an Irn-Bru for the dog.'

It is more fun walking with company!

Frost nip

As we debate which route to take today, breakfast as a team takes longer than a solo one, but is far more enjoyable. The weather is allegedly to be better than it was yesterday, so we select the circuit of the two Munros of *Creag Mhor* (big crag), and *Beinn Heasgarnich* (peaceful mountain).

The route up Creag Mhor offers excellent terrain as we start the climb, and offers wide panoramas too. Away across Glen Lochay, the rounded hilltops are sprinkled with light snow that eventually grades downwards to the dark, rich sienna-brown of the lower slopes. The chocolate cake ranges look edible!

But once again, as we near the summit ridge, winter sets in. Even in summer, you can plan on losing 10°C with every 1,000 metres you climb, and keep the change if you are lucky. With at least a foot of snow, and winds skirling, we find a large boulder and shelter behind it – though Daniel is more intent on angling his seven foot frame precariously into the wind to capture the stunning conditions on video.

We pause to discuss the conditions and the snow-covered route ahead, deciding to press on to the summit, but we decisively rule out a continuation to the so-called peaceful mountain Beinn Heasgarnich, four kilometres away.

Once over the summit, we continue to the grid reference advised for the start of the descent, and attempt to glissade down. In doing so, however, so much snow piles up between my legs that I suffered quite severe frost-nip. Though I feel no pain as we tramp through the peaty valley back to the car, the blue streaky marks along my inner thighs were to stay with me for several weeks. Fortunately, there are no further complications...

Jumping Blackberries!

I am glad that I have now installed into my Blackberry a detailed GPS mapping system, for without it we would not have found the summit of Beinn Heasgarnich, nor perhaps the way back.

We set off next morning for the huge massif. From near our base in Glen Lochay, a road runs over to the neighbouring Glen Lyon with its reservoir and dam, and we leave the car at the highest point of the intervening hills. As we cross undulating and sometimes boggy ground we are soon in snow and ice, as we had been yesterday.

Some mountains have pointed tops, and their summits are easy to find; or domed ones, in which case it may take slightly longer to find the summit in poor conditions. On other mountains, the summit lies on a ridge and can be found, at worst, by a full traverse of the ridge-line. But Beinn Heasgarnich belongs to a fourth class of mountain where the top is 'complex': it undulates, is grooved and furrowed, lures you to dead ends. Fortunately the Blackberry GPS serves its purpose well. Step by step, the coordinates of its digital readout clock up and eventually lead us to the true summit, though we are there treated to a white-out rather than a view.

It is perhaps to be anticipated, then, that on our return the handy device would jump of its own accord from my pocket as I am springing across a stream. I had heard of spontaneous combustion, but not spontaneous drowning; I would have to think of a good excuse to give the IT department. Fortunately the unit has served its purpose for the day.

The Highlands would claim further Blackberries before I had finished the round. My friends kept telling me to get a proper outdoor GPS unit, but a Blackberry will keep tracking for over 15 hours if you turn off the phone receiver, while a normal Garmin GPS or similar at that time was heavier and had a far shorter continuous tracking time.

Always carry Diclofenac

I am now walking solo again, since Neels and Daniel have completed their allotted three-day stay, and I decide to climb the Munros of *Meall Glas* (grey-green hill) and *Sgiath Chuil* (back wing), from Glen Dochart to their south.

Though a relatively easy stroll, the glaciated valley that intervenes between the two Munros means there is a demanding 300 metres to be lost and re-gained. It is a slog, but I make it to the top of the second Munro and pause for a quick bite.

I am often asked what I am thinking about as I walk, and enquirers are never really satisfied by the truth: that when walking on rough terrain most people are thinking of nothing other than placing each foot safely on the ground in front of the other one. The dangers of not doing so will be familiar to any experienced walker and I am reminded of this every three to four outings.

Descending Sgiath Chuil I suffer an extreme version of the lesson, for I fleetingly wonder merely, 'what shall I think about now?'

And that is sufficient. On innocuous ground that slopes only slightly I lose concentration for a split second. The heel of my boot gains traction on the grass, but the grass then loses its grip on the rock beneath. I slide a metre or so – or rather, most of me does. I should fall over, but unfortunately I just manage to maintain my balance – which leaves my left thigh extended in a position that it has not previously experienced. I badly pull a muscle in the front of my leg and my limp back to the road is severe. All very well near the bottom of this last hill of the day, but what if it had happened in the midst of one of my remoter walks?

That is why I try to think of nothing as I walk the hills, and why I now always carry Diclofenac: a fast-acting prescription anti-inflammatory drug.

The Silence of the Lambs

Some dismiss *Ben Challum* (Calum's mountain) as an uninteresting peak, and it is true that the path straight up and down from Strath Fillan is unremarkable – though I could not help lingering at the graveyard and wondering whether it matters (or not) to be buried in such a remote spot.

From its peak, however, the outlook over Glen Lochay is admirable. Though the surrounding hills do lack the gravitas and authority of the mountains further north, the wide and ranging glen guarded by its four sentinel Munros is an impressive and memorable sight on a clear and crisp afternoon.

On my way down I pause again opposite the graveyard, as the sun has come out and the air is warm and the breeze is still. I sit on a grassy bank as, from around a bend, a herd of ewes approaches. The lambing must have just finished, as the black and white collies cajole the ewes and the newborn lambs outside for perhaps their first time. Behind, a farmer paces with his crooked staff, and small boys tag along in imitation of the collies. The girls sit in a row on the worn little bench that rests against a whitewashed wall of the croft and point and giggle first at the collies and then at the boys.

* * *

Missing my companions and my now defunct Blackberry, I decide to head home a few days early – as usual paying ScotRail dearly for my change of plans.

▲▲▲

Clockwise or anticlockwise?

'Never walk a circuit anticlockwise,' warned the ranger at the Ben Nevis Information Centre, shaking his head slowly and looking very much like a Celtic Druid, 'for that way lies Destruction.'

Many routes across the Munros are circular rather than linear. For example, three-quarters of the 131 Routes that Cameron McNeish describes in *The Munros* involve some sort of circuit.

A circular route clearly raises the question of whether to prosecute it clockwise or anticlockwise. Even when guidebooks agree on a direction I have often found the opposite direction to be better, and there are good reasons – as well as flippant ones – why a party should make an explicit decision on direction before setting off.

Safety. Especially on long walks in uncertain weather, circulate so as to complete the hardest parts soonest.

Direction of cragginess. Most people do not climb the In Pinn up its sheer face and down its angled spine (though some have!). For some routes this consideration forces the decision.

Ascent / descent profile. Most parties prefer 'steps' up even if steep, and a more gradual descent for weary knees at the day's end.

Keeping boots dry and light. An extra pound on the foot is as heavy as an extra five pounds on the back: opt for the direction that keeps your boots driest and hence lightest for longest.

Ease of return. Some routes such as the circuit of the four Strathfarrar Munros require a walk, cycle, or lift back along a road. The likelihood of thumbing a ride, or ease of biking, may be a factor.

Best views. The South Glen Shiel Ridge, for example, is normally trodden from east to west along its crest, to take in views over Loch Duich, Knoydart and Skye (though some may prefer the other direction).

Clearest warning of impending weather. Occasionally I have walked the high level segment of a route in a direction that allowed me to see the approach of an expected weather front, without having to keep looking over my shoulder.

Wind at your back. Aim to walk along the ridge with the expected wind at your back. (In extreme wind, walk-in and out via the floor of the glen, ascending via a headwall for the summit only.)

Time of day. If the initial ascent is long and steep, for example, circulate in a direction that avoids the heat of direct sunshine at the start.

Watering holes. The need to re-fill water bottles and bladders may suggest the best direction.

Religious affiliation. Some religions favour clockwise (e.g. Hinduism), some anticlockwise (e.g. Islam), and some favour both (e.g. Taoism – with clockwise taking energy from the Universe, and anticlockwise giving it back).

Brain asymmetry of dopamine distribution in the mammalian brain. Studies in rats reveal a higher concentration of dopamine in the left side of the brain, biasing movement towards the right. Applying this theory to shopping for example, market researchers have suggested the retail outlets should guide shoppers in a clockwise direction (which they indeed typically do).

Leg asymmetry. Few of us have legs of exactly equal length. Those with longer left legs may favour clockwise, and *vice versa*. This seems identical to the haggis principle but is in fact a subtle variation of it. (For

Sassenachs: before being culled, some haggi live their lives traversing hills clockwise and hence have longer left legs (and *vice versa*).)

▲▲▲

In four years of climbing Scotland's hills, I have still not climbed a Cairngorm and in late May I put that right. As I am still decidedly in bagging mode, I calculate that the intended six-day trip should net me 21 Munros, up from my previous record of 16, in a trip the previous year.

By the Shank of Drumfollow

Glen Clova, 70 kilometres north of Perth, is a long lush valley with verdant meadows and lofty pines. All the flora there benefits from growing in the southern margin of the Highlands with its warmer climate and richer soils. The glen is also a little-used back door to the Cairngorms National Park, from which you can walk the whole way via Braemar to Aviemore.

Alongside the road that provides access to the glen, the unhurried driver can peer down at the meandering river, and guess as to the stock of fish therein. Further up, perched high above Glen Clova and its extension Glen Doll, two Munros peer out over the six corries squeezed into just a few kilometres of valley below: *Driesh* (bramble) and *Mayar* (plain, or possibly my delight).

I spend a pleasant half-day there, along tracks with names intriguing (Jock's Road) and resonant (Shank of Drumfollow), and through ample forests of conifer, bearing the scent of late spring. But these hills are really just a preamble to the other Munros that lie to the north of Glen Doll and south of Braemar.

An optional snout

Arriving in Braemar, 70 kilometres further north, I check into the Schiehallion Guest House and am immediately made welcome. This is to be my base for the next four days, but I am confused: why is a house that is situated miles from Schiehallion named after that hill? It turns out that the house was built by a man whose favourite hill was Schiehallion, and who had named all six houses he had built after the hill! Perhaps there are people even more obsessive than Munro-baggers.

Ten kilometres down the road south of Braemar, I reach the Cairnwell ski slopes. Without snow the area looks stark, scarred, and unkempt, but not nearly as bad as I had expected given what others had written regarding 'the hand of man on the hills'.

And anyway, once up the initial slope, the ridge-walking from *The Cairnwell* (hill of bags – from *Carn Bhalg*) to *Carn a' Gheoidh* (hill of the goose) is wonderful, snaking along above corries that face both north and south. The ridge is only three and a half kilometres long, as the crow or goose flies, but my legs notice the extra kilometre that the path's wiggles impose.

I now have a choice. I can either return to my starting point, or spend a few more hours on a route that doubles back along the ridge, and takes in an additional hill. On such a glorious spring day it seems a pity to miss it out, and I feel strong enough to include the optional extra destination. This involves an off-path traverse of yet another U-shaped valley, up to a quartzite ridge and along it to *An Socach* (the snout). I guess the Gaels spent a lot of time with pigs, since a 'glen of the pigs' appears on many a Highland map, and there are three Munros called 'the snout'.

The replaced Blackberry with GPS serves me well across the traverse. I do not strictly need it, so good is the visibility, but there is a river to be crossed and I want to hit the recommended spot precisely.

Once up on the quartzite ridge, the vast extent of the high Cairngorm plateau becomes apparent. Clearly visible about 20 kilometres to the North, though still covered in snow, are five of the six highest mountains in Britain, including Ben Macdui (whose summit is a mere 40 metres lower than that of Ben Nevis). These mountains do not soar as the West Coast ones do, rather the intervening chasms lend them shape as they swoop and cut through the glacier-scarred tableland.

Returning across the valley and past a small lochan, I reach *Carn Aosda* (hill of age) and civilisation close below. On the way I am already contemplating tomorrow's outing and the highlight of the week's trip.

Lochnagar

Queen Victoria bought Balmoral in 1852 and would spend up to four months a year there after the death of Prince Albert. Thus was established the Royal presence in the southern Cairngorms. Lochnagar is the closest Munro to Balmoral, just ten kilometres away, and, not surprisingly, a favourite of Prince Charles and Camilla. I have met several walkers who have bumped into the royal couple there; all agree that they are charming and engaging conversationalists.

Technically, Lochnagar is a ridge rather than a peak, and its highest point is *Cac Carn Beag* (little hill of the faeces – though most books are demure and refer to the name of the Lochnagar ridge instead of the hill).

From the east end of Loch Muick, I set out on the 26-kilometre circuit of Lochnagar and the four further Munros that surround it. This loch is not so much a jewel of a loch – it is more of a vast and glittering Koh-i-Noor diamond of a loch. Queen Victoria even had her own secret bothy on its shores. It is strange that the name of such a beautiful loch should mean 'loch of the pig'.

My circuit is to include Lochnagar and four further Munros, and I set out in an anti-clockwise direction, mainly to arrive as soon as possible at Lochnagar, in case the weather deteriorates. The approach is via a wonderful pastoral walk at loch level, replete with herds of deer that look surprisingly tame, and then up a curving path into the folds of the mountains.

This area boasts many breasts! For the path winds around a minor peak called Meikle Pap (big breast), opposite which is Little Pap, and close by is Coire na Cìche (corrie of the breast). Although many hills do look fairly breast-shaped, the appellation does seem over-represented across Scotland!

With little warning the corrie, crags, and cliffs of dark Lochnagar appear over the crest of a ridge and this process of revelation undoubtedly adds to their impact. The black sheer face of Lochnagar rises grimly and resolutely from the even blacker lochan that echoes its name. Whether blackened by intense weathering, or merely darkened by its northerly aspect that ensures it sees no sun – or perhaps the combination of these factors – the rocks arrest even the casual observer. The chiaroscuro of white snow on black rock creates an even starker effect.

Mounting the edge of the corrie upon The Ladder – the disguised steps laid out for Queen Victoria – I reach Cac Carn Beag and loiter for a while to take in yet again the vastness of the Cairngorms National Park.

Then I am off, over the undulating plateau to *Carn a' Choire Boidheach* (hill of the beautiful corrie), *Carn an t-Sagairt Mor* (big hill of the priest) with its remains of a crashed aircraft, *Cairn Bannoch* (peaked hill), and finally *Broad Cairn*. The final stretch home is still a further eight kilometres, but in perfect conditions I am not complaining. The last section of the path boasts a magnificent view down over Loch Muick to Queen Victoria's royal lochside bothy, Glas-allt Shiel.

A bike missed

Straggling an hour to the east of Braemar is *Mount Keen* – the easternmost Munro and named from the Gaelic *caoin* meaning gentle, smooth, pleasant, or beautiful. The hill does show all of these attributes, but Lochnagar is a hard act to follow. I walk rather than cycle the 24 kilometres of approach and exit alongside the Water of Tanar, and after

seeing two people who have taken bikes right to the top of the hill, I wish
I had too.

The braes and burns have an easy pastoral beauty, but I am saving my
full attention and energies for the bigger day tomorrow.

A long tour

Some people say it is a con: the circuit of six Munros to the south-east
of Lochnagar that traverses *Creag Leachach* (slabby crag), *Glas Maol*
(green-grey hill), *Cairn of Claise* (hill of the hollow), *Tom Buidhe* (yellow
hill), *Tolmount* (hill of the valley), and *Carn an Tuirc* (hill of the boar).

Those who say it is a con claim that these hills are not really Munros
and point out that the whole round includes only 1,100 metres of ascent
– an average of a paltry 200 metres per hill. Their naysayers point out
that even after reaching the plateau there is over 100 metres of ascent on
average between the hills. Either way it promises to be a big day, as the
route extends over nearly 30 kilometres – assuming you don't manage to
hitch a lift for the last stretch back to the car.

I start from the ski centre car park at The Cairnwell, forgoing other
routes that start a kilometre to the south. The ascent is a pleasantly
winding track that eventually steepens and rises up a vertical kilometre
onto the southern Cairngorm plateau.

The day provides a brilliant gallery of Cairngorm scenes: great sweeps
north-west to the even higher, snow-capped hills of the Cairngorm
plateau proper; great cleft valleys and corries, the more imposing for their
ice-sculpted roundness, and views that are miles long over wind-stunted
grass, across which my route treads.

I had hoped to hitch a lift back to the car at the end of the route, but this
proves to be false optimism, and I plod the extra four kilometres on foot.

A last-minute addition

On this trip, my second of the year, I have already trodden 115 kilometres, yet I am still looking forward to just one more day on the hills
before returning southwards.

To climb *Glas Tulaichean* (green-grey hillocks), and *Carn an Righ*
(king's hill) I start as most people do from Spittal of Glenshee, which lies
on the road from Braemar down to Perth.

The route up the glen to the first top is straightforward. Nicely graded,
it makes full use of a disused railway line that once took guests and victuals
to the old lodge, the ruins of which stand defiantly before you.

Visibility on the summit is nought, but the GPS saves me useless roaming and I make it to the cairn. There I am joined by two other walkers – fit youngsters on vacation from the Royal Bank of Scotland, with whom I tag along until we reached the second top, much of the time in mist.

I then decide to add a peak to the route since it will not create much of a detour. My map does not extend to *Beinn Iutharn Mhor* (hill of the edge), but my trusty GPS map does. It is not too far away so on this occasion I take the risk of going without a paper map (NB: ALWAYS take a hard-copy map that is waterproof or in a waterproof container). I cannot see much through the mist, but later, back at home, I realise that this addition has been a lucky one. For the only other realistic route to climb that hill involves walking four kilometres over the boggiest peat I have heard described.

I circumnavigate a few hillocks and return down a long glen that extends ten kilometres or more, and as I start talking to myself I realise it is time to go home!

* * *

Thus ends my ninth trip to Scotland's hills. With the two large circuits of this expedition I am surprised to see that I have now climbed 86 Munros. I am still not presuming I shall get around them all, but a single trip to add a further 14 Munros will bring me to a nice round tally of 100, and there are worse ways to spend five days...

▲▲▲

Shock and Awe: the legacies of volcanic activity

Lochnagar, the vast high Cairngorm plateau, Glencoe, Ben Nevis, Skye: many of Scotland's most dramatic landscapes owe their origins to great upwellings of volcanic and plutonic rock.

Of the Cairngorms, Nan Shepherd says,

> the plateau is the true summit of these mountains; they must be seen as a single mountain, and the individual tops, Ben MacDhui, Braeriach and the rest, though sundered from one another by fissures and deep descents, are no more than eddies on the plateau surface. One does not look upwards to spectacular peaks but downwards from the peaks to spectacular chasms.

Like the bubble in one of those hot-oil lamps from the 1960s, boiling magma had welled up through fault-lines that had been stressed and flexed by colliding plates (the three-plate pile up of tectonic activity 400 million years ago). In the vast triangle between Fort William, Aberdeen and Inverness, and to a lesser extent beyond this, plutons rose and solidified into vast nodules of hard granite that have flouted erosion in the Cairngorms and beyond.

In some places the intrusions became extrusions: towering volcanoes spitting and spewing lavas that remain as some of the rocky faces of Glencoe, Ben Nevis, and even of the most northerly Munro, Ben Hope.

It is impossible to imagine the scale of some of these volcanoes. Geologists now rate events using the Volcanic Explosivity Index (VEI). The ancient eruption at Mount Vesuvius, and the more recent one at Mount St Helens in the USA, spewed up about one cubic kilometre of rock, giving them a VEI rating of five. The Krakatoa eruption was ten times bigger, with a rating of six. The Thera explosion that destroyed the ancient Minoan civilisation was ten times bigger again at a rating of seven. And it is thought that the Glencoe volcano may have spewed out ten times more rock than that: over 1,000 *cubic kilometres* of rock; almost enough to trigger a global volcanic winter.

There are volcanic landscapes of more recent creation, too. One day a friend and I had paddled across Skye's Loch Scavaig, silent and still in the morning cool, and dragged our kayaks up into Loch Coruisk ('Cauldron of Waters'). Vertical, sheer, the rocks frowned down upon us, and we trespassers wondered whether that was their perpetual demeanour, and if so for how many millions of years they had kept it up. Those rocky slants, created in a later volcanic era, are more poetically described by George and Peter Anderson of Inverness in their 1850 travel guide:

> The Bay of Scavaig, into which Loch Coruishk discharges itself, is a scene of almost unexampled grandeur; and, being less confined than the latter, presents an interesting difference of character. It is flanked by stupendous shivered mountains of bare rock, which shoot up abruptly from the bosom of the sea. They are of a singularly dark and metallic aspect, being composed of the mineral called hyperstein. On the left are three shattered peaks: – Garbshen, or 'the shouting-mountain', Scuir-nan-Eig, 'the notched peak', and Scuir Dhu, 'the black peak'; and on the opposite side is a similar and very high hill, called Scuir-nan-Stree, 'the hill of dispute', or 'the debateable land'. A little island at the base of Scuir-nan-Stree is styled Eilan-nan-Lice, 'the island of the slippery step', from a dangerous pass in the face of the rock, which makes it imprudent in a stranger to visit these scenes by land.

These great mountains, and others that lie along a huge north-south arc from the Faroe Islands to Arran, and on to Ailsa Craig, are also born of tectonic shifts. Those shifts date back a mere 65 million years and so are far more recent than the shifts that led to the Caledonian plutons and volcanoes.

Scotland at that time was literally sandwiched between Norway on one side, and the plate that would become North America on the other. Wedged onto the northern margin of both land masses was the plate that would become Greenland. Deep rumblings started to force these plates apart, hot magma shooting up between the plates and into (and sometimes through) any existing land that was sufficiently faulted.

The magma is still bubbling up – though now, of course, the active margin lies at the bottom of the mid-Atlantic trench, which has been opening since the start of its journey at a rate of four centimetres per year. (Scientists have dated and hence paced the expansion by matching the stripes of alternating magnetic polarity that run down both sides of the mid-Atlantic crest.)

Yet for 12 million years that explosive margin lay on Scotland's northwest coast. This was the laying of the foundation stones of Skye's Black Cuillin in grippy gabbro and smooth basalt, when the roots of the Red Cuillin welled up in plutonic blobs to become coarser granite, and when lava spewed out in Skye, Mull and beyond to form vast flat headlands. In addition to the pyrotechnics, less dramatic but more pervasive upwellings saw the intrusion of dykes and sills that in their dotage were to become mere Tourist Paths up Ben More in Mull, or jointed and weathered relict walls at which generations of school children on science outings would stare dutifully (or not).

'Remember: gabbro is good and basalt is bad,' said my guide during my first excursion on the Cuillin ridge. This meant that gabbro is rough and grippable whereas basalt is smoother and more slippery. I did remember his advice and was eventually to discover why it was true: basalt was originally extruded out into the air, cooling and solidifying quickly into a kind of glass, while gabbro was of the same raw materials, but had remained buried. The gabbro cooled more slowly, allowing time for larger crystals to form and a rougher texture to develop.

While later Ice Ages would create the detail of arête and corrie on Skye, Mull, Harris and beyond, the essential character of the landscape was set by the igneous bedrocks of this magmatic arc, laid down long before the ice came.

▲▲▲

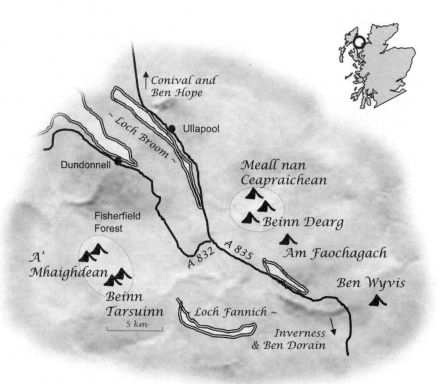

The North-West, South of Ullapool

CHAPTER 7

The Utter North

From the lone shieling of the misty island
Mountains divide us, and the waste of seas –
Yet still the blood is strong, the heart is Highland,
And we in dreams behold the Hebrides.

CANADIAN BOAT SONG

I SMOOTH OUT the colourful A3 map of Scotland that serves as my overview of where to go next and survey the great expanse of *terra incognita* that covers its northern third.

The ancient landscapes that are older than life itself are remote and hardly populated, apart from along its thin shoreline. 'Here be dragons,' the map should state, or as the Romans wrote on their maps of Scotland: *hic sunt leones* – here be lions.

A return to Scotland's north appeals for several reasons. Firstly, it is now mid-June, and long days can be used to good effect in northern latitudes. Secondly, I want to settle a score with the elements and gods regarding the previously aborted circuit of Fisherfield Forest, and the advent of High Pressure over the whole country promises sun. A productive tour will also allow me to have visited all the Munros north of Loch Maree. Such logic is becoming a hallmark of my choice about where to go next – it is spurious logic but at least vaguely convincing.

A Wet Orchy

Whenever I have been to Bridge of Orchy, about 80 kilometres north of Glasgow, it has been raining. This time is no exception, despite the fine forecast, and as I finish stop for lunch en route to the Far North. And as I set off up boggy slopes, the rain threatens to turn to hail. I must confess that the ascent to the bealach that sits between *Beinn Dorain* (hill of the small stream) and *Beinn an Dothaidh* (hill of the scorching) is feeling like a slog.

The rain has transcended the local vocabulary, from smirr to dreep, from plowtery to gandiegow, from pish-oot to sump, from attery to thunder-plump. In worsening weather I dump the pack at the bealach for greater speed, flip an imaginary coin, and turn right to head for Beinn Dorain's top. With no visibility to manage my expectations along the ridge walk of two and a half kilometres, it takes longer than I anticipate. And on the return, I am beset all round by little gullies, having strayed into unfamiliar terrain.

Correcting my course, I regain the bealach (and my sandwiches), then head up the other hill. It is boggier, it is wetter, and it is windier. I claim the cairn and descend quickly, glad to reach the warmth of the car. So much for summer! Friends sometimes ask why I bother to go out when it is raining – I reply that Scotland's fabled 'four seasons in a day' means you might as well go out – even if it is wet when you start. On balance, my optimism has paid off.

I have not booked a bed for the night, since I was unsure of how long the combination of driving from London and climbing the hills would take. But my friends Dario and Lesley at the Altguish Inn past Inverness are able to offer a last-minute room, and are kind enough to accept my return at 11pm.

The Inn, lying between Inverness and Ullapool, would be my base for the next week, apart from planned visits to the lands far to the north.

Gale-y goalie

The huge sprawling mass of mountain called *Ben Wyvis* (*Glas Leathad Mor*, hill of terror) is the first line of defence from the north-easterly gales which can blow in from the North Sea, as they did on the day of my visit. The range lies sprawled at an angle like an ice-hockey goalie trying without success to stop the Cromarty Firth scoring a cold and windy goal.

But don't let me discourage you; despite the wind I find this to be a grand circuit, starting through Nature Reserve woodlands, climbing high above a wonderful broad deep glen and, after gales on the summit, offering a descent through enormous sweeping braes that flank a farther glen.

It is just a pity that, to assure a clear view from the top, you would have to go and live in Inverness and head out at the first sign of guaranteed good weather. The fifth time you do that you might strike lucky…

The famine wall

You may recall that almost exactly a year previously, I had walked up alongside the River Lael, on to Seana Bhraigh, and during my return included a trip up Eididh nan Clach Geala in wet and windy conditions in which I could see nothing at all. Now I am returning to Inverlael to take in three neighbouring Munros, in what promise to be better conditions.

I should have used a bike, for on this excursion I have to go all the way to the top of the glen that the River Lael has carved – a good ten kilometres even before the serious uphill work begins. The first stretch is through forest – or rather, through lumbering activity of industrial scale. But once the farthest plantation gate is passed, the valley opens up to reveal slopes that tower 300 metres above you: to the left, smooth and vegetated inclines; to the right, craggy vertical rock-faces set firm and unwelcoming.

I now reach the first segment of the upward path, and it brings me to a high, rocky table-top area at about 850 metres in altitude, around half a kilometre square, and home to three small lochans. If you too follow this route, you will reach the source of the River Lael, and having tracked it from sea to summit, can claim to have bagged a Highland river – perhaps your first.

From this hub I take three spoke-like routes, the first to *Meall nan Ceapraichean* (hill of the stubby hillocks) where the mists are still tantalisingly close to lifting but still too low to allow a view. Back to the hub, I then climb *Cona' Mheall* (joining hill) up scree slopes to its summit. The air has cleared now, to expose little Loch Tuath, overshadowed by the massive bully of a curtain wall behind it.

Again I return to the table-top and segue around its edge, to reach the steep rocky steps that lead up to the top of *Beinn Dearg* (red hill). If there were a competition for the most spectacular dry-stone wall in Britain, then the one up and along Beinn Dearg would surely win. About three kilometres long, it rises to two metres high in many places and is about one metre thick. These hundreds of tons of rock have been man-handled into place, to build a wall, the altitude of which never falls below 800 metres. Even more remarkable is the fact that this and other 'famine walls' across Scotland were built by men living off a meagre 650 grams of oatmeal a day, as the government and a few benevolent landlords tried to tide crofters over the potato famines of the 1840s. Nominally to demarcate land and prevent the straying of sheep, the famine wall was the ultimate version of what happens when an 'odd job' meets 'spending your way out of a recession'.

About to return down the glen, I am suddenly accosted by two elderly ladies armed with stout walking sticks and stouter brogues. We strike up conversation and they say that, rather than go straight back down, it will be far better if I take the route that slopes gradually down the long ridge – the one that forms the edge of the hill and overlooks the glen, and that eventually drops down easily to join my route of approach.

I follow their advice. But as I near the end of the ridge I find no alternative but to slither – kicking and screaming – down several hundred metres of heathery and rocky slope. I feel that their idea of 'dropping down easily' was far different from mine, or perhaps they belong to that breed of bionic pensioner to be found wandering the hills when their families say they should be playing bingo instead.

For Queen and Clearance

The next day I head north to climb two of Scotland's most northerly Munros. About *Ben Klibreck* (from *Cleith Bric*, hill of the speckled cliff) itself, there is not much to say: a flattish walk to a lochan, a very steep slope up to the ridge along a path that I am grateful to find, and a short walk to the summit cairn.

But two specific views from the top intrigue me. Twenty kilometres to the north is Ben Loyal (so-called 'Queen of Scottish Mountains'). In aerial perspective, its coronet-like silhouette is an attractive mauve-blue, and I wonder whether I should instead be climbing that non-Munro rather than Ben Klibreck. I am still firmly in Munro-bagging mode, however, and conclude that the best picture of the Queen is probably from a respectful distance rather than from a perch upon her shoulder.

Just visible 25 kilometres due east are the upper reaches of the Strath of Kildonan. This is the setting for Neill Gunn's classic *Butcher's Broom*, in which he portrays with vivid and heart-rending eloquence the later stages of the Highland Clearances of the 18th and 19th centuries.

▲▲▲

The Highland Clearances

There are few events more tragic than those that were visited upon the Highland folk as they were cleared from their lands.

Families lost their freedoms, not in battle against some powerful foe, but via lawyering and bullying to sate the sneaky greed of those who had for generations been their respected kinsfolk and elders. Sons did not lose their mothers to infirmity, nor their sweethearts to rival lovers, but to the threatening sword and staff of an English government for whom those sons were now off fighting in distant lands. Children lost the roofs over their cots not through storm and tempest, but as they were thrown out on snowy nights: their homes destroyed, and roof-timbers burnt to make the long walk to the coast more attractive to their parents than the prospect of re-building with worn-out tools. This was not quite ethnic cleansing, though the Catholics suffered worse than others – it was economic cleansing, but it tasted no better.

In looking for the roots of this inglorious story, we are led into a matrix of events political, religious, military, technological, and economic.

The political rumblings had started with The Tenures Abolition Act 1660. Across Britain this Act marked a shift away from feudalism, towards a greater fealty required to the Crown, and towards the introduction of national taxation. For Scotland, this meant in theory the end of feudal loyalty to the clan chief. Most crucially, it saw the chief's role start to degenerate from that of leader to that of landlord.

A few chiefs with allegiances to the south sensed which way the wind was blowing and started to cultivate and curry favour with those they thought were in the ascendant. Most, however, were roused to rebellion, further inflamed when James VII of Scotland and II of England was deposed. James had originally unified the two countries' Parliaments, but with his pro-Catholic and anti-Protestant position increasingly clear, influential peers invited William of Orange to assume the throne in his stead, and James was forced into exile.

This of course led to the Jacobite movement, which aimed to re-install James, and then his heirs, as monarch of Scotland and England; and predictably that ratcheted up England's resolve to suppress its neighbour. Thus, after the 1715 Jacobite Uprising, General Wade was despatched north to build the roads (250 kilometres of them) and bridges (more than 40 of them) to allow access for English forces. When this infrastructure was used against its constructors by the returning Bonnie Prince Charlie and his forces to strike to within 200 kilometres of London, the English backlash was more decisive, leading to the establishment of Forts William and Augustus, and further military strongholds.

Some Highland folk had already started emigrating to North America. But it was a surge in the demand for food, and the prospect of greater riches through using new agricultural technologies, that drew the avaricious chief-turned-landlord to evict his own clansmen in ever larger numbers.

Southern appetites were growing in line with the increased affluence of the Industrial Revolution, and with the hunger of an Army at war on many fronts. Growing demand, coupled with the new technologies of improved animal feeds, and new practices such as the outdoor wintering of sheep, vested each acre of glen with much greater value than a simple crofter could ever return. In the rhetoric of the time, the unproductive crofts were merely wasting the land. As the Lady of Lawers, with her gift of Celtic 'second sight' had foreseen 150 years earlier, the land will first be sifted and then riddled of its people... The jaw of the sheep will drive the plough from the ground... The homes on the Lochtayside will be so far apart that a cock will not hear its neighbour crow.

The expulsions of the Highlanders escalated during the mid-19th century and the potato blights and famines made life harsher still. Under the banner of agricultural improvement, many tens of thousands of men, women and children were eventually displaced, brutalised, deported, sold into servitude abroad, or killed by Factor, Constable and Sherriff emboldened by a newly-drawn lease and the Riot Act. The lyrics of the Canadian Boat Song illustrate the lament of those who would never again see their lone shieling upon their misty Hebridean island. At last the vested interests were content: the lands were clear now for the sheep, and later for the deer and gun. Crofters would be later afforded greater security through various Acts of Parliament, but their forbears' ruined homes, strewn across the Highlands, are the crumbling bookends that remind us of the tragic personal stories that they once framed.

▲▲▲

As far as you can go

Half a billion year ago, hot magma welled up beneath a fault-line that now runs through *Ben Hope* (mountain of the bay). Its hard resilient rock withstood the erosion that later stripped the neighbouring land, leaving us with this northern-most Munro.

At the crossroad village of Altnaharra, there is a road sign that points with optimism and encouragement to 'Hope'; surprisingly, no joker has yet attached one pointing in the opposite direction to 'Despair'. I follow the sign and soon sense an imposing sill of rock crowding out the sky on my right-hand side. It is no surprise therefore to arrive at the start of the route and immediately to encounter a no-nonsense climb that zigzags steeply up the cliffs of that rocky outcrop.

Quickly I am rewarded with an excellent vista across some of our most archaic landscapes – down the wide strath that leads to Loch Hope and Loch Eriboll to the north-west, and if I had better eyesight and could see around corners, to the Faroes, Iceland, and Greenland. Some people climb Ben Hope up its steep north face, and as I edge gingerly to the northern margin of the summit arena and peer over the edge, I am glad that I have not arrived from that direction.

Inevitably, a clammy mist starts to close in and I race the cloud-base down the hill: knowing that I shall be sleeping in the back of the car tonight, I am determined to stay dry.

Rocks of Ages

In search of the stump of another ancient volcano to climb, I drive across the top of the country, past Cape Wrath, and southwards down the coast of Sutherland to Inchnadamph. I awake to a grey and drizzling day in Scotland's far north-west. But despite the conditions, I am not yet complaining, because the windscreen of my improvised accommodation frames a superb picture of Castle Ardvreck not 100 metres away, and the stretch of Loch Assynt beyond.

The walk up to *Conival* (from Cona' Mheall, joining hill) proceeds on a gradient that steadily increases, winding alternately left and right up the luscious Gleann Dubh. Eventually I reach the track that climbs more purposefully up to a wee lochan, heralding the start of the short further ridge to the first summit and beyond. The views are once more obscured by cloud, but there is plenty to keep the mind occupied. For the ridge to *Ben More Assynt* (big mountain of Assynt) requires in a few places a sure foot and good forward momentum; teetering and hesitation are not recommended. I do, however, think others have been too flattering to this ridge when they compare it to the Aonach Eagach in Glencoe. This ridge is not as hard, though in winter conditions would be a serious proposition.

As I reach the end of the ridge, the clouds rise for an instant, and I realise I am standing on the highest point of a landscape that looks prehistoric – and indeed is. From here you are looking across a billion years to the Lewisian gneiss, but even if you knew nothing about geology, you would surely know this landscape was older than the Ice Ages. Three times older than the dinosaurs even, created before the first dinosaur was even a twinkle in an amoeba's eye... for this land was laid down hundreds of millions of years before the first saw life.

There is apparently a good route back down a craggy path which skirts the loch to the south of the hill, but mist and rain are closing in, and I return via the quicker path of my ascent.

With the heater at full blast and all vents covered with wet clothes, I head 25 kilometres south to attend to some unfinished business.

The Best View in Scotland

I mentioned that, on Midsummer's Day last year, a storm had forced me off Sgurr Ban and chased me out of Fisherfield Forest. I am determined to return now: not merely out of revenge, but also because one of the remaining hills promises what many call 'the best view in Scotland'.

The four Fisherfield hills that remain to be climbed are inconveniently spread out, and require either a two-day journey or an extremely long one-day expedition. With the weather now suddenly set fair, I opt for the one-day version, particularly because this will be a Munro-bagging challenge *par excellence*.

At 8am, leaving my improvised car accommodation at the dog-leg bend of the A832, I set off on what is to be the longest continuous walk in my Munro-bagging experience. The sky is already light, and I happily tramp the four kilometres along the delightful Loch a' Bhraoin, heading into the folds of the mountains ahead. Reaching the bothy at the end of the loch, the path becomes rougher, and evidence of a past Ice Age is evident as I am routed through channels excised by melt-waters ancient and modern. Rounding a turn in such a channel, I suddenly spy a cow blocking my path, and on closer inspection it turns out to be a bull. I remember the bull running in Pamplona, and now feel I am heading the wrong way up a one-way meltwater gully.

I climb discretely up the grassy side of the channel, which is only 3-4 metres high, only to find that I am right on the margin of a vast herd of bovines, most of which appear to be bulls and some of which – even from a kilometre away – sport bulging musculature. I skirt the herd but throughout the day the nagging vision returns of having to make my way back at night through their valley; there is no other way…

I press on to make the straightforward but lengthy climb up the steep flanks of *Mullach Coire Mhic Fhearchair* (peak of the corrie of Farquhar's son), and from there via a reasonably easy, if stony, connection to *Beinn Tarsuinn* (transverse hill). This hill has an extraordinary 'landing pad' of completely flat and almost level rock about several football pitches in extent, with sheer drops on all sides. Upon this table-top I spread out my lunch and take stock: five hours gone, ten remaining.

Resuming my trek, I try for the line of least descent down to a col then up to *A' Mhaighdean* (the maiden). As an etymological aside: although the Gaelic and English words *look* similar, the Gaelic is pronounced 'uh vay-jin' – almost identical to 'virgin'. It seems that the Gaelic has frozen the precise point at which the words 'maiden' and 'virgin' have morphed.

I reach A' Mhaighdean up fairly easy grassy slopes, and count my blessings as the sky is cloudless and I know what is in store over the crest of the hill, since I have seen it many times in other people's photographs.

But even the photos cannot prepare me for the stunning picture out to the west. Fionn Loch sparkles white as its name requires of it, separated by only the merest filament of causeway from its nemesis Dubh Loch (black loch). A knobbly limb curves down there from my summit's right-hand side, and on the other side rise high peaks – some named and some anonymous. Beyond Fionn Loch glints the thin streak that is Loch Awe; and farther away the darkened rim of horizon that is Harris joins the sky. Farther still, but beyond sight and at the very edge of memory, must be the island of St Kilda, 100 kilometres even from Harris. And then nothing – just icy ocean, all the way to Newfoundland.

But more spectacular still is the dappled pattern of the vast lochscape. Dark pools in ancient hollows: small puddles here, larger lochans there, all joined up into some elaborate fractal medley that somehow just emerged; became.

I spend an hour here, and eventually tear myself away to the final hill of the day, *Ruadh Stac Mor* (big red stack). There are several ways up, and I take the most popular one, which inevitably is the most eroded. The path is navigable and can be scrambled up to reach the top, though I am careful to keep track of the way-marking cairns: I would not want to have to find the path of descent in mist.

The weather is holding up well, but it is now 6pm and I still have a long way to go: four kilometres back to the base of Beinn Tarsuinn, a further six contouring around Tarsuinn's outer flanks – probably through heather – and then a further five back to and through that herd of bulls.

By the time I reach their territory, the bulls have fortunately scattered to the higher hillside, and I live to tell the tale. After 15 hours, 45 kilometres travelled horizontally, and nearly three kilometres of vertical ascent, I reach my in-car bed and at 11pm, with the sky still light, fall immediately and utterly to sleep.

I dream of my revenge on the bulls, little knowing that I will reap it conclusively in several years' time as I eat one of them (while staying with the herd's owners in Inverlael)!

* * *

Those vistas of incomparable beauty are a fine way to end my trip, and my tally of Munros has soared to 100. I am in full-swing collecting mode, but little do I suspect that my next visit to the hills will have to be so brutally aborted.

▲▲▲

Older than life as we know it

The Cambrian Period is the great dividing line of prehistory: from before then we have only rocks, from after then we have rocks and life. Named after the Latin for Wales – where the first fossil evidence of ancient life was discovered – the Cambrian started about half a billion years ago.

But for two and a half billion years before that, the Earth's mantle and crust had been slowly churning away, powered by the heat of its core. And of course if you heat a blob of viscous fluid from its centre, you can't have the 'hot air rises' phenomenon happening *everywhere* on the blob's surface: something's got to give. The result is a vast swarm of creeping, circulating, synchronised cells – with liquefied mantle broiling slowly up in some places and churning slowly down in others. Viewed from the surface all we see are 'plates' in motion – born on one margin and destroyed on the other. But beneath, all is circulating.

Within the Mordor-like zones of broiling and churning, huge pressures and temperatures for aeons wreak acts of creation and destruction. Rocks that once lay at the surface and were eroded, weathered, and deposited are now folded, fractured, sheared and crushed: clay to schist, sandstone to quartzite, granite to gneiss. All this churning resulted in a patchwork of mini-plates called 'terranes', at the edge of the vast tectonic plate called Laurentia.

Beneath what is now the Hebridean Terrane of Lewis, Harris, Skye and the far north-west of Scotland, these processes created the rock-bottom of all basement layers – the Lewisian Complex of gneiss.

Churned, shot through from below with igneous injections and re-churned, these tough timeworn metamorphosed rocks are the old boot-leather of geology. And when exposed and eroded, the scenery to which they give rise is in the words of an early geologist:

> characteristic. It nowhere rises into a hill of any considerable height, but represents a monotonous landscape of grey rock, now rising through the heather in rounded hummocky knolls, now sinking into hollows occupied by lochans.

Smoothed ages later by ice, this is the Flow Country of the north, and knock-and-lochan terrain of the north-west, that look just as ancient as they really are.

Though the precise nature of the transformation is still uncertain, similar processes were rumbling on deep beneath the other two terranes that comprise the Highlands: the Northern Highlands Terrane (the north- western slice of the Highlands north of Loch Ness), and beneath the Central Highlands Terrane (from Loch Ness south to the Highland Boundary Fault).

The regions overlying these three basements have endured slightly differing fates, and recent analysis of the minerals within each terrane confirms that they – and indeed some of their component parts – were created separately, and only later conjoined via a smaller local replica of the global tectonic motions.

The tough old Lewisian Gneiss of the Hebridean Terrane was gradually eroded to yield hill and vale. This terrane was then submerged so that over the course of millions of years, sand was deposited to at least three kilometres deep, compressing eventually into hard resilient sandstone. The area was then uplifted and the Torridonian sandstone in turn eroded almost completely, but left behind were several notable expanses of mountain in a geological equivalent of Darwinian survival of the fittest.

These are some of Scotland's best-loved hills: An Teallach, the Fisherfield Munros and more than a score of other non-Munro mountains such as Suilven and Ben More Coigach. Wizened old rock faces scored up and down and side to side with a billion years of aging, witness to a dozen Ice Ages but still standing mellow ochre as you leave them at day's end for a warm whisky in the pub.

But there is more: for visible across Loch Maree is a truly unique sight. Beneath Slioch's rugged heights, a valley of ancient gneiss is clearly visible and preserved by the sandstone that was deposited into it; and as you squint to see the dividing line you are looking back two billion years – nearly half the age of the planet...

Across the other two terranes of the north-western and Central Highlands, similar processes of deposition occurred, this time of muds rather than sands. Here too the ground was uplifted, but unlike in Torridon, these two terranes were intensely metamorphosed creating the Moine and Dalradian schists respectively.

All these rocks have been mapped onto The British Geological Survey's map *Bedrock Geology: UK North*. It might seem an unlikely candidate for the Royal Academy's Summer Exhibition, but its variety of colour alone would give it a chance of selection. A symphony of colours swirls in intricate patterns as it traces outcrops and bedrocks of different ages. The map's legend codes the rocks: you'd think that X, Y, and Z would stand for the oldest rocks. But much of the North-west is even older still, and coded A for Archean.

▲▲▲

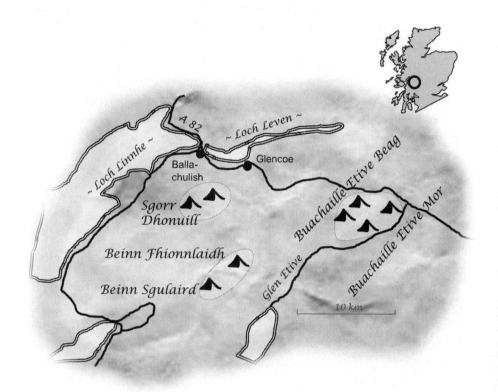

Some of Glencoe's Munros

CHAPTER 8

The Point of No Return

Go, climb the rugged Alps, ambitious fool,
To please the boys, and be a theme at school.

Juvenal Satires Translated by JOHN DRYDEN

GLENCOE: DARK, TOWERING, brooding, glowering. The mountains' spurs and spires overhang and hover like an eagle scrutinising its nest. The hills dwell moodily on something that somehow does not seem quite right; they enthral for good or evil. They challenge description, then defy it. They exist on their own terms, and admit no other. They glare and glout and en-gloom the observer. Glencoe is Gormenghast Castle built by Nature to exceed the horrors of any Creator's misguided whim. Glencoe demands to be experienced with all your senses.

The death of my father earlier in the year has brought home to me in a way previously unimaginable how short life is, how transitory health may be, and how goals may eventually become unachievable.

With those thoughts in mind, and having reached the psychological waypoint of my 100th Munro last year, I now want to see whether a hard push can bring the final target of 283 within closer reach. The Americans would have called this year 'The Year of the Surge'.

Glencoe at last?

It is April and I aim towards Glencoe, with a plan to claim about 25 summits. By this stage in my Munroing vocation I have developed several sophisticated checklists to ensure I do not leave anything behind: a checklist for rucksack contents, one for clothes in which to walk and climb, one for electrical equipment and chargers, and so on.

I duly tick everything off and brave the Friday traffic northwards, aiming to park near Beinn Sgulaird, just south of the Glencoe area and – since there are few B&Bs in the area – decide to use my in-car camping technique as described earlier.

Eight hours and 450 miles later I am parking next to the start of the path up Beinn Sgulaird, breathing the clear Highland air, and having earlier grabbed a quick dinner, start readying the sleeping bag and previously-inflated Lilo for my slumbers.

It is while moving things around in the back of my car that I first sense that my boots may be missing. But the car is jam-packed with bags small and large, so I am sure I shall find them somewhere. I take everything out of the car – even the spare wheel, and several awful truths dawn on me in terrible succession:

First, I have left my boots in London; second, I have left my high-quality walking jacket in London; third, I have left my maps (annotated with intended routes) in London; fourth, I am miles from any decent outdoor shops in which to spend £300–400 on replacements; fifth, any shops in the neighbourhood are likely to be closed since it is a Bank Holiday weekend; sixth, even if new boots are, it would be unwise to walk in them without breaking them in first.

I spend an hour trying to improvise togs to last me a few days until more advanced shopping is feasible: a waterproof jacket made from orange plastic rubbish bags, courtesy of The Royal Borough of Kensington and Chelsea? Sneakers instead of boots? GPS maps instead of paper maps? It isn't really going to work.

I sleep on the problem but sleep brings no insights – just the memory of the most important bag of luggage, duly ticked off, especially left until last, still sitting just inside my front door at home.

The next morning I extrude myself from the sleeping bag, into the driving seat, and head back south; eight hours and 450 miles later, I am back at home.

* * *

That evening I realise the extent of my addiction to those hills – for in deciding not to unpack the car, and deciding instead to drive all the way back up to Glencoe again the next morning, I feel I have crossed some kind of threshold… I am passing a point of no return.

Psychologists talk of 'cognitive dissonance': the discomfort that prevents us from changing a course of action that we have previously decided must be right. How can we admit we could have been wrong? How could I not now compleat the full round?

Glencoe again?

The next day, en route from London to my second attempt at experiencing the full beauties of Glencoe, I break my journey at Carlisle, a stop I shall regret.

My trusty Salomon boots are becoming tired and leaky and I decide to treat myself to some new reserve footwear. I have previously used Brasher boots – not the most macho ones, but definitely the most comfortable I have ever worn, and wearable 'straight out of the box' as the forums say, and as I had experienced. I find a shop, buy the Brashers – a fine, light-weight pair – and head off to the B&B at which I shall be staying tonight.

Beinn Sgulaird (possibly hat-shaped hill) and *Beinn Fhionnlaidh* (Finlay's hill) are both relatively solitary hills, which I have decided to unite in a day's walk.

I slip on the Brashers that feel oh-so-comfortable and head towards the farm at Glenure. There the cheery farmer gives me a few pointers and I set off up the glen, then striking uphill to Beinn Sgulaird's summit. Even with the benefit of the farmer's inside knowledge, the path is always elusive and evasive, but I reach the summit, and the views to Mull and beyond live up to their outstanding reputation.

It is at this first summit that I feel the first signs of blistering heels, and immediately administer Compeed patches, knowing they will do the trick.

The farmer's route now continues north-east, then over several minor tops, across the River Ure, over boggy and heathery slopes, and up to Beinn Fhionnlaidh.

To cut a long story short, this was a day spent contouring around crags with no paths, plodding across hummocky heather, and occasionally slithering up wet grassy slopes.

This was definitely not the way to break in new boots, and despite having tended my feet as well as possible along the way, I knew the dark truth before I gingerly slipped off my boots at the circuit's end and then saw it face-to-face.

There was virtually no skin left on either heel. It would take at least two weeks for them to recover enough to hillwalk on, and I could not stay in Scotland that long. I never did break in those boots.

A second aborted trip, and four wasted days of merely travelling to and from Scotland. Perhaps it was time to give up… On the other hand, if I could just shift this now-aborted holiday slot back a few weeks…

The Thunderbolt

A few weeks later, I again aim for that tract of legendary Scottish mountaineering: Glencoe.

This time, I'm really going to grab a bag-full of Munros. To warm up, I start slightly to the west of Glencoe from a town called Ballachulish. The town's name is illustrative of Highland etymology, and is an English bastardisation of the Gaelic *Baile a' Chaolais*. *Baile* means town (as in bailiwick), and *Chaolais* means 'of the straits' (as in Kyles). Ballachulish really is the town by the straights, and has the bridge to prove it.

Sgorr Dhearg (red peak) and *Sgorr Dhonuill* (Donald's peak) rise from opposite ends of a broad rounded ridge called Beinn a' Bheithir. This name is translated as Hill of the Thunderbolt. But every hill in Scotland is by default subject to thunder sometimes, so it has always surprised me that the hill should have acquired such a non-unique label. True, there are many hills called, for example, *Mor* 'big' – which in a way is an even less unique attribute. But at least in a given locale it is possible to see which the biggest mountain is. Beinn a' Bheithir is not obviously the most thunderous one...

Anyway, having set off at about 8.30am as usual, I start up a Land Rover track. The informally laid out woods soon turn into denser forest and plantation, and the route divides several times. The relatively new tracks no longer match those shown on the Ordnance Survey map, and I am now lured by a path that dives into a forest and promises a shortcut. Tugged, tweaked, and thrashed by branches and twigs that refuse to snap, I soon learn the hard way to avoid forest paths unless you know them to be both wide enough and tall enough... for their full length.

Past the forest, the path is straightforward up to the bealach: the fulcrum of the T-shaped route. There I dump the rucksack apart from essentials and claim first one and then the other summit. The views from the two tops are famous for being glorious and stunning, sweeping over Loch Leven to the north-east and over Loch Linnhe to Strontian (where Strontium was discovered) to the west. But alas, I am not to experience these sights today, since both peaks have their heads firmly stuck in the clouds.

The return is relatively easy, and with an outing behind me that I give only a one-or two-star rating, I start thinking about tomorrow's route that promises six stars out of five.

The Herdsmen

There's nowhere like the Pass of Glencoe – nowhere even similar, even in Scotland. There is the history of course, familiar in detail or in outline to all those who visit. But even if you had not known of the Massacre, genocide, and ethnic cleansing, you would be struck by the spirit of the place and never forget it.

Towards the eastern end of this place is the Kingshouse Hotel: recommended as a place to stay, but seemingly always booked up, perhaps because the West Highland Way passes so close to it. From its front terrace, however, is visible *Stob Dearg* (red peak). You will almost certainly have seen this mountain before. Its image, which from a certain angle looks like a perfect cone, is portrayed widely. The mountain is the playground of climbers, even in winter, and despite the fatalities. It was also a favourite of WH Murray, mentioned earlier.

Stob Dearg and its brother *Stob na Broige* (peak of the brogue) sit on adjoining shoulders of a rounded ridge called Buachaille Etive Mor (the big herdsman of Etive). On the other side of a very wide U-shaped valley that appears to have come straight from a geography textbook, lies the herdsman's brother: Buachille Etive Beag (the little herdsman of Etive) with its two peaks *Stob Coire Raineach* (peak of the bracken corrie) and *Stob Dubh* (black peak).

While these two parallel ridges of four Munros are often climbed on separate days, the weather is set fair and I decide to 'tramp hay while the sun shines'.

I will not go into the details of the expedition itself, since the route was smooth of curve and gradient, and there were no major obstacles. Enough to say that I was blessed with outstanding conditions and virtually unmatched views north-east to the long black gash of the Blackwater Reservoir, and south into the heart of Glen Etive.

The only surprise of the day was that the snow was still lingering on a few nearby peaks, and that my legs felt uncharacteristically stiff after the day's exertions.

A test of mind over matter

Bidean nam Bian is the highest mountain in the old county of Argyll, and gives its name to the whole majestic range of mountains that runs along the south side of Glencoe. Jutting northwards are further dramatic ridges known as the Three Sisters, visible from the road at a parking spot where a lone piper in kilted regimental attire is often seen – and from where the moan of drone and lilt of chanter often drift. The highest summits of the range are hidden away behind the Sisters – a layout that was to prove unfortunate for my next trip.

From the parking area deep in the Pass of Glencoe near the Meeting of the Three Waters, I cross boggy moorland and ascend a valley that parallels the famous Lost Valley to reach a ridge. This in turn leads me to an intermediate peak high above a lochan, up which for three perspiring hours I scramble. Clinging to the top of this peak, however, my spirits are dashed – for as I search for the line of the route ahead, I can see no exposed ground whatsoever. On this hot and sunny day in early June, invisible from the road far away, the swoop and soar of the several hundred metres that must be traversed to reach Bidean nam Bian's summit is completely covered with snow.

In 1969, Eric Langmuir wrote the definitive book *Mountaincraft and Leadership* and it is still a classic. On page 399 of the 2004 edition is a drawing that has always haunted me. It shows how snow can sheer off a mountain ridge at a much shallower angle than you would expect. This means that on some ridges there is no truly safe path for the traverse: neither side is immune from the risk of sheering. Today I have no ice axe, no crampons, and no climbing colleague. To continue or to turn back? My intentions lurch back and forth. Continue and risk a slip, or return and have to climb that thousand metres all over again? I see-saw for 15 minutes, straining to see whether there is a path up through the snow and ice even if I make it to the foot mountain's north face.

In the end I defer to Langmuir. This is the first time I have set out and not climbed even a single Munro. All that work and 'nothing' to show for it!

Nothing? Perhaps this is another turning point in my journey: recognising that enjoyment does not necessarily require the achievement of ticking the summit?

Either way, my legs are still stiff after tackling both Herdsmen yesterday, and with so much snow lying around I grumpily head back home. My last three outings have barely warranted the journeys north. This relationship with the Munros has become a love-hate one.

▲▲▲

The language of the glacier

Much of Scotland's hillscape is written in the language of the glacier: the undulating vowels of the U-shaped valley set between the hard consonants of the corrie, capped with the pointed circumflexes of the arête, and embellished by the sibilant meanders of meltwater rivers. If we know the language of the glacier, we converse more fully with the landscape and hear better what it has to say.

'The Ice Age' is actually 50 ice ages that spread across Europe during the last two and a half million years. In Scotland, the last full-scale ice sheet (extensive enough to link Scotland to Scandinavia) persisted from 29,000 to 22,000 years ago. A mini-ice age then held most of Scotland in its grasp between 15,000 and 14,000 years ago, and finally the 'Loch Lomond Stadial' – centred on that loch and covering the central half of the western half of Scotland – brought a return of ice-driven erosion from 13,000 to 11,500 years ago.

The impact of glaciation is easiest to see in the western Highlands, where greater rainfall contributed to larger amounts of ice. Here glaciers carved out corries, charged through mountain ranges to reshape river catchments and networks, eroded valleys into U-shapes, and sculpted the landscape through transport and deposition of debris. The fluctuating weight of Scotland's ice cap and the rise and fall of sea levels combined to create both raised beaches such as in Skye, and sunken valleys in the form of the West Coast's numerous sea lochs.

Pre-glacial landscapes, which you can see in eastern Scotland and parts of Wester Ross, show where landscapes avoided recent glaciation. These may show features, such as ones you can see along the shoreline of Loch Maree, that include *domes* and *bowls* of bedrock with *erosion surfaces* from earlier times; ancient *pre-glacial valleys* and latent *fault-lines*; and rocks that have been weathered but not later glaciated. The latter include *deeply weathered granites* that crumble at the touch, *nunataks* such as the sharp spires of An Teallach that probably kept their heads above the glaciers, and the jointed *tors* of hard but rounded rock atop many Cairngorm hills, which have been exposed but not removed by the passage of ice.

Erosion by glaciation created a host of landforms, most pronounced where the ice was thick and in motion; thin or relatively immobile ice may not leave much of a mark (as in the more recent glaciation of Cairngorm mountain tops).

Glaciers either gnawed the rocks by freezing-and-plucking or sand-papered them using embedded cargos as scraping tools. At large scale, glaciers can chisel whole mountains into 'crag and tail' profile such as Castle Rock on which Edinburgh stands. At smaller scale, they create 'knock and lochan' landscapes where flocks of streamlined *roches moutonées* (sheep-shaped boulders) alternate with eroded hollows.

Other features visible in the majority of mountainous Highland landscapes include *corries, hanging valleys* (as in Steall where a younger but deeper glacier has cut across a higher older one), *truncated spurs* (The Three Sisters of Glencoe, where a glacier has carved across a sequence of valleys), *arêtes* (the sharp ridges often along the headwall dividing two glaciers, and *trimlines* (separating the deeper marks of scouring and the upper marks of weathering where a glacier part-filled a valley). The clutter of rocks frequently seen at the foot of a corrie cliff (e.g. at Ben Eighe) delights in the fancy name of *pro-talus rampart*.

Deposition and meltwater action. As glaciers retreat, they leave a range of features familiar to the hillwalker, primarily through dumping rock and soil that they had been carrying in ice or in their melting waters.

Moraines are perhaps the most evident deposition feature – most typically deposited across the mouth of the retreating glacier (e.g. near Am Foachagach), but sometimes running along the edges or centre of the glacier (e.g. the medial moraine that aids the ascent of the headwall to Beinn Liath Mhor).

Clusters of hummocks and hillocks (called *drumlins*, from the Gaelic *druim* meaning ridge) are also prevalent forms of deposition (e.g. the Corrie of a Thousand Hillocks in Torridon). Longer sinuous *eskers* result from deposition in meltwaters, typically as they burrowed tunnels through the glacier, and *kame terraces* are often visible as stepped landscapes carved into valley sides by more energetic meltwater.

And of course there are the *erratics* – rocks that can be up to the size of a house, left stranded on hilltop or valley floor as their transport melted away.

But the bane of the walker is the *kettle-hole*: a depression formed when a block of the glacier remained frozen while soil and till was deposited around it. Later this hole would fill with water to create a loch or lochan, or if smaller would become an oozing bog patch awaiting the leg or torso of the unwary.

Periglacial structures. Finally in the vocabulary of glaciation are the periglacial features. These are formed by intensely cold conditions adjacent to an active glacier, or after a glacier's departure.

Most mysterious are the graded and patterned formations of stones, created by 'frost heave' – though you would swear they must have been laid out by human hand. Nets, circles, polygons, lobes, stripes: they come in a range of shapes.

▲▲▲

Phase 3 – Trophies

MY PREVIOUS FEW years of hillwalking have clearly become ones of blatant bagging. I gained summits voraciously, with my chief interest becoming the count of Munros climbed. I had pushed myself to days that claimed four, five and six hills, and days of 15 hours' almost continuous walking. I had tested some of my limits. And the biggest boon of all, at least in terms of 'body': the Munros had provided my ultimate incentive for giving up smoking. For good. I have never smoked another cigarette since quitting them for the Munros.

Yet still, I had climbed neither Ben Nevis, nor Glencoe's very best peaks, nor other recognised classics such as Liathach and Ben Alligin. Subconsciously my attention now turned towards the 'Trophies' Stage of my development, and rather than go for Quantity I would seek Quality.

In the language of the hunter, I am now after bigger game; I now seek to claim Munros where the journey is further, the vistas more striking, the landscape more legendary, or the mountain more iconic. Of course, there are neither definitive criteria for these 'best mountains' nor definitive lists of them; it is all subjective.

Nevertheless, *Trail* magazine does hazard a go at a list of the 'best 100 mountain walks in Britain', and hillwalker forums often conduct polls in which usual suspects do recur. A few of those trophies are already in my bag, of course: The Ring of Steall, The In Pinn, perhaps Ben Lawers, certainly An Teallach. But I now set out on a mission more clearly focused on experiencing the supposed best of the Munros.

The following chapter, *Torridon*, describes a return to the north-west and to its ancient sandstone giants. These giants stand defiant and uncompromising, proudly laying claim to the surrounding lands. They are mountains that would argue with you if they could speak and could be bothered to. This chapter also offers you an introduction to mountain ecology.

The Cairngorms Proper tracks across the central Highlands and to the vast Cairngorm plateau. I had nibbled at the Cairngorms' edges on an earlier trip, but now I wanted to experience it more completely: Cairn Gorm itself and Braeriach, and in between the Wells of Dee and the drove road of the Lairig Ghru. This chapter also traces the food chains that typify mountain habitats from lichen to eagle, and further examples.

Finally, *Glencoe, Ben Nevis and More* takes us back, firstly to the most haunting of glens, and then to our country's highest summits. I also offer some suggestions regarding safety.

* * *

In pursuing our mission, we eventually start to focus on Quality instead of Quantity. Many bottles of wine have been consumed: now it is time for the Chateau Margaux. And with this stage comes a growing awareness and understanding of what we, personally, choose as the criteria that define our trophies, and the hallmarks by which we will recognise them.

Schiehallion from across Loch Rannoch

The Torridonian giants

Chapter 1: The back of Ben Nevis, seen from the Ring of Steall

Chapter 2: Ben Lomond and its loch, from the shoulder of Beinn Dubhchraig

Chapter 3: Two figures atop the In Pinn

Chapter 4: The ridge of Ben Lawers

Chapter 5: Water pouring 500 metres down the haunches of Sgurr Ban in Fisherfield Forest

Chapter 6: Queen Victoria's 'bothy' from near Broad Cairn

Chapter 7: Ben Loyal, from the steep flanks of Ben Klibreck

Chapter 8: Sunset over Loch Leven from Glencoe

Chapter 9: The Horns of Alligin

Chapter 10: The sphinx-cairn atop A' Chailleach

Chapter 11: Ben Starav as it looks down on Loch Etive

Chapter 12: Monument at Glenfinnan to Bonnie Prince Charlie

Chapter 13: Late afternoon from below Beinn Achaladair, towards the Black Mount

Chapter 14: The infant River Dee, with Bod an Deamhain (right), from the shoulder of Ben Macdui

Chapter 15: Rime on Nicholson's Chimney

Are we there yet?
Friends and family on a
determined mission to
help bag that last Munro.

CHAPTER 9

Torridon

Climb the mountains and get their good tidings.
Nature's peace will flow into you as sunshine flows into trees.
The winds will blow their own freshness into you
and the storms their energy
while cares will drop off like autumn leaves.

JOHN MUIR *My First Summer in the Sierra*

THE TORRIDONIAN AREA of north-west Scotland is all that a geological playwright could wish for. A robust stage-set with a floor of the most ancient rocks in the world, dappled grey-green, and interspersed with black lochans that turn blue or white as the sun's stage lights are trained on them. A few scattered mounds and ramps for seating. The ingress of Upper Loch Torridon as the doorway. And the ancient actors, standing proud and patrician, wizened of rock-face and Herculean of limb...

These well-bred hills are to be my next trophies: Liathach, Alligin, Slioch, Eighe. Visiting these 'extreme' mountains will also surely dull the memory of those last three trips, which were so unproductive. A month after my last trip, therefore, I am back in Scotland again. Having analysed the Met Office data, I can see the trend that local residents have recounted: sunny May and June are the new high season, as July and August have become wetter. Presumably, globally-warmed air is picking up water from the Atlantic sooner these days. From now on I will factor that into my planning.

Frost-shattered peaks

Arriving in the huge natural pass that is Glen Torridon, the weather is good, though rain threatens to follow. I decide to climb the two peaks of Beinn Eighe today, and leave Slioch to visit tomorrow. I have already seen many of its views from Fisherfield Forest further north, so it won't matter too much if it does indeed rain tomorrow.

In glorious sunshine I head off from the glen's car park and around the roots of the Beinn Eighe massif. This route leads to the back-stage entrance of a giant opera house. Out to the left are the now-familiar ancient landscapes, from which erupt the occasional relics of primeval sandy sea-bed. But the true spectacle lies on a bearing to the right: mounting up beside a substantial waterfall, I eventually peer over its upper lip. I had known of the triple buttresses that would face me – huge cliffs 200 metres high, rounded ramparts in general form, yet sharply cragged for surface texture.

What surprises me is their distance, for between me and them is half a kilometre of lochan stretched out across the corrie. Such high-level lochs do not normally come at such scale. Even more astounding is the 200-metre rock-fall to the right that has spilled down into a perfect semi-cone from mountain peak to corrie floor. From across the lochan it is hard to gauge distance and height, and it is only when I later zoom in to my photo that I spot at the foot of that cone a tiny figure sunbathing and realise the enormity of the place!

What I think is the back-stage of the opera house is actually the main front door, and as I press on alongside the lochan I try to burn the images upon my memory indelibly; they are too fantastic to lose.

A long scree slope soon confronts me, reaching hundreds of metres up across the corrie's head-wall. The scree is clearly at its critical angle of repose – the maximum gradient that the scree granules can sustain, so that when you add but one more grain the whole pile slips or even avalanches. Since the path promises five steps up to four steps back, I opt instead for a slightly dodgy scramble up the rock-face to the right of the screes.

The ridge finally attained, I soon reach *Ruadh-stac Mor* (big red stack), and then retrace my steps to continue to *Spidean Coire nan Clach* (peak of the stony corrie). The route to this top is along a path that sometime tiptoes, sometimes frolics, often romps, and is nearly always exposed: take care if the wind is gusting.

Nearly at the top sits a trig point. Painstakingly built by the hand of man, its careful geometric construction looks out of place amidst the acres and acres of chaotic rock that almost match it in colour. There I meet a lass in plimsolls who looks too overweight for the hill, but who nevertheless sprints ahead, intent on showing how the true top, a hundred metres on, should be tackled.

My vote for the Best View in Scotland still goes to that from the top of A' Mhaighdean, as previously recounted. But a very close second must come that from Spidean Coire nan Clach. This latter vista comprises mountains almost exclusively, and the lack of sea is why it does not quite earn top marks. But what mountains they are! I gaze out over the magnificent life-sized map of the week's later peaks: the mighty Liathach just five kilometres away, and Ben Alligin beyond. Slioch and An Teallach to the North. And looking back to the first Munro of the day, it appears now as a huge promontory, its sides riddled with hollows and pock-marks as if it had been used for some sort of celestial target practice.

Back at the trig point again, the clearer path down lies to the left, but I choose the one to the right to take me more directly – and with some exciting scree-running – back to the start.

Looking back to the massif, I now realise that its most impressive features lie hidden on the far side from which I had approached. But I only appreciate the vast extent of its shattered quartzite range when I come to see it from afar, from other peaks.

The spear

A new day dawns, and the rain has set in as expected. I shall be soaked, yet there is a consolation prize: the romantic view along Loch Maree, from the start of the hike.

Down the loch the little tree-clad islands are clearly visible, including the Island of Mary, who gives the loch its name. The clouds hang heavy but not yet grey, draped across the loch; somewhere a greenshank calls out wild and proud.

Although no two mountain routes are identical, the route up *Slioch* (the spear) is similar enough to others on a driech and low-viz day that a summary is probably sufficient. It matches one of the generic patterns: the lochside promenade leads to a gentle incline up to a glaciated hollow, then up the ice-smoothed burly shoulder, around the lochan, to the final pull with a false summit or two, to the top. On a clear day I would have had A' Mhaighdean's 'Best View in Scotland', seen from a slightly different angle – one day I shall go back for it.

Liathach

Liathach – the Grey One – demands respect, even if you're too scared to see it from the traverse of its high ridge. Standing tall and authoritative above Upper Loch Torridon and its glen, it is an ultimate mountain. It rises so sheer from the loch that in photographs you'd swear the row of tiny houses at its feet must have been shrunk using Photoshop. Liathach is also an extreme geological specimen; on its slopes I look sidelong and count the ancient and serried ranks of stacked-up sandstone terraces, and determine their number to be what mathematicians call 'uncountably infinite'.

Meteorologist and local alike predict the cloud-base will be below the Munro tops for the next few days. This gives me the excuse *not* to traverse Liathach's notorious ridge with clammy hand upon wetter rock, and instead I climb its two peaks – *Spidean a' Choire Leith* (peak of the grey corrie) and *Mullach an Rathain* (peak of the row of pinnacles) – in separate outings.

The first of these expeditions involves a relatively straightforward ascent from the roadside up 1,000 metres to the ridge, with a slight dodge rightward when the path appears to disappear headlong into a huge vertical slab of rock. Once aloft, I have a foretaste of the difficulties the ridge can present in wet and slippery conditions. It is half a kilometre to the peak of Spidean a' Choire Leith, though nowhere is it treacherous. Views on the return are intermittent through cloud – a pity since the high altitude of my perch combined with the steepness of the slopes makes for potentially tremendous vistas.

Those vistas are available the next day, however, when I tackle the other end of the ridge. Instead of ascending from the roadside, I take a path that winds around the back of the massif, and climb more gradual slopes in the company of other classic hills to my left.

I reach the top in swirling mist and cloud, and see a group of three spectres – they have, like me, been staying at the Torridon Youth Hostel, one of the few accommodations in the immediate locale. Touchingly, they are there to spread the ashes of the father of one of the group.

The mists abate on my descent and allow a classic west coast sight to emerge. As the late afternoon air warms you slightly more than you expect of it, you kindle your undazzled gaze at the full beam of the declining sun (to borrow a phrase from Milton) and dance your scrutiny from Ben Alligin, to Skye, to Lewis, and then across the sea like a skipping stone; and you cannot help the unexpected shiver that tingles your spine as you think of Bonnie Prince Charlie, and your old Scottish forbears. And there's also the afternoon tea with shortbread waiting for you down below...

Bejewelled horns

Ben Alligin looks like the last man standing from a vast geological slugging match. Handsome and brawny, it bears the mark of an axe-stroke or worse, which would have cleaved most mountains in two. A corrie has gouged out a huge chink of the hill's rock-face. The mountain has clearly been mauled by a giant.

Ben Alligin means 'jewelled hill' and since 1997, bears two designated Munros. It is to the newer one – *Tom na Gruagaich* (hill of the maiden) – that I first head, all the time wondering whether I will dare to take the infamous Horns.

The attractive walk-in brings me fairly swiftly to the mouth of the corrie. The path then tucks in behind its western wing to follow a wee burn that with melted snow would surely be a torrent.

Without warning in this relatively remote spot, I am suddenly aware of someone approaching me from behind, then running past me. 'No way he'll keep up that speed,' I think. But I am wrong: he does keep it up – at least for the 200 metres of ascent during which I can check on him.

When I eventually reach the top, the runner has disappeared, and so has the path. I tip-toe down over an exposed edge which is in roughly the right direction, and regain the path inelegantly.

The ridge itself is then well-pathed. As the Horns edge closer from the distance, the high surround of the Chasm of Doom rears up to block my way. From its top, I gaze down thousands of feet to the bottom of the cleft hill.

Farther on, I reach *Sgurr Mhor* (big peak) and I can no longer put off the decision about whether or not to descend over the Horns of Alligin. The Horns constitute a huge serrated fin of ancient sandstone that you would swear is about to overbalance – along the chiselled top of which a path supposedly runs. Unless you are an experienced climber, it looks at least a little daunting. And then there are the conflicting stories about 'definitely do it clockwise' and 'definitely do it anticlockwise'; the alleged slabs, with no handholds, that are taller than two basketball players; and so forth.

Although the Horns now appear close enough to touch, this is clearly an optical illusion: they are so far away that I cannot make out a route across their tops, nor the more dangerous path that bypasses it by snaking down the near-vertical sides of the fins.

I think you can guess by now that I bottle out and return by the route of my ascent – I can only plead that I am travelling solo and am not sure what the implications would be of becoming crag-fast or a casualty on the Horns.

A raspberry ripple of a mountain

I am keen to see *Beinn Liath Mhor* (big grey hill) in person because it is a prime example of an 'imbricate' structure. Think raspberry ripple: red Torridonian sandstone was laid down a billion years ago; then a creamy quartzite layer was spread on top; later the whole lot was concertinaed into undulating ripples; and then erosion finally sliced off the top. You are left with an entire mountain made of unusual vertical stripes of alternating orange and grey rock. I had heard much about it when I was studying geology in my youth, and now I will get to touch it.

Today is due to be windy, so I approach via the sheltered valley created by the River Lair, and as I pass this mountain's flanks and make for the valley's headwall, the imbricate stripes appear, just as promised.

From the col, I head up into the clouds of the first peak, return, and then look for 'the grassy ramp' that guidebooks promise will take me steeply up the other side. The ramp located, I continue to climb for about an hour, finally reaching the top of *Sgorr Ruadh* (red peak) and the company of four pensioners out for a stroll.

We chat and break bread together, but I soon press on since I am keen to assess the potential to add on a route over to a neighbouring Munro: Maol Chean-dearg. Upon closer inspection, however, the drop down into the glen, the three kilometres across the glen and up the other side, and the difficulty of getting back to the car afterwards all seems too much. I leave that hill for tomorrow; it would be a glen too far today.

A dreadful thought, and a summit of two halves

I approach that neighbouring Munro, *Maol Chean-dearg* (red-capped hill) the next morning, up the glen that runs parallel to yesterday's glen. Passing a well-maintained bothy, I strike up the hillside and eventually reach a bealach about a kilometre from the top. Looking west, the very shapely Corbett called An Ruadh-Stac presents itself. A Corbett is a Scottish peak between 2,500 and 3,000 feet high, with a drop of at least 500 feet all round; there are 221 of them. If yesterday's hill was a raspberry ripple ice-cream, then this Corbett is a Mister Whippee: with a seemingly spiral structure to its whipped-up quartzite top.

So beautiful is this hill that I stop and loiter for a quick lunch, and a thought too dreadful flits through my mind: *if I do ever compleat the round of Munros, will I be lured into climbing all the Corbetts too?*

Shaking my head to banish this thought, I press on, and 20 minutes later reach the top of Maol Chean-dearg with mist closing in. Just visible all about are the huge sandstone hills, their tops elegantly draped in quartzite. But this summit seems to be one of two halves: half red sandstone, half white quartzite – and the unusual two-tone cairn incorporates both types of rock.

A bad rap

Fionn Bheinn (pale-coloured hill) has a poor reputation, and I am expecting a quick and slightly monotonous hill – one that will occupy a morning before heading back home at the end of my trip. Three and a half hours will see me up to the top and back, with time for lunch on the summit too.

But I have underestimated the hill, for the paths to the top soon traverse wide open moorlands that are a pleasant change from the hard quartzite and other cooked remnants of metamorphic activity on which I have trodden for so long this week. I also enjoy the novelty of a high-level route that can be completed in a morning.

With its excellent vistas over its north-facing corrie to the familiar Loch Fannich, and north-west towards Slioch and its neighbours, Fionn Bheinn is a fitting full stop to a great week on big hills and an appropriate *adieu* to the mountains. Having climbed 11 Munros on this trip, and more importantly having scaled several classics, I feel I am resuming my momentum after the three setbacks earlier this year; but nothing can be taken for granted on the Munros.

▲▲▲

Munro ecology: flora

Tall swaying pines, flowing banks of purple heather, checkerboard muirburn, bare mountaintops: certain aspects of Munro ecology are pervasive and make for mountain scenery that is so typical of Scotland – even though each hill has its own unique ecology based on its shape, rocks, microclimate, groundcover, and legacy of human intervention.

Baldness, for example, is a hallmark of Scotland's mountaintops. Indeed, many a hill includes in its name the word *Maol* – Gaelic for bald. And, like the monk's bald tonsure, the hill's transition from hairy forest to bald pate is abrupt. There are special reasons why the demarcation of the treeline in Scotland is characteristically more sudden than in other countries, and these are explained below.

But to review the flora that greets the Munro-bagger, let us follow the example of a fascinating lecture by Charles Gimingham – past President of the British Ecological Society and still a world authority on heathlands and heathers – and travel up the hill, not down it.

We start our walk near a belt of broad-leafed woodland that clothes the riverbank and valley bottom. Eleven thousand years ago, after the snows of the last mini-Ice Age receded, algae and lichens were the first colonisers of the gravelly eroded rock. These species absorbed and retained water, quarried minerals, and created a decaying organic floor on which further colonising plants such as mosses and grasses took root and developed.

Later stages of succession saw the spread first of heather, then of shrubs such as juniper and rowan, and then of trees such as oak (more predominant in the South), birch (in the North), and Scots pine (in the East). Depending on the nature of the underlying rock, heather, blaeberry, ferns, grasses, and flowers came to carpet the floor of the open forest. Across floodplains and along river bottoms and banks, rich alluvial deposits started to support an even greater variety of cover.

When man began to colonise Scotland about 10,000 years ago, woodlands covered roughly half the land. With Britain still connected to Continental Europe, the ancient Caledonian Forest was part of the vast wooded *taiga*: a biosphere that still extends across Canada, Alaska, Russia, Mongolia and beyond, larger than the world's rainforests combined.

For 5,000 years, Scotland's forests continued to expand, ultimately covering 80 per cent of the land. But then unfavourable weather patterns took hold, and the demands imposed by a growing and developing population whittled away at the woodlands until, by the 18th century, they covered a mere five per cent of the land. (The Bonawe iron smelter alone consumed two acres of woodland a day; and there were up to 100 such smelters across Scotland in the 18th century. The furnaces consumed so much timber that it was cheaper to bring the heavy iron ore all the way from quarries in England, than to ship the Scottish timber there.) Patches of the original Caledonian Forest do remain, albeit vastly out-spread by industrial-scale plantations of imported Sitka Spruce. Between these extremes of ancient and modern forest, the avid walker will want to be able to identify alder, sessile oak, hazel, willow and both types of birch (silver and downy).

As we continue the hard slog uphill, we next reach the timberline – the highest altitude at which trees grow tall and straight. This altitude varies with conditions and tree species, and in the Highlands is typically in the range 300–550 metres above sea level. Beyond the timberline, we pass briefly through the Montane Scrub Zone, before reaching the treeline. The treeline in Scotland is low, rising to only 650 metres in the Cairngorms, and to only 500 metres on the west coast. Yet in Norway trees grow at up to 1,000 metres altitude, which would completely cover most of a Munro; in the Alps to 2,200 metres; in Canada 2,400 metres; and in the Andes to 5,500 metres!

Scotland has one of the lowest treelines in the world, and two factors have caused those upper regions of the Munro to remain so tree-less. First, the strong influence of the sea cools the Scottish summers and at high altitudes restricts tree growth during those months of peak development. The influence of the sea is especially strong on the west coast where the coastline is highly fretted, with more than 80 sea lochs bringing the sea far inland. In contrast, you would have to ascend twice the height of Ben Nevis if you wanted to see the bare and furrowed brow of a hill in Tyrol, because the warmer summers allow higher treelines there.

The second factor that keeps the treeline low in Scotland is a mix of agricultural practices that have all but eliminated the Montane Scrub Zone. This zone normally occurs on the forest's uphill edge and is a habitat that can foster the upward spread of trees. This zone has been largely nibbled away as estates have allowed sheep, and the deer herds sustained for sport shooting, to graze the saplings. Estates have also kept down the scrub through the practice of muirburn: burning large areas of mountain heather in rotation, to provide tender regenerated heather buds for red grouse fodder. The vast patchworks of earthy-coloured swatches that drape across many hillsides are thus the result of modern muirburn, rather than any older influences that you might have imagined.

In a few areas in Scotland (typically designated as Sites of Special Scientific Interest) and more extensively abroad, this scrub zone is intact and stretches between the timberline and the treeline. Here we glimpse a landscape in which shrubs and trees – usually pine, birch and juniper – are short, twisted and scrubby. Where soils are rich in lime (perhaps as underlying rocks originated from the deposited shells of marine life), a richer variety of plants grows, including the woolly and downy willows.

Farther up the hill, we spot a rowan in splendid solitude, rooted atop a huge erratic boulder, and another that clings to a cliff's rocky projection. How did they get there? Of course, the rowan is one of the few trees that has berries on which birds and martens gorge – and what they drop, ready-manured, often sprouts successfully.

As we now gain the shoulder of the hill, we enter the Montane Heath Zone. Here the effects of cold, wet, wind, and soil acidity show strongly in the familiar combination of heather, moss and peat. This trio prevails at lower altitudes too, where the bog also hosts Scotland's carnivorous plants: sundews, butterworts and bladderworts. But the trio is more extensive higher up where rain falls faster than it can evaporate, causing the ground to waterlog. As the soil derives from granite rocks, and as the water leeches out the bases and minerals, the soil becomes acidic – nutrient-poor conditions that few plants other than heathers and mosses can tolerate. And as the heather and moss decompose, in anaerobic waterlogged conditions, peat is formed. Peat develops at the rate of about 1mm per year; with banks often building to depths of 6–10 metres, they clearly hold a fascinating historic record stretching back many millennia. Some of those white stripped branches – the bridges on which we teeter so as not to sink into the bog – can be as much as 1,000 years old.

Other plants that grow in these wet patches include the golden spiky bog asphodel, white fluffy cotton grass, and sweet-scented bog myrtle. If you tread on them, you can expect to sink in to the bog beneath them: at least to an ankle and perhaps to a knee.

At last, we reach the upper heights of the hill, which from a distance looked bare; on closer inspection, however, we find a complex yet fragile eco-system. Plants here are low-growing and have deep roots to reach washed-down nutrients (as crowberry and blaeberry do); leaves that are waxy (crowberry) or are shed entirely to reduce water loss by transpiration in high winds (blaeberry); or are hairy to retain moisture as far as possible (alpine lady's mantle, moss campion). Where the snows lie longer, moor mat grass, stiff sedge and some of the 14 types of sphagnum moss predominate. Where the snow is regularly blown away, expect to see the three-leaved rush. And where lime-rich rocks and soils outcrop, the range of flora expands further still. Here, high up, are glorious Alpine-Arctic flowers: starry and tufted saxifrages, rock speedwell, alpine milk-watch and alpine cinquefoil – often loitering in the gravelly stripes, lobes, or polygons. Though these geometric shapes look man-raked, they are in fact created by centuries of alternating temperatures, and the processes of solifluction and winter frost heave.

As we head back down the mountain and avoid the forest, we notice that the moorland extends down to around 300 metres. But soon more species are viable at these lower altitudes, and the groundcover is determined by a more complex interplay of environmental factors. Unfortunately, the damp bog reappears at the foot of the hill to mark the end of the trek. At least the carnivorous bladderworts are too small to cause us harm.

Worth a visit is Beinn Eighe National Nature Reserve (NNR). Established in 1951, it was the first NNR in Britain and its protected flora are now well-established, as are its fauna. Scotland offers over 50 NNRs:

see www.nnr-scotland.org.uk, which itself is a site of great beauty! And worth a read is *Hostile Habitats: Scotland's Mountain Environment* published by the Scottish Mountaineering Trust.

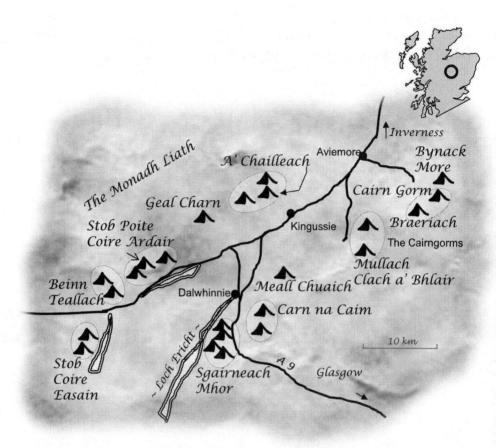

The Monadh Liath and Northern Cairngorms

CHAPTER 10

The Cairngorms Proper

*After looking at the Alps, I felt that my mind had been
stretched beyond the limits of its elasticity, and fitted so loosely
on my old ideas of space that I had to spread these to fit it.*

OLIVER WENDELL HOLMES, SR
The Autocrat of the Breakfast-Table

GLENMORE LODGE IS Scotland's national outdoor training centre, set in the forest that surrounds Loch Morlich, near Aviemore. This is to be a perfect base for the next two days as I make my first visit to the trophy mountains of the Cairngorms Proper.

I say 'Proper' because there are many who claim the term Cairngorms should be reserved for the hills around Ben Macdui, and that the southwards reach of the Cairngorms National Park to include Lochnagar and beyond results in a misnomer. Certainly the huge pluton of granite that includes Braeriach and the other hills near Ben Macdui has a character of its own, and it is at least ten kilometres to the separate granite nodule that supports Lochnagar.

Regardless of the etymology, I have four weeks of carried-forward vacation this year, and ten days after my last trip, I am back for my fifth outing of the year. Preceded by the Munros of Drumochter Pass, and followed by selected hills of the Monadh Liath, I expect the Cairngorm Mountains to be the centre-piece of the expedition.

Past the Boar and the Sow

To anyone who drives along the A9, the Balsporran cottages are familiar as lonely white dots out to the west of Drumochter Pass, a few miles south of Dalwhinnie, and I will have the pleasure of staying in one of them at the start of my late July tour.

From the nearby layby number 79, I cross the railway line and am soon strolling up the glen that carries the Allt Coire Domhain river, between the two non-Munros vividly named the Boar of Badenoch and the Sow of Atholl. Looking back to the Pass, it is easy to imagine how it was created by a glacial bulldozer that tried to join the Spey to the North with the Tay to the South.

The paths here are well-maintained and the weather excellent as I come to the first riddle: how to cross the river that I have so far been merely following upstream. I resist the temptation to cross bare-foot, and eventually find luxurious, five-star stepping-stones upstream, and from there find the path to the top of *Sgairneach Mhor* (big boulder-field). Despite the hill's name, its summit, at least, is not heavily bouldered, and promising views emerge of the day's circuit ahead.

The area has an affable character: the hills are broad but not over-powering, they have some cragginess but are generally grassy under foot, they populate the area well but do not jostle each other too closely. I make a note: 'scenic tops and curvy links', and though the paths undulate strongly, they never do so to excess. The continuation to *Beinn Udla-main* (lonely mountain) and the out-and-back to/from *A' Mharconaich* (the place of horses) is straightforward and devoid of equestrian evidence. To add some excitement to the day I drop, in a free-style bowed path, down to the bealach from which the smooth rise to *Geal-charn* (white hill) starts.

The only real challenge of the day is the unavoidable bogginess of the final descent, though the welcome at the cottages makes up for it.

The Quaich and beyond

I am keen to move on to the Cairngorms, and so the next day climb the linked Munros of *Carn na Caim* (cairn of the curve) and *A' Bhuidheanach Bheag* (the little yellow place) in the morning, and *Meall Chuaich* (hill of the quaich) in the afternoon.

These hills are somewhat mediocre – as is the weather – but I share an enjoyable *quaich* (a traditional Scottish drinking vessel, used to offer a guest a drink of welcome or farewell) with three fellow walkers I encounter. Two of the girls have just started on the Munros, but their friend has only 15 to go. I feel a pang of envy, and the perennial question arises: *shall I or shan't I try to climb them all?*

Mind the gap

With some trepidation, I reach the national outdoor training centre of Glenmore Lodge – a few kilometres from Aviemore. Although I am just there for a bedroom, I feel I am re-living a first day at school, for this is where Mountain Leaders are trained and assessed. Leaders of many of Scotland's other outdoor sports are made here too. The crampons, ice axes and other paraphernalia prove the serous intent of the place.

I soon take to the hills, and the path to *Braeriach* (brindled brae) starts quietly with little hint that the next 21 kilometres will require 1,200 metres of up and down. But soon I am crossing a gorge by way of the handy bridge, and once over the rise on the far side, the long and winding route to the Chalamain Gap becomes apparent.

It is hard to convey the rocky mayhem that this boulder-strewn Gap presents: a ravine of angled rhomboids of granite, seemingly stable, yet somehow elbowing you even though they do not move; a relict toy-cupboard left over from some giant's misspent childhood.

With this difficulty negotiated in due course, I head on towards the crossing of the famous Lairig Ghru. Although used for centuries as a road to drove cattle, this route is probably even more ancient; part of a network of low-level routes that cut across the granite massif, and which doubtless allowed access and transit for many centuries.

The river that runs along the Lairig Ghru has excavated downwards for about 80 metres, and as I look up from between the vast yet all-enclosing sides, I experience a weird sensation of ground-rush in reverse: perhaps I have over-exerted myself! I claw up the rise of over 80 metres on the other side of this valley, then proceed along a ridge that parallels the drove road, finally reaching the peak of Braeriach – poised at the last remaining scrap of ground where five glaciers once met and carved out their corrie thrones. I am tempted to continue briefly to find the Wells of Dee. This is the ultimate headwater of the River Dee, which oozes from the ground later to swell to maturity and unite with the North Sea at Aberdeen 125 kilometres away. But with cloud closing in, I forgo the opportunity, for now at least.

As the route back treads the same path as the route out, I am glad to share it with a man and his dog, now heading the same way I am.

'I started at Braemar,' he explains in due course, 'reached Ben Macdui, and just kept on going.' I comment that this seems a very laid-back approach to a serious hike, especially with the added weight of tent and dog-food. He replies that his wife did not allow him much time off for the hills so he had to make the best of it!

We eventually part ways at the Chalamain Gap as I turn off to try a path that rises steeply beside and around it. It turns out to be only marginally easier than re-traversing the Gap itself.

Cairn Gorm

I return from Braeriach mid-afternoon, and so have just enough time to drive the few miles up to the Cairngorm ski centre, keen to investigate the lie of the land.

The paths up to *Cairn Gorm* (blue hill) appear an easy proposition despite the hot afternoon sun, and instead of climbing it tomorrow as planned, I set off immediately. Compared with the impact of this mountain's huge brand name, the ascent is unremarkable, even industrial, through the paraphernalia of the ski resort and railway. But from the top the entire vast plateau of the Cairngorms stretches to East and South as far as the horizon, rifted intermittently by the scars from slash of ice and slurry of snow.

To the West, however, is a sign that is of great concern to any hill-walker: an entire hemisphere of dark black cloud that with alarming speed is consuming what remains of the bright blue sky. The weather front is approaching fast, and I only just manage to out-run it and find shelter.

The barns

Atop the solitary ridge of *Bynack More* (big shawl), rise several clusters of granite tors that have resisted erosion. I find them as I walk the ridge the next morning, from the back door of Glenmore Lodge. By some miracle, the weather has cleared, though the picture-postcard Strath Nethy and its river are working hard to shift the remnants of yesterday's storm.

Once atop the ridge, Beinn Mheadhoin stands in the middle distance and beckons from across the mystical sounding Fords of A'an. It nags at me: if I don't climb that hill today, it will be a far longer walk-in on some other trip via Braemar. But I resist the mountain's call, as my plans have been arranged otherwise.

The Monadh Liath

Straddling the centre of Scotland lies the range of the Monadh Liath: the Grey Mountains. Whenever I see or hear its name, I imagine the evocatively-named range must have escaped from a Tolkien novel.

I have read that these hills can attract continuous rain, and as I arrive at about 3pm to climb the most westerly of the range's nine Munros – *Geal Charn white hill* – not to be confused with the other three Munros called Geal Charn – the clouds duly roll in.

I spend the next three and half hours becoming completely drenched from the top down, as well as from the boots up. Marshy; swampy, boggy, plashy, quaggy, muddy, sloppy, squashy; paludal, moorish, fenny: every one of Roget's 'boggy' adjectives would have found an appropriate subject here.

The hill will eventually rate as my least-enjoyed Munro – the rating influenced heavily by the weather, but also by the need for a winding, bumpy, single-track journey of about ten kilometres from Laggan to reach its start, and back to Laggan as dusk draws in.

A lucky break

The next day I hope to find slightly better weather as I back-track about 30 kilometres towards the Cairngorms. Having turned off the A9 and headed down Glen Feshie, I soon don my boots and start up the path to *Sgor Gaoith* (peak of the wind).

I stop half-way to chat briefly with a mountain-biker who has ridden – or rather pushed – his bike all the way to the top, and I then resume the track, finally reaching the vast table that surrounds the summit.

Part ridge, part plateau, the area is completely shrouded in mist. I pace around for 15 minutes awaiting a view, then decide to leave. But the clouds lift in the nick of time, merely ten metres or so, though that is sufficient. And there, staring across the huge valley that contains Loch Einich, is the entire western end of the Cairngorms in full stereoscopic view. A kilometre and a half away, it is a remarkable sight, as if I am an insect staring into a mint and pistachio ice-cream from which an unknowable hand has just taken a huge slice.

I am granted five minutes of prime viewing, and then the peak of the wind lives up to its name again and blows the mists back in. In hope of further views I tread onwards, to *Mullach Clach a' Bhlair* (peak of the stone of the plain) but there are no more lucky breaks to be had that day. Indeed, there is the very *unlucky* break of not finding the alleged shortcut path down – which costs me a kilometre of rubble, heather, and steep gradient for 300 metres of descent... I wish I had taken the longer but more obvious track.

The sphinx

The weather is unsettled, albeit predictably so. It alternates by day: the good then the bad, the good then the bad; the ugly is yet to appear.

Today is the return of the good as I set off to circumnavigate the three hills that lie slightly to the north of Geal Charn. I leave the car park and skirt a plantation, then climb steeply up beside the Allt a' Chaorainn river. I manage to spot a small cairn about two kilometres further on, which leads down to a helpful bridge across the water. Then I am onto long stretches of a peaty hike, up the easy gradient to the top of *A' Chailleach* (the old woman).

The hill is bulky, so I cannot yet see the day's journey laid out, but the summit cairn is impressive. I am no expert on the ecology and evolution of cairns, but this one has clearly evolved, with the helping hand of man, into a sphinx. Just as when I had noticed the cairn-face on Stob Daimh five years earlier, and the cairn-meerkats on Carn an Righ, I kick myself for not having created an album of unusual cairns. Perhaps someone else will, or has? I head down the steep drop to a small col, and rise the other side to reach *Carn Sgulain* (hill of the basket), a mere two kilometres away.

The next section of the walk would be a seven-kilometre drag in poor weather, but visibility remains excellent on this outing, and my interest picks up when the line of bent fence posts at my side peters out and gives way to the first glimpses of the corrie ahead.

On top of *Carn Dearg* (red hill) there is a party going on: a couple, a group of four quite portly men, and two lively dogs. The sun brings out the best in us, and we chat for an hour over an unholy mix of sandwiches, beers, and Snickers bars.

The route down becomes a marvellous wide spiral that skirts the edge of the corrie to set me down in a huge open basin about one kilometre wide and many times that in length. Somehow the brown and black mottled peat has dried out, which makes for easy walking.

Good company

Thirty kilometres down the road towards Spean Bridge lie the most westerly of the Monadh Liath Munros: *Beinn a' Chaorainn* (mountain of the rowan) and *Beinn Teallach* (mountain of the forge).

It is misty and cloudy as I set out from the roadside and through the forest, but it is not yet raining. After a few junctions and turns on good tracks, I emerge from the pine trees onto a consistent upward slope. There I meet a party of three: Ivan from Glencoe, a minister from Fort William and the latter's brother-in-law. Normally a meeting on a hill is a more or less brief encounter, but I am happy in the company of these amiable fellows, and we walk together for well over an hour.

I'm sure Ivan is far younger than the relatively advanced age he claims. He has walked the hills for many years, is one of the few people to have climbed all the Munros, Grahams, Corbetts, peaks higher than 2,000 feet in the Lake District, and higher than 3,000 feet in Ireland and is a leading figure in the Marilyn Hall of Fame. It is with reluctance that I eventually leave them as they stop for lunch, and we exchange telephone numbers – for which I am to be thankful next year.

The day's route is in the shape of an oval that is oriented north-south, and as I arrive to the first summit, I am halfway up the northbound edge, with the views of Loch Laggan behind me gradually obscured by hill and cloud. I am now entering the gym for the treadmill: hard work and no view, as the cloud base has dropped to about 600 metres. While there is a tiny sliver of visibility along the glen at the northern tip of the oval, and long sweeping views they are, my head is back in the clouds again as I continue the roller-coaster route uphill along the oval's other side.

The final descent down open and smooth slopes is instructive from the point of view of hillwalking technique. My guidebook has warned me 'not to be drawn off course by the transverse angle of slope'. So in the mist and without even an occasional stone as a sighting point, I set the compass bearing and *really* concentrate on following it. I check the GPS five minutes later and I have indeed veered off downhill to the left. I repeat the experiment, with the same result. Only when I continuously 'bounce' from one sighting point to another, or when I watch the compass absolutely non-stop, am I able to counteract the hidden force pulling me at right angles to my path. This example of gravitational pull is a useful lesson that I keep in mind for similar situations on future hills.

The National Nature Reserve

Just north of Loch Laggan lies the National Nature Reserve (NNR) of Creag Meagaidh. Part of it was designated a Site of Special Scientific Interest as early as 1964, because of its importance in presenting part of the Dalradian sequence of rocks. In 1986 it was also designated a NNR due to its botanical richness. There were protests from those who did not want deer excluded, nor forest plantations denied, but they were unsuccessful and the park took shape. It now presents a full Highland ecology.

There are various routes onto the three Munros of *Creag Meagaidh* (bogland crag), *Stob Poite Coire Ardair* (peak of the pot of the high corrie), and *Carn Liath* (grey hill), and I choose the one that follows the river and corrie to a very steep headwall above a lochan. I repeat two steps forward (despite one slipping back), often enough to at last arrive at a high col between the first two Munros. Though the weather below is still dry and warm, at 900 metres altitude there is driving hail and shivering wetness. I should therefore be surprised that the two lads approaching me have chosen to wear shorts – but I have become used to this type of spectacle in Scotland.

After a quick visit to the first top and then a return to the col, I mount the slightly steeper slopes to the summit of the second Munro. From there the long traverse high above a succession of three corries – often with fence posts to guide me in the mist – brings me to Carn Liath.

I am always wary when the guidebook says, 'find the feint path down', since those paths are often too feint to be found. Wiser than in my impatient, early days of hillwalking, I know it is worth scouting around for the path – but still I fail to find it. That is how I become entangled in the undergrowth of special scientific interest, and transgress my old rule of never entering a forest unless you are sure that the path will take you out the other side!

Loch Treig

A branch of the West Highland train line runs along the eastern banks of Loch Treig (pronounced *trayck*), and I have travelled it many times in both directions.

For almost its entire ten-kilometre length, the loch is guarded on its west by huge cliffs that seem to plunge 1,000 metres from ridge to loch. While the drop is indeed that long, the angle of view from the train creates the illusion of a plummet, whereas the braes in fact slope at about 45 degrees to the vertical. Viewed from any direction, the loch is a place of stunning beauty.

I am now approaching the end of my nine-day tour. The weather is deteriorating, but my periods of holiday are hard-won, and I am keen to squeeze in one more day on the hills. This is the perfect opportunity to climb the two Munros that make up that western ridge which rises above Loch Treig. If the rain and clouds do close in, I can gain the obscured views on a later trip, by climbing the two hills mirrored on the east side of the loch, in sunshine if I am lucky.

Even as I park near the few houses that collectively call themselves Fersit, the clouds are gathering, and as I set off to track the east side of the loch for a few minutes, I feel a droplet of water in the air. By the time I reach the level of the first ridge and zigzag up a long nose to the upper ridge, the rain has set in.

The rain drizzles on as I reach *Stob a' Choire Mheadhoin* (peak of the middle corrie) and then drop down to a col and up again to *Stob Coire Easain* (peak of the corrie of the wee waterfall). The drop is just over 100 metres, but despite the continuous downpour, seems much less on the helpful paths.

Rather than return over the previous summit, I choose the alternative path that drops quickly from the col to the Allt Laire river, and follow its course along boggy paths, through a forestry cutting, to the car park.

Along the way I realise that even the best waterproof pockets are not entirely waterproof, and in the process destroy a second Blackberry.

* * *

This tour has been moister than usual, but despite this and the particularly sodden conclusion, it has had its highlights – especially in the Cairngorms, to which I look forward to returning.

Though I am trophy-hunting, not number-bagging, the tour has encompassed 23 Munros, my longest trip so far. I feel that I could have added more, and wonder again whether I really should now push hard to compleat them all.

▲▲▲

Munro ecology: fauna

The Golden Eagle settles on its lichen-covered crag: the top of the food chain perched upon its base.

I described earlier how pioneer lichens and mosses established a habitat that heathers, shrubs and trees would colonise in later years. From these beginnings, thousands of species of plant and animal have surged, and the keen naturalist might spend a rainy afternoon or two sketching out the intricate food web that connects them.

Below I highlight a few subsets of this web, particularly those that involve the fauna most visible to the walker. But a few general points will first help to illuminate the Munro's eco-system. First, as we saw earlier, we are often tramping acid soils that cool damp conditions have eroded from granite rocks. At a macro level, this acidity in part accounts for the relative paucity of animal life on the higher slopes. For acid soils do not contain much calcium, which means that molluscs and vertebrates have little to sustain their shells and skeletons. Young Highland cattle grazed on high acidic soils, for example, do not develop well – and mature ones can at best merely maintain their size.

At the micro level, acid soils scare off soil fauna such as earthworms; this not only reduces soil aeration but also denies a food source to certain animals such as moles.

The vast, intricate food web that sprouts from this soil can, at its simplest, be boiled down to a few simple steps: 1) Foliage or seed or insect or worm → 2) Bird or mammal → 3) Bird or beast of prey. A few examples follow, which include the most visible of our mountain fauna.

Sapling → Red deer → Man. Since the last wolf in Scotland was killed in about 1700, adult deer have had no predator apart from man. They have multiplied dramatically as the growth of the sporting estates a century and a half ago encouraged their grazing and breeding to the detriment of re-afforestation. It would be easy to think that deer do not exist in the vast numbers claimed, since entire days of hillwalking can pass without a sighting. Of course, the deer have simply fled because they scented you long before you sighted them. Occasionally, however, you will cross a corrie where the whole grassy bowl bears the tell-tale hoof marks of a large herd. It is no easy task to poach and retrieve a deer, but in our hard-pressed economic times, poaching is apparently on the rise.

Heather → Red grouse → Golden eagle. One of our hardiest mountain birds is the red grouse, and like the ptarmigan, it has evolved to lay eggs that resist being split by frost or ice. Grouse feed on heather sustained by the practice of muirburn mentioned earlier – though their sudden up-rush when alarmed makes them a natural enemy of the deer stalker.

The Golden eagle is the ultimate raptor, opportunistically preying on several hundred types of mammal and bird including, the grouse. It will also feed on carrion, if nothing else is available. With a wingspan of six to seven feet, the eagle typically takes prey of half its own body weight or more.

But was that really an eagle you saw circling above Loch Etive? Though the eagle is twice the size of the raven, and the raven has far glossier plumage, these differences may not help to distinguish the birds when they are far overhead. More helpful pointers include style of flight (the eagle is more likely to wheel slowly in great circles; the raven to perform high swoops or even to fly upside down); tail shape (the raven has a lozenge-shaped tail; the eagle a more conventional wedge); or wing-shape (the eagle's wing having a straighter leading edge, and more defined 'fingers' at the wingtip).

Lichen → Bark louse → Crested tit → Pine marten → Red fox. Scotland boasts over 400 species of lichen, and they support large colonies of bark lice. In summer the lice spin webs that completely engulf a tree and create a ghostly appearance. In turn the lice are eaten by bark-gleaning birds such as the crested tit. The latter primarily inhabits older forests, which have more lichen. With a distinctive crest and striped markings, the tit is often seen foraging in an upside-down position. This bird also feeds on the larvae and caterpillars of the pine looper moth, which, unchecked, becomes a serious pine forest pest.

The tit's eggs and chicks are often taken by the inquisitive pine marten. This mammal can grow to exceed the size of a domestic cat, and has recovered from near extinction during the last century. Its presence is most often noticed by its droppings; these vary by season because of its versatile eating habits, and in summer, for example, are often visible as a blaeberry blue on the path or adjacent rock.

The red fox is the most widespread and abundant land-dwelling carnivore in the world, in part due to its versatile diet, that includes the pine marten. Like the marten, the fox's droppings are more conspicuous than the fox itself; the droppings are typically grey-tinged, and may contain small bones.

Berries → Ptarmigan → Sparrowhawk. The hillwalker has probably seen more ptarmigan on the hills than any other animal. They alarm the walker as often as the walker alarms them, for they are the masters of disguise: hiding behind rock-coloured plumage in summer and snow-coloured plumage in winter. They have also evolved feathers that cover their feet to conserve heat and allegedly (though implausibly) to spread their weight when on snow. Interestingly, the word *ptarmigan* comes from the Gaelic *tarmachan* meaning croaker, with the silent initial *p* added in 1684 by physician Robert Sibbald to echo the Greek *pteron* (meaning wing, as in pterodactyl). In contrast, sparrowhawks are harder to spot because they fly low and fast, skimming bushes and trees to surprise their prey, which is typically other nimble birds.

Fish → Polar bear → Siberian tiger. The bear, tiger, musk ox and several hundred other tundra animals do indeed roam Scotland's hills – though only in the Highland Wildlife Park near Aviemore, which offers intriguing sights on a half-day visit.

▲▲▲

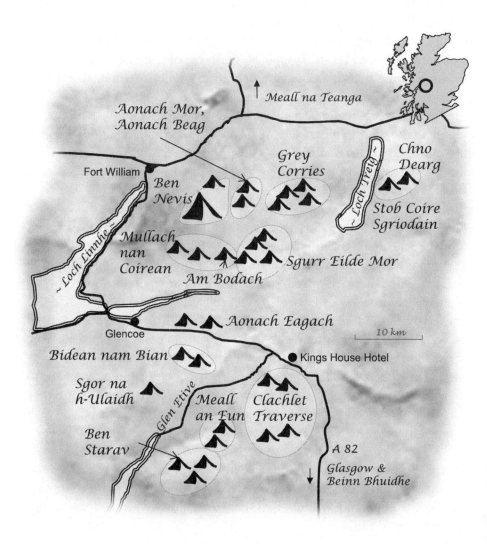

East of Fort William, and Glencoe to the South

Ben Nevis, Glencoe, and More

He who climbs upon the highest mountains
laughs at all tragedies, real or imaginary.

FRIEDRICH NIETZSCHE *Thus Spoke Zarathustra*

BEN NEVIS IS obviously the Mount Everest of Britain, but I have not yet climbed it, nor have I climbed all the trophy mountains around Glencoe's famous Pass.

I now decide, for my sixth trip to Scotland this year, to focus on these two iconic areas, while also tackling The Mamores and The Grey Corries. This journey aims to include 34 Munros, so in recounting the events I will be briefer and more impressionistic than in earlier chapters.

Since my introduction to the Munros five years earlier, my routes have taken me across 1,000 kilometres of hillside and mountain path, and up 80 kilometres of ascent, and for the first time I seriously consider trying to compleat a full round of those hills, while age is still on my side.

Yellow hill

The north end of Loch Fyne lies 15 kilometres from the viewpoint of the Rest And Be Thankful, which itself is 60 kilometres north of Glasgow. I stay the night there as a staging point to Glencoe, and as a base from which to climb *Beinn Bhuidhe* (yellow mountain) tomorrow. Sixty-five kilometres long, Loch Fyne is the longest sea loch in Britain, and at its northern end sits its world-famous oyster bar, where the oysters are indeed fyne. The views down the loch and across it are also worthy of exploration.

Many people trudge up Beinn Bhuidhe begrudgingly, yet I believe it is an under-rated hill. True, the seven kilometres of walk-in do have a feel of same-ishness about them, but they are nowhere near monotonous, and the admittedly ugly earthworks do not impose severely nor for long.

Near a ruined lodge at the end of the track, I strike left through waist-high bracken and grasses that threaten to overpower the path, then flank the river back up to its first waterfall. Now I am on my own, steeply and pathless, through hummocks less benign than the map markings indicate, to eventually reach the ridge and the cloud.

I return by the same route and high up on the track encounter a couple with a gaggle of their own and others' children. The couple had themselves played here as children, and despite now living in London have brought the kids here to play. All skipping stones and digging up insects with sticks, the youngsters look like characters straight out of a Gerald Durrell book.

The Clachlet Traverse

The Clachlet Traverse is a 25-kilometre hike, which embraces the entire massif that abuts the south-east end of Glencoe. I had pored repeatedly over the details of this route, and am now about to start that trip. This will require nine to ten hours, starting after an early breakfast from the Inveroran Hotel near Bridge of Orchy – about 50 kilometres north-ish from Loch Fyne – and ending with dinner somewhere yet to be determined.

The first challenge is the midges – the ones near the start of this walk let you know where the top of the food chain really lies! I brush them off and speed up for a while, which seems to do the trick.

Having passed a lodge and bothy on easy tracks, I turn uphill and start the first workload of the day. With the help of well-cut steps in a protruding spur of hillside, I am soon on top of the world – or at least on top of *Stob a' Choire Odhair* (peak of the brown corrie).

Much of the excitement of life happens at borders and boundaries, and the same is true of landscapes. Stob a' Choire Odhair is one of several peaks that flank the 130 square kilometres of flat, brown, Rannoch Moor. This largely featureless moorland nevertheless sports mucky lochans and bog-pools that dress themselves up as pristine in the sun's reflection, their vivid blues contrasting, tartan-like, with the earthy tones of the surrounding land. Against this background, the neighbouring mountains stand proud and clean-shaven, as if above the daily ooze of botany and zoology.

Still shaking my head in disbelief at the perpetually stunning beauty of this place, I march on, scrambling along the Aonach Eagach (not to be confused with the ridge of the same name in Glencoe), to reach the top of *Stob Ghabhar* (goat peak).

The weather still sunny, I connect to the second part of the route. This is usually walked on a separate day, and I find out why: after the drop down to an intermediate bealach, the ascent is 300 metres of steep and pathless grind.

After traversing two further gentle cols, I am on *Creise* (meaning unknown), with spectacular views over my friends the Herdsmen of Etive and beyond. I have to retrace my steps for about half a kilometre, then head down along the sharp-looking edge towards the final Munro of the day. Fortunately, the edge proves less sharp than it looks, and I soon land on *Meall a' Bhuiridh* (hill of the bellowing). With late afternoon clouds gathering, and unsure whether I would make it down in time for the last bus to the hotel, I hurry off the summit on a line that is direct but probably not the most comfortable. On skis, the natural bowl of the corrie would be exhilarating; in boots, it is just a long hack.

From on high, I am keeping a close eye on the road. If I miss the last bus I might need to hitch a lift for the 15 kilometres back to the start, and little traffic suggests little prospect of a lift. But underfoot the ground is firm and dry and I make swift enough progress that I can stop off at the Kingshouse Hotel for the tastiest and fastest ale pie ever, before catching the bus to do battle again with the midges.

Rather than stay on at the hotel, I reclaim the car and move on to Glencoe where I was anyway intending to book in with Ivan, the walker who had given me his telephone number on Beinn a' Chaorainn last year, and his charming wife Thea, at Heatherlea Bed & Breakfast.

The Lost Valley

Ten kilometres east of Glencoe village, from where the piper sometimes plays against a backdrop of the Three Sisters, I set off for the Lost Valley. This hidden vale is reputedly where the Clan MacDonald hid its rustled cattle, but man and beast must both have been agile if that were true.

I am now on my second attempt to climb up *Bidean nam Bian* (peak of the hides); you may recall that I had been snowed off on the first try. Up through the shadowy gorge, I at last stumble into daylight and the wonderful hidden plain that is the Lost Valley. I can just about imagine cattle grazing and children playing, though if the place ever had grass then the cattle obviously did a thorough job of eating it all!

Into this haven a river enters with force, then courses in unruly braids as it is suddenly unleashed: ill-disciplined, and un-channelled. I miss the correct point to cross the waters, spend 20 minutes trying to build a causeway of stepping-stones, make a note never to bother trying that again, and later cross the river with an easy hop higher upstream.

The route up the headwall of the corrie is a trough that is sandy and extremely steep, but with the ridge at last attained, I climb onwards to reach my elusive goal of Bidean nam Bian.

The view from the top makes you feel you are standing on the conductor's rostrum of the London Symphony Orchestra. Arranged around you in almost concentric rings are the ensemble of mountain ranges and ridges. To one side the massive double bass of the Glen Etive granites, to the other side the high-piping Aonach Eagach, in between are the strings of the Buachailles, and in the background, the big bass drum of Rannoch Moor. The strident chords and harmony are visible, palpable and almost audible.

But eventually I have to step from the rostrum, retrace my path back to the top of the headwall, up *Stob Coire Sgreamhach* (peak of the dreadful corrie) and back down to the road again. Though the orchestra was imagined, the man in full Highland attire who pipes me across the valley is real enough.

The lost treasure

Sgor na h-Ulaidh means 'peak of the treasure', but on a day when the wind is blowing at more than 75 kilometres per hour on the ridge, and when I am forced to give the summit cairn no more than an unashamed touch-and-go, the treasure is nowhere to be seen.

As the mists close in, however, it becomes an instructional day. It is easy to get lost when low visibility meets complex terrain. For then you can navigate neither by sight nor by compass-assisted 'line of slope'. In these situations, a GPS unit is invaluable and I thought I had learnt my lesson regarding their safe-keeping. I had lost one Blackberry GPS to a stream, and a second one to atmospheric water vapour. I now carry this valuable instrument in a heavy-duty waterproof and hermetically sealed pouch tethered firmly to my belt.

Lost in descent, I grab the Blackberry, press the button to turn on the display, and am greeted by the message 'Keyboard Locked'. The wind and rain press more urgently, and I fiddle around only to discover that the keyboard has not been locked by the normal button of the Blackberry handset – but by the specialist application that runs the mapping software. As the unit bumped around in my pocket, it must accidentally have registered some unknown series of keystrokes. I have no idea how to unlock it. How could this be happening, after I have taken so many precautions? I try all sorts of keystrokes, all to no avail.

As my shivering starts, I have one last idea: turn on the phone's network connection, pray for mobile reception, and ask Google how to unlock the application.

By a stroke of luck, I find reception and the required answer. I now carry a backup GPS unit – though this combination will doubtless prove fallible too!

Aonach Eeeeegach

There is a video in which a youthful Muriel Gray relates the perils of crossing the Aonach Eagach, while screeching the word 'Eeeeegach' and tipping backwards in mock-topple. Such is the reputation of that traverse.

I had planned to walk that ridge today, but the weather is very wet, which is unfortunate for two reasons: first, I shall remain an unbadged and immature hillwalker who has not yet undertaken this essential rite of passage. Second, I shall just have to climb separately the Munros at each end of the ridge: more effort for less scenic reward in the mist.

I duly climb the eastern *Meall Dearg* (red hill) via a lesser-trodden 'back door' path from Loch Leven, and then the western peak *Sgor nam Fiannaidh* (hill of the Fiann warriors) via the Pap of Glencoe. Visible and instantly recognisable from afar, the Pap is – or should be – a brilliant National Monument with an engaging route of access. Instead, the normal route uphill passes through a ramshackle gate on which roughly scratched capitals declare merely: PAP.

I reach the Munro summit, and from its southern edge take in the outstanding aspect of the Three Sisters, seen across the great swoosh of Glen Coe. On the way down, however, the long, ranging view that stares along Loch Leven to Loch Linnhe proves just as commanding.

That night I stay at an inn that turns out to be very noisy. In fact, it is so noisy that I cancel my subsequent nights' reservations, and plead with Ivan and Thea to take me in again. They kindly oblige, and even allow me to stay when they leave on vacation!

Nearly cragfast

Past the Herdsmen of Etive there are 16 kilometres of winding and undulating one-track road to get from the Pass of Glencoe into the heart of Glen Etive. But of course, if it weren't so hard to reach into, the glen could not have remained so stunningly unspoilt.

It rains all day for my first visit, which makes the immediate and steep ascent of *Stob Coir' an Albannaich* (peak of the corrie of the Scot) harder. The climb up the gorge-like route does reveal, however, how the power of Chinese water torture can carve a cleft deep into 1,000 metres of solid granite pluton.

The route along the top to *Meall nan Eun* (hill of the birds) undulates unpredictably and navigation there requires close attention to detail, especially in cloud and rain.

As always, descent from a summit in poor visibility is fraught with danger, and I confess to poor judgement on my way down. Descending

too early through cliffs and crags, I suddenly reach a drop I cannot negotiate. My foolishness is not so much in walking into this situation, but
rather in persevering with this line of descent. I am just too lazy to climb
all the way back up. After much thought, I figure that if I can traverse a
ledge of about ten metres length and 15 centimetres width, then I can get
to a step-like area that will let me down. I edge along the ledge, but soon
feel the cliff pushing against my back. Recalling an overheard story about
how a cliff had actually pushed someone off in this way, I return to the
start of the ledge, remove my rucksack, and take a seat on the ledge.

Bingo! As I sit down, I suddenly realise I can safely negotiate the
ledge, if I slide sideways on my bottom. Gingerly I let the rucksack drop
an anticipated three metres. To my horror, the torso-sized object drops,
bounces, then rolls and trips for a further 30 metres down the crags. Two
immediate thoughts: first, that could have been me; second, I now have
no access to any of the emergency equipment I carry.

I eventually make it down, glad to be in one piece. The rain pours, but
I would have other chances to see Glen Etive in sunshine. The highlight of
the day is to see the staggering cascades of recently rained water tumbling
and drooling down the granite slabs that make up the slanting headwalls
of the return glen.

Return to Loch Treig

By contrast, the next day is hot and summery as I travel north-east to
return briefly to Loch Treig. Stalking has started, and I had called the
estate to be told that I may indeed walk the designated hills. But when I
turn up at Fersit, I notice a fancy Land Rover with a personalised registration plate, loaded with people who look like paying guns. As I park,
I strike up conversation with a local chap who had been straining with
binoculars to scan the horizon. 'Just keep to the ridges,' he says, 'and ye'll
be ok.' I follow his instructions, though this standard routing along ridges
during the stalking season always makes me feel like an easy target for a
wayward gun or empty-handed deer-hunter.

Before starting out I am tempted to lighten my pack by removing
the heavier gloves and the extra thick fleece, in recognition of the sunny
weather. But in these situations I always recall how rapidly the weather
changed on Beinn Sgritheall...

I set off, past the parked guns and along the farm track. Led by the
course of the tumbling stream towards its source, I attain the knobbly
metamorphic ridge, and then the summit of *Chno Dearg* (red nut, or red
hill).

I mentioned previously my view from a train of the great curtain wall that flanks Loch Treig, and I can now see it from the best of angles. One huge sheet of rock-face: a giant billboard on which nothing has yet been posted, save for a fault here, a hollow and a bump there, and a crag over in the corner. I am greedy, and hope for a view of Loch Ossian too, but the intervening hills preclude that and I would have to wait until next year for my first full view of it.

The stillness of the day is interrupted by a polite flurry of a breeze, quickly followed by a more insistent and intrusive tugging at the sleeve and tousling of the hair. By the time I reach the rim of the corrie that extends to *Stob Coire Sgriodain* (peak of the corrie of the scree), the air is shot through with icy blasts from no direction in general, yet from every direction in particular. I stop to pull on all my extra layers, now glad that I had not jettisoned them.

In descent, I avoid the huge bowl where the deer would have gathered, keeping downwind as far as possible along the vague ridge that stretches down to the corrie's lochan.

As I pass the houses at Fersit, portly men bulge fat and flat against the windows of the 4x4s, glowering looks shot towards me over polystyrene cups, no doubt blaming me for their lack of sport that day.

The eagle

Summer rains have revived the Eden that is Glen Etive, and now the sun is perking every blade of grass and sprig of bracken erect. Morning has broken – like the first morning.

I cross the River Etive by the well-made bridge, turn right and skirt the newly fenced-off croft to head for the imposing bulk of *Ben Starav* (mountain of noise). This hill is a vast sumo wrestler of a mountain with a low centre of gravity – but benign paths and terrain lift me quickly up its side. Halfway up, I loiter to collect myself and to collect the features of the scene: high hills crowding deep glens, rounded tops rising over sharp-edged ravines, black lochs fed by white rivers. What the passage of time and the elements have done to Glen Etive is wonderful; it is still an Eden, viewed even more clearly from the summit.

I press onwards, dropping down the sharp yet negotiable ridge to a high col, then out and back to take in *Beinn nan Aighenan* (hill of the hinds). Back at the col I rest to gird loins and Snickers bars for the remainder of my nine-hour hike that would total 20 horizontal kilometres, and 1.8 kilometres of ascent.

Perhaps the Glen Etive eagle knows to associate a seated hiker with subsequent crumbs and morsels, for as I lay on my back for a few minutes I see it spiralling slowly, slowly above me with end feathers spread like fingers. I recall having seen such an eagle from the higher vantage of Ben Cruachan four years earlier, and wonder if it is the same one.

The ascent to the day's final Munro of *Glas Bheinn Mhor* (big green-grey hill) is straightforward, though its topography can only be described as 'baggy', and this tends to obscure the views along the way rather than to enhance them. In continuing fair weather, I press on, with five kilometres still to cover. But with the infant and then adolescent Allt Mheuran as my babbling pal, and helped by the stalkers path past the Robber's Waterfall, I return safely to my start.

*   *   *

Though I shall again pass through Glencoe and feel its magic and its majesty, I have now completed my round of its Munros, and so make my way towards the Nevis and Mamores ranges. And yes, the latter range is indeed named from the Gaelic *mam-* meaning mammary-shaped.

The CMD arête

After years of *not* climbing Ben Nevis, I want to do so on a day that is clear; I am, after all, still in Trophy-hunting mode. Today is one such day, and I set off, initially up the well-trodden tourist path.

My first destination is the Munro of *Carn Mor Dearg* (big red hill) and to reach it requires turning off the tourist route at the Halfway Lochan, and skirting around into the deep cleavage of Ben Nevis's bosom. Having then crossed the river, I head up steep and path-free slopes to the summit cairn. With five years of hillwalking in Scotland, I think I know what 'hill-fit' means, but I am suddenly passed by two lads who have both fitness *and* youth on their side. We chat briefly and then they speed off, apparently armed with some inside knowledge about a better point at which to cross the river. I slog on, and it is of some comfort to the old dog (me) that when I do reach the top, the two speedy youngsters are still struggling up. Their progress has been hastened by the enthusiasm of youth, but also diverted by its recklessness.

I now reach the centrepiece of the day: the traverse along the sharp arête that joins Carn Mor Dearg to The Ben. I wouldn't want to do it in snow or high winds, but on a sunny summer afternoon it is not too scary, and of course the views are superlative: south to my first ever Munros of the Ring of Steall, and north into the Ben's corrie. Inevitably, there is a sting in the tail: the final leg-sapping climb up to the summit of *Ben Nevis* (possibly meaning venomous mountain).

As the summit plateau comes into view, I am astounded. *WARNING: SPOILER – don't read the rest of this paragraph if you have yet to make your first visit...* the plateau looks like something from Tibet or Burma – the pure white ground, the multiple spires (cairns to remember those who have died on the mountain and beyond), and the other-worldly light. I am expecting the tourists, of course, since this is one of Britain's most-climbed mountains, but the spires come as a huge surprise. Yet, as in my descent off Liathach and many other hills, it is that view way out to the north-west that is the ultimate boon: to Skye, to Knoydart, and beyond into the sun.

The time comes to descend, in the company of scores of fellow walkers. There is not much new to see on this descent, save for the stones that I have not previously tripped upon – but there is good conversation to be had with fellow hikers, old and young.

Beyond Kinlochleven

It is pointless to pick favourite routes, but if I have to then the circuit of the four Munros above Kinlochleven will be near the top of the list.

I start from the Mamore Lodge Hotel, which is closed as I pass it, the chap painting the windows saying it was because of a dispute with the landowners. But from there the path is nicely inclined all the way to the high lochan, about seven kilometres farther on.

It is a full day of seven and half hours, 18 kilometres and 1,600 metres of ascent. But it is worth every bead of sweat as I make the circuit of *Sgurr Eilde Mor* (big peak of the hind), *Binnein Beag* (little peak), *Binnein Mor* (big peak) and *Na Gruagaichean* (the maidens).

My brief notes of the day, written up in the pub that evening, read:

> Highs: great ancient lumbering hills gathered around the lochan watering hole; sweeping vistas across the back-country; amazing straights of Loch Leven framed by the AE [Aonach Eeeegach] on the L and un-named hill [actually Beinn na Caillich – hill of the old woman] on the R – look like great sentries guarding the entrance to a land of pharaohs or that bit from Lord of the Rings. Lows: none.

A *real* whaleback

Such fickleness! Yesterday, brilliant sun; today, thick, low, mucus cloud that blocks the sinuses of the glens like snot.

In such conditions I almost don't bother going up the huge whaleback ridge that lies to the east of Ben Nevis, and which includes *Aonach Beag* (little ridge) and *Aonach Mor* (big ridge). I almost succumb to the temptation of taking the unusually convenient gondola up, instead of walking. I nearly stop halfway up instead of continuing to the summit. And once on top, I almost can't be bothered to find the cairn. Everyone has their ultimate pointless hillwalking experience, and this is probably mine.

But don't let me put you off, for on a good day the views of The Ben and beyond would make it worth expending every one of the required 5,000 calories.

And there's always the pleasure of the chance encounter: I have a most enjoyable half-hour chat with a chap who had operated the chair lifts for years, and is now out in the freezing rain 'just for fun'. When I seek his expert opinion on boots (since mine are starting to leak), he extends a leg and nods at his yellow footwear, 'sailors' wellies,' he says, '… can't beat 'em.'

So much for Goretex!

Loch Lochy

The next day the whole country is suddenly blessed with High Pressure. I am torn: having been walking the hills for 11 days without a break, I am now looking forward to the comfort of my own bed and the conversation of my friends and colleagues. Yet on the other hand, who in their right mind would pass up the opportunity of guaranteed sunshine on the mountaintops? 'Another few days,' is my compromise.

Yesterday was a fairly hard day. So, on my principle of alternating hard and easy where possible, I now decide on a more relaxed day. This is how I come to fully appreciate the 15 kilometre-long Loch Lochy, and the two Munros that overlook it: *Meall na Teanga* (hill of the tongue) and *Sron a' Choire Ghairbh* (nose of the rough corrie).

While the walk-in yields delightful forest promenades and the summits offer excellent views, I admit that the true high points of the day are, surprisingly, the views from the roadside up and down the vast rift that is Loch Lochy – sweet holiday postcard, severe lines of perspective, and distant vanishing points all-in-one. Definitely a Beauty scene.

An old friend

With skies still bright and blue, I return to the scene of my first Munro outing: Glen Nevis (around the back of Ben Nevis). The nearby Mamores can be climbed in a huge variety of permutations, and my route today aims to take in *Stob Ban* (pale peak) and *Mullach nan Coirean* (summit of the corries), with a special sideways extension to climb *Am Bodach* (the old man). (You may recall that five years earlier I had had to detour past it as I rounded the Ring of Steall.)

Initial paths take in dark forest, tinkling-twinkling burn and boggy hillside to bring me to the summit of the day's first Munro.

Accompanied by a raven – more laggard scavenger than spirit guide – my path skirts corrie after corrie, six in total, to bring me to the second summit. Passing shattered peaks, along crumbling ridges, and past thick sills of brilliant marbleised limestone, I eventually reach the col that marks the start of the normal descent.

But the Old Man beckons, and soon I am back on the Ring of Steall again, travelling anti-clockwise to Am Bodach. As I scan along the ridge for three kilometres to where I mounted it on my first Munro day, I see a party picking its way along it. Tiny ants, almost invisible: such an image once again screams out our tiny-ness in these vast landscapes.

Looking down into the corrie, I am five years older, and my legs have tramped a thousand more kilometres, but the glaciated valley has not blinked.

The Grey Corries

Sheared and folded strata draped with grey: weathered and shattered quartzite that a billion years ago was sand, laid down in some now extinct sea: I gaze out through the picture-window of The Braes Guest House to the huge rocky rampart in the middle distance.

I have been talking to myself for several days now, and resolve that this really will be my last outing before returning to home, hearth, and mental health.

After parking a bit too cautiously and thus too far from the true start of the trek, I nevertheless make good progress along the Lairig Leachach – an old road along which cattle were once droved 40 kilometres, from the Great Glen to Kingshouse Inn in Glencoe.

At a well-maintained bothy eight kilometres from the start, I turn right and head up a petite valley to a col. The valley is gorgeous but boggy, and I wish afterwards that I had taken the path that ascends the ridge to the south of the valley. As I leave the col to ascend *Stob Ban* (pale peak), I bump into a smarter walker who has overtaken me by using that better ridge route. After a brief chat, Bill continues on while I still face the slog up the white shattered quartzite.

Returning to the col, and climbing the zigzag path to *Stob Choire*

Claurigh (peak of the corrie of brawling), it is a pleasure, for a change, to have someone tracking ten minutes ahead of me. For to judge scale and distance in the Highlands seems much more difficult than elsewhere, and a human-sized ruler ahead helps greatly.

The ridge path on to *Stob Coire an Laoigh* (peak of the corrie of the young deer) offers wonderful variety: switching to left and then right, on fine gravel and then crumbling quartzite, atop flat tramlines and then the exposed edges of slanting beds of rock. And the views surpass many of the trip so far, especially to the west where Ben Nevis plays hide-and-seek, dipping behind intervening ranges when my path sinks.

Atop the third Munro I meet Bill again and we share a late lunch. He had planned to return to his car, but we persuade ourselves that there are enough hours of daylight to include *Sgurr Choinnich Mor* (big peak of the moss) in our outing. This extension requires some exposed moves, and a perhaps ill-considered decision to contour around the final top on our return, rather than to re-ascend it.

All that remains is a ten-kilometre ramble over hillock and through glen to bring us to Bill's car and, with thanks and adieus, to mine.

On this sixth trip of the year, I have claimed some Trophy hills. I have also bagged 34 Munros in 14 days, though the effort required seems less than for equivalent previous trips. I am ready to enter a new phase of hillwalking.

▲▲▲

Staying safe on the hills

'What is the leading cause of death when hillwalking?' asks the instructor on the Wilderness First Aid course I am attending. Hypothermia? Fall? Stumble? But my fellow participants and I all guess wrongly: being hit by a car is the most likely cause of fatality, as we walk to or from the start of our route. You have been warned!

Lurking in glens and rivers and on ridges and slopes, however, are other dangers that must be taken seriously. Each year during the period 1996–2005, an average of 187 people were injured and 26 met their deaths on Scotland's hills, and most of those incidents were preventable (see the Mountain Rescue Committee of Scotland site: www.mrcofs.org/pages/statistics.php).

Below I set out the leading risks and relevant precautions. Please take them seriously on every trip. Accidents *do* happen. I confess to having been in fear of my life at least twice on the hills, so now always carry two GPS units. I have seen a fit person break two ankle bones just through misplacing a foot, so I now tread with extreme care.

Causes

It is clear from the table below that poor navigation is the prime cause of those incidents that required the attendance of the Mountain Rescue Service in Scotland between 1996 and 2005. Any kit that will prevent you from getting lost is worth taking. I used to navigate using only a compass and map. Then I supplemented these with a map-enabled GPS and a spare. When hearing of this, a former colleague, a member of the Territorial SAS, claimed this was making life too easy (not precisely the words he used), and said I should be able to navigate in zero visibility using 'line of slope' alone. He has yet to accept my challenge of negotiating several square kilometres of Ben Alder's undulating summit plateau in mist...

Causes of mountain incidents (percentage of 2,466 cases)

23%	Poor navigation
18	Bad planning
11	Inadequate equipment
11	Medical
8	Poor timing
7	Group separation
5	Inadequate footwear
4	Inadequate clothing
3	Rockfall/hold gives way
3	Poor level of fitness
2	Inadequate skill
2	Avalanche
2	River crossing problem

Safety rules

The risks on the hills derive mainly from failing to plan for three factors: weather, terrain and remoteness.

The weather, for example, can change in minutes even on low-lying hills. There *will* be four seasons in a day. Specifically, the higher you go:

- the lower the temperature ($1°C$ per 100 metres)
- the stronger the wind (2–3 times the speed in the valleys)
- the greater the rainfall (3 times than in the valleys)

- bigger the risk of mist and cloud (mist on the tops three days out of five).

Terrain too can differ from your expectations – exposed paths perhaps more eroded, rivers deeper or swifter and the ground harder to read. And the sudden absence of a phone signal can plunge you suddenly into more remoteness than you had bargained for.

So, sensible precautions must be taken (the following is adapted from Registers of Scotland: www.ros.gov.uk/pdfs/hillwalking_safety.pdf)

Preparation
- Consider attending an approved mountain skills course
- In remote settings, only attempt half the distances and elevation gains that you have comfortably achieved in safer environments
- Learn how to cross a river or stream; streams in flood are particularly dangerous and may need to be avoided
- Know how many of your paces on rough terrain equal 100 metres
- Never walk alone if possible

Planning
- Decide where you are going and how long it should take, and get a weather forecast for the area
- Ensure that you will be off the hill well before dark
- Always leave word with some responsible person: where you will be walking and at what time to expect your return; update this as needed; set an electronic reminder that you must announce your return (people do forget)
- Take a compass and map (waterproof or in a waterproof case); mark your route on the map in advance; have safety routes and know how you would reach shelter or a road if needed
- Take a GPS unit (based on satellite, not a telephone network); keep it in an *airtight* container as humidity alone can destroy a unit; potentially take a backup too
- Take a fully charged mobile phone; but do not assume you will get reception and never do anything that you would not do if you did not have the phone with you
- Use walking boots with good ankle support
- Wear suitable clothing and carry spare warm clothes at all times. Essentials include a waterproof hooded jacket and over-trousers, headgear (and spare), gloves (and spares), fleece (and spare one)

and probably an extra layer too, *irrespective of the weather on starting out*

- Use a rucksack for spare clothing, food, drink and reserve high-energy snacks; consult relevant sources to estimate the amount of water you need to carry; plan on doubling consumption on a hot day
- A small torch and first aid kit are useful; a whistle essential. Also take a biro (its ink will not smudge) to note grid references if needed, or to write emergency notes

When walking

- Know where you are in the hills at all times. Keep checking, and collect 'markers' along the way
- Place your feet carefully on each step of the way as there is always the risk of concealed holes, rocks, slippery ground and soft bog; be particularly careful when descending steep ground
- In a genuine accident or emergency, contact the emergency services and ask for Mountain Rescue. A sequence of six blasts on a whistle, or flashes of a light, at one-minute intervals is the recognised distress signal which may be picked up by rescuers of other walkers

A final point: technology has moved on, and legislation now allows walkers to use a PLB (Personal Locator Beacon). This can be used to alert emergency services, and if it is a 406MHz unit, uses geo-stationary satellite communication (not mobile networks) to receive your GPS location automatically and very quickly. About the size of a cigarette pack, weighing about 200 grams, and costing around £200, these devices are a great insurance policy. I always carry one – even if I have left the rucksack, to make a side-journey off the main route.

▲▲▲

Phase 4 – Flow

IN THE LANGUAGE of the oriental philosophy of Taoism, there is a principle called *wu wei*. This is the principle of 'effortless action'; and approaching it becomes the next and penultimate stage of my journey. Rather than merely claiming the summits of hills designated as High-Quality icons, I seek to go further. I now aspire to having High-Quality *experiences* on those hills, or with them. This is subtly different from my previous stages of hillwalking, for now my journey takes me on a more spiritual tack.

Wu wei, 'effortless action', is a doctrine neither of passivity, nor of mere acceptance… nor even of simple efficiency. Rather it is a principle of extreme focus cleared of clutter and distraction; of passion vested completely in an activity but not wed to a pre-conceived outcome; and of intimate engagement with the action itself.

It is what makes the golf-swing that, with the ultimate 'ping', drives the ball further than you have ever driven it before, though with apparently less force than you have ever previously exerted on a swing. It leads to the perfectly arcing tennis ball that flies from the sweet-spot of your racquet as if sent by the strings alone, rather than propelled by your arm. It writes the computer programme that works perfectly first time. It spawns the unexpected pun or one-liner that has everyone in tears of mirth or rolling on the floor laughing aloud. It is being in a mode that allows you to act in complete concert with your surroundings, with maximum connection. It is about being alive to experience an opportunity. It is about being alive.

In contrast, a bad *wu wei* day is when you struggle endlessly and achieve nothing, or notice nothing. All effort and no action, no result and no experience.

Wu wei appears in the psychology and philosophy of both west and east. In the west, *wu wei* is what Mihály Csíkszentmihályi has famously described as being in the Flow: completely immersed, with focused energy, time passing though you are unaware of it. In psychology, it is akin to Jung's individuation, and to Maslow's self-actualisation. In the Zen of the east, *wu wei* is the 'mind of no mind' (*mushin*), when anything can be realised because although you are purposeful you are also flexible, and not bound or diverted by preconceived goals and strategies. In retrospect, I see that little by little, step by step, this was the attitude with which I came to approach the hills.

In the following chapter *A Pound on the Foot*, I start the year with the dramatic Munros that girdle Lochs Eil, Affric, Arkaig and Mullardoch. I come to understand the significant effect that lightweight boots and equipment can have on speeding or extending the day's journey: *wu wei* of the body.

Zigs and Zags recounts a criss-cross route across the Highlands as I 'mop up' the scattered Munros I had not yet climbed. It also tells of how I come to understand the best angles of zigzag and gradient to follow: *wu wei* of the mind.

And in *May the Road Rise up to Meet You*, I revisit the Cairngorms Proper and explore Glen Shiel, hoping finally to attain *wu wei* of the spirit: to literally conspire with the landscape, to breath with it, in a lasting epiphany.

* * *

Whatever our mission, we eventually reach a stage where the passion is in the technique and in its perfect execution: technique first employed consciously, and then lived unconsciously. It is at this stage that the Journey becomes more important than the Destination...

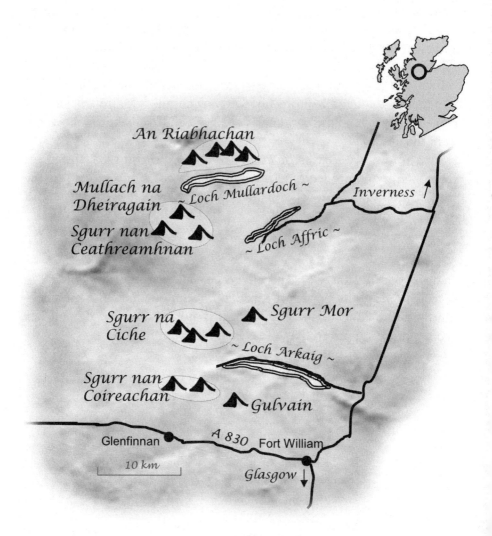

An Riabhachan

Mullach na
Dheiragain
~ Loch Mullardoch ~

Sgurr nan
Ceathreamhnan
~ Loch Affric ~

Inverness

Sgurr na
Ciche
Sgurr Mor

~ Loch Arkaig ~

Sgurr nan
Coireachan
Gulvain

Glenfinnan
A 830
Fort William

10 km
Glasgow

North-West of Fort William

CHAPTER 12

A Pound on the Foot

Man of the plains, why do you climb the mountain?
So I can see the plains better.

CHINESE SAYING

THE TWIN-ENGINED Otter DHC–6 suffers only slight turbulence as we cruise between the peaks of the high Himalaya. We all breathe a sigh of relief that the clouds have stayed at bay, because landing at Lukla airport, once voted the most dangerous in the world, is not something you want to do in poor visibility.

Having taken a leave of absence from work, I am on a year of travel, and next on the itinerary is trekking the 120 kilometres from Lukla to the Base Camp of Mount Everest and back.

Though the mountains are huge, I feel they do not match those of Scotland in terms of allowing you to truly engage with the landscape. The Himalaya are Hollywood, but a too distant spectacle; in Scotland you are in the landscape, not just on it; you are exclaiming with the hills, not at them. And of course there is the old adage, 'climbing Everest is good preparation for Scottish winter mountaineering!' But from observing closely the footwork of the porters, bearing loads that often exceed 100 kilograms, I do learn much about the *wu wei* of walking.

Our entire party of ten make it to Base Camp and back, and while everyone else suffers broken or twisted limbs, severe stomach problems, or altitude sickness, I am still fit by the end. I feel pretty proud of myself – until I land back at Heathrow to find I have acquired a severe lung infection from wandering around Kathmandu's dirtier streets.

I had, however, already booked a three-day, 12-Munro trek in the Highlands, and in early May, ten days after my return to the UK, and with the course of antibiotics coming to an end, I am back in Scotland getting in a few days' hill practice in Glenfinnan and Glen Dessary before the trek I have booked with Steven Fallon. Steven has climbed all the Munros a staggering 15 times (at the time of writing), and holds the current record.

Heroes

Glenfinnan is home to heroes both ancient and modern. At the head of Loch Shiel stands the solitary tower that remembers Bonnie Prince Charlie, who landed nearby from France, raised his standard, and led the 1745 Jacobite Uprising that saw a Scottish army strike within 200 kilometres of London. More recently, it was Glenfinnan's famous viaduct that saw Harry Potter aboard the Hogwart's Express, hurtling at full speed.

Near these sites, today's Munros are more remote than on some of my earlier trips, and for the first time I use a mountain bike. It helps me to gobble up the four and a half kilometres from the start of the route, under the viaduct, to the beginning of the path that leads up to *Sgurr nan Coireachan* (peak of the corries) and *Sgurr Thuilm* (peak of the hollow).

Several years ago, I had started to take an interest in the effect of boots' weight on the walker's *wu wei* and stamina, and was finding that having wet boots was not merely uncomfortable, but it also created noticeably more fatigue. So the twin considerations of keeping boots dry and light for as long as possible, and of traversing the ridge with the wind at my back rather than in my face, suggest a circuit clockwise. Several people are taking the opposite route for no particular reason that I can see, apart perhaps from the fact that most guidebooks suggest that direction.

The paths are clear and the terrain firm and I make good progress. The literal high point of the day is the northward sight of Glen Dessary and the intensely deformed metamorphic rocks that give The Rough Bounds of Knoydart its name and its extremely rugged character, as I would later experience. It is almost incredible that it was across these inhospitable lands that Bonnie Prince Charlie made his escape after Culloden, somehow navigating in the dark of night and sleeping rough in tight-drawn plaid.

I tear myself away from the view, and on the way down, I practice the techniques of Geisha and Water. I discovered these walking techniques by accident five years ago, and they have kept my knees pain free since then, on all descents, however steep or arduous. The former technique requires making your steps quick and *tiny* (not just small); like a geisha your feet are practically overlapping as you step. The latter technique requires taking a slalom line that you would imagine water taking over the terrain. Taken in combination, these techniques allow you to glide serenely down almost any slope.

* * *

The bike comes out for the next day too as I tackle *Gulvain* (*'Gaor Bheinn'*; possibly meaning filthy hill) from Glenfinnan. From the foot of this hill the route to the top seems straightforward, but it is a long slog with a false summit that is most misleading, and thus highly demoralizing, especially as I am overtaken quite rapidly by a walker who has both youth and fitness on his side. But as so often in brilliant weather, the fantastic views make it all worthwhile – even though today they are almost identical to those of yesterday.

Return to Loch Laggan

Monarch of the Glen was filmed near Loch Laggan, so as I park nearby the area seems vaguely familiar from occasional TV scenes. Here, 50 miles inland, just past Fort William and Spean Bridge lie three Munros I have not yet climbed: *Beinn a' Chlachair* (mountain of the stonemason), *Creag Pitridh* (possibly Petrie's crag), and *Geal Charn* (white hill). They are often to be found – or rather, not found – clothed in cloud, and since the weather now looks set fair, I take the opportunistic step of climbing them today.

The bike soon takes me to the Lochan na h-Earba, lying just south of Loch Laggan. On a sunny morning with the shimmering blue of the loch reflecting the even bluer sky, the west end of the loch is the perfect spot at which to stop – for no reason other than to absorb the view and wonder whether there really was a sentient God. For everything is so perfectly arranged: a perfect loch between two such perfect ranges of hills, and the long-past flight of the bird that dropped a seed from which a solitary rowan tree would sprout beside the path with such perfect positioning.

But a breeze stirs, and I move on to Beinn a' Chlachair, standing guard over its north-facing corrie, still snowy. To the south, the Ben Alder massif 12 kilometres away looms surprisingly large. But the wind is now screaming in my face, so I turn and via easy ridges am gusted along to the two further Munros of the day. From the last of these (Geal Charn), the northward aspects to Loch Laggan and the Creag Meagaidh Reserve are particularly impressive.

The Rough Bounds

For hundreds of years, Knoydart has borne the epithet 'The Rough Bounds' because of the lumpiness of its metamorphic rocks, and the deeply incised nature of the fjord-like sea lochs that slash inland.

The Knoydart peninsula is a huge tract of remote land between Loch

Hourn and Loch Nevis that juts out towards Skye, and its features reflect practically the whole geological history of the Earth – from Lewisian gneiss originating several billion years old to the glaciation of the last mini-Ice Age 10,000 years ago.

Not surprisingly, therefore, the 30-kilometre drive deep into Glen Dessary along the northern shores of Loch Arkaig is one of stunning beauty. The majesty of the scenery continues as I bike up to the further reaches of the glen and then take to foot and hillside up a path to *Sgurr nan Coireachan* (peak of the corries), from where I can appreciate the delightfully shaped Loch Quoich.

As expected, the ridge walk to the next two Munros of the day – *Garbh Chioch Mhor* (big rough breast) and *Sgurr na Ciche* (peak of the breast) entails a rough and knobbly path though without serious difficulty or obstruction. The route is accompanied by another amazing 'famine wall'. Although the wall is somewhat smaller in all dimensions than the one near Inverlael, it is far more remote. Again, one is forced to wonder how many windswept and ice-riven nights its builders could really have spent on the hill as they constructed it.

From the last of the day's peaks the whole of the Knoydart peninsula stretches out below, with the islands of Skye, Rum, and Eigg shimmering in the distance. Lounging against the ample windbreak are two couples, with one pair of the walkers embarked on the mission of climbing every Marilyn in mainland Scotland. The Marilyn List is a cousin to the Munro List, but includes all mountains that have a relative height (a measure of their prominence from the surrounding land) of more than 150 metres, and there are 1,214 of them in Scotland. The couple apparently moved up from England for this sole purpose, which suddenly makes my own Munro goals feel far more manageable.

The route back from this last outlying Munro is a lengthy one, and I am glad of the bike to speed my return. With the prospect of a 60-kilometre drive along single-track and undulating road out of the glen and back in again the next morning, I decide instead to bivvy on the mountainside on the route to tomorrow's peaks.

Having bathed in the ample bathtub of the ice-cold loch and consumed a bite of early high-carb dinner, I retrieve my sleeping mat, borrowed bivvy-bag and some food from the car. Since my pack is slightly heavier than usual this evening, it is lucky that the bike ride is not too lengthy; and I am again soon clambering up heathery slopes to a col.

In principle, cols can be too exposed and windy for a good night's kip, but this col has plenty of large boulders and furrows behind which to shelter. The beauty of the bivvy is its simplicity: find flat ground and remove or trample any bumps, lay out the large bag, insert the sleeping mat and shove the sleeping bag in on top of the mat. Optional extra: lay out cheap polythene sheet underneath, potentially adding soft vegetation beneath if it is available – which on this occasion it is not. I have a surrogate dinner, and inject myself into the bag.

Since I have committed few crimes of any importance – and perhaps because I am too insensitive to have a guilty conscience – I generally fall asleep quickly, often within 15 seconds of hitting the sack. But I am also quite a mobile sleeper, and twisting from one side to the other does not work well in a bivvy bag. I cannot pretend that I slept well.

Which rock is which?

I awake with the dawn, glad that the midge larvae buried beneath me are still hibernating, but damp from the condensation that has built up inside my bivvy bag. Fortunately the weather looks set fair for today, and I treat myself to a cup of coffee, brewed in my kitchen of titanium Esbit stove (just 13 grams), a pot made from a beer can, and a hexamine fuel tablet. Breakfast is pitta bread and jam; then I am off.

Mor means big in Gaelic, and from the col, the great curtain wall of *Sgurr Mor* (big peak) does indeed seem over-sized. Just when I am expecting a small hill nestling tidily amongst others, I am instead confronted by a long, steep, pathless climb up the side of a ridge that had apparently been plonked down as yet another barrier that hinders access into the secretive peninsula of Knoydart.

I lighten my load by hiding my bivvy bag, sleeping bag, and other paraphernalia beneath a huge rock of unique and unforgettable shape. The lightness speeds my step, and I duly reach Sgurr Mor's summit without excessive sweat. The views are similar to those from yesterday's vantage point five kilometres to the west, and so I am not complaining!

However, on my return I find that the 'huge, unique and unforgettable' rock no longer seems so large nor so unforgettably shaped. I was so sure I would recognize the spot; but even when I regain the patchy path, it takes me 15 minutes of searching to find my deposited items. (Tip: write down the grid reference from the GPS when depositing kit.)

* * *

I do not usually take rest days during walking trips, but since returning from Everest, my lungs feel they are operating at only 75 per cent of their normal effectiveness. In addition, I am about to start three days of trekking with the famous Steven Fallon, so I take the next day as a vacation from the vacation, driving slowly to the rendezvous 60 kilometres further north near Loch Mullardoch.

At the Tomich Hotel that evening, the team assembles: Steven himself, another guide by the name of Adrian, two other walkers and me; a friend of mine having had to cancel at the last minute for personal reasons. I had decided to climb these hills with a guided group both so that I could enjoy more company than usual, but also because the logistics of climbing the next Munros would be more complicated than normal. As the plans for the next three days are set out over a beer, I realise I have made a great choice of guide.

Mullardoch

The next morning, Steven drives us to the dam at the east end of Loch Mullardoch where we meet Carl the boatman. Carl is a Norwegian who moved to Scotland many years ago because he 'likes deer'. He has a motor boat into which eight passengers can squeeze, and which he then pilots five miles up the loch to deposit us on the shore. This saves us having to walk the heavily eroded path along the northern shores of the loch. Ten quid very well spent.

Fortunately, we three clients of Steven's seem to be equally fit (though Steven himself is a hill-runner and fitter by far than most, and Adrian also runs hills, including the Everest Marathon, which he has completed four times). With the guides throttled back from their maximum speed, we keep together well on the circuit of the four Munros: *An Riabhachan* (the brindled one), *Sgurr na Lapaich* (peak of the bog), *Carn nan Gobhar* (hill of the goats), and *An Socach* (the snout). Even by the high standards of May, the weather is excellent and the views therefore stunning. The highlight is definitely the northward view across Loch Monar, to lands that I would explore later in the year. Down in England, East Anglia is already suffering the drought of the century...

Glen Affric

The next day is tougher. We start with the 16-kilometre bike ride in from Glen Affric car park, along a track that is both undulating and stony. We dismount the bikes a mile or so before reaching one of Britain's most remote youth hostels at Alltbeithe. Legs are burning even before the climbing starts.

Our route takes us first to a further *An Socach* (the snout) which already has its head in the clouds. Returning to a col, we next ascend the ridge to *Sgurr nan Ceathreamhnan* (peak of the quarters) and with the wind at our backs, continue the ridge walk to *Mullach na Dheiragain* (peak of the sparrowhawk). As we reach the summit, the cloud conveniently clears to expose dramatic views over the broad glens below on both sides. Adrian, a highly qualified ecologist, 'brings the ground to life' throughout the day: the 16 different types of sphagnum moss; the insectivorous plants; the crag where – more than likely – the eagle would perch (but not build his eyrie), and so on.

We avoid the easy route back, instead taking a straight 'Roman' line down for 300 metres into the massive glen that bars our path, then up the other side, eventually reaching our original col and later our bikes, and the 16-kilometre ride back to the cars...

I start to notice that my breathing is becoming more laboured than usual, and I mention this to Adrian. It turns out that he normally takes a month's rest after his Everest Marathons to allow his lungs to recover. This reassures me that I was not merely lacking general fitness, but makes me wonder whether I, too, should have rested for longer after my return.

* * *

My sleep that night is fitful, and I am unable to draw full breaths. So in the morning I decide that prudence should trump bravura – and with bitter regrets opt out of the final and most strenuous day. When I return home and look up the details of that route, I realise I had made a good decision, since the day would have been about 50 per cent harder than the previous one.

My trip thus concluded with a tally of 17 Munros, and a mental note to rest for the next month.

▲▲▲

Does a pound on the foot really weigh five on the back?

I once read the claim that carrying an extra pound of weight on your feet (i.e. half a pound on each foot) is as tiring as carrying *five* extra pounds of weight on your back.

As I was about to buy a new pair of boots, I thought I should research this properly. Should I consider super-lightweight boots? Do gaiters impose a significant hidden burden when walking?

It turns out that the first evidence for the claim comes anecdotally from the successful 1953 Everest expedition.

> ... the expedition came to the conclusion that in terms of physical effort *one pound on the feet is equivalent to five pounds on the back*. A consensus of informed opinion now seems to support that assessment.[1]

There is further anecdotal evidence from veteran long distance hiker Chris Townsend, whose hikes include the 5,000-kilometre Continental Divide Trail, amongst many others, in *The Advanced Backpacker* (2001): 'The often quoted adage that a *pound on your feet equals five on your back is true* in its overall implications.'

More scientifically, from Soule RG, Goldman RF (1969) Energy costs of loads 27 687–690 carried on the head, hands, or feet. *Journal of Applied Physiology*: '...energy cost is about *five times greater* if you carry a weight on your feet compared to carrying it on your torso.'

SJ Legg & A Mahanty. Study conducted in part fulfilment of an MSc in Human and Applied Physiology, London University, Ergonomics, Volume 29, Issue 3 March 1986, pages 433–438. (Affiliation: Army Personnel Research Establishment, Hants, England): '... indicating that [in terms of energy] it was 6.4 *times* more expensive to carry weight on the feet as compared to the back.'

Somewhat to my surprise, the maxim is confirmed overwhelmingly by both anecdotal and scientific evidence, and I experienced similar results as I exercised on an inclined treadmill, carrying varying weights of pack and boots, and using my pulse rate as a rough measure of effort.

Another rule of thumb asserts that: 'A pound *off* the back adds a mile to the day'. Given that lightweight boots can be two pounds lighter than conventional boots, those lighter boots are equivalent to ten pounds off the back – or put another way, should allow you to hike a further ten miles or 16 kilometres in a day. It is clearly worth considering the lightest footwear consistent with sufficient ankle support.

▲▲▲

---

1   Quoted in *The Complete Walker* IV (2002) by Colin Fletcher and Chip Rawlins.

Glen Etive

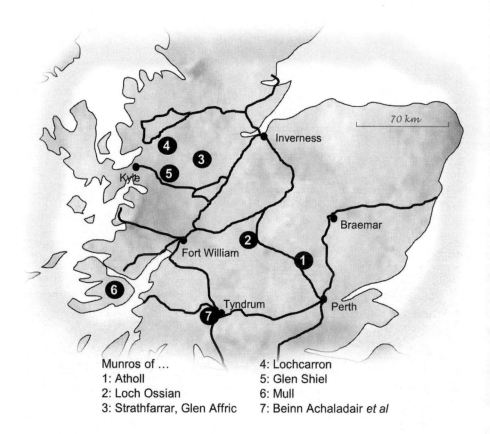

Munros of ...
1: Atholl
2: Loch Ossian
3: Strathfarrar, Glen Affric

4: Lochcarron
5: Glen Shiel
6: Mull
7: Beinn Achaladair *et al*

A tour of selected remaining Munros

CHAPTER 13
Zigs and Zags...

The noise of the world does not touch me. I live too far
inland to hear the thunder of the reef. To this place no
postman comes; no tax-gatherer. This region never heard the
sound of the churchgoing bell. The land is Pagan as when
the yellow-haired Norseman landed a thousand years ago...

ALEXANDER SMITH *In a Skye Bothy*

ALTHOUGH THE EXACT centre of Scotland lies near Drumochter Pass, 70 kilometres south of Inverness, Loch Ossian feels more like its true centre of gravity. The Loch's name also links it to a literary centre of gravity, in that the mythological poems of the Gaels were supposedly authored by the eponymous Ossian. His work lent impetus to the development of Scottish literature and indeed to the whole Romantic Movement. Fans included Byron, Wordsworth, Goethe and Thomas Jefferson; devotees included Napoleon Bonaparte and the painter Ingres. If there were a list of trophy lochs, the picture-postcard Loch Ossian would, for varied reasons feature prominently.

The loch is also the geographic centre of my ante-penultimate expedition across the Munros. This will be a large circuit that takes in Atholl, the nine Munros in and around Loch Ossian, vile accommodation, the site of a Spanish invasion 200 years after the Armada and the drama of the volcanic island of Mull.

This June expedition is one of rich diversity and also juxtaposes vastly differing landscapes – creating an album within an album of memories. My aim is to sweep up those Munros that lie outwith the few core areas that will see my final ascents.

Fifteen hundred miles of driving (and an unwarranted speeding ticket) would be the small price to pay for 16 amazing days on the hills and the trophies experienced along the way.

Blair Atholl

Few areas within the Grampian Mountains region are flat, but the land around Blair Atholl is one of them. The evocative place name derives from *Blar* – Gaelic for field or plain, and *Atholl*, Gaelic for Old Ireland.

Heavily populated in comparison to more remote areas in western Scotland, its history is entwined with the Jacobite Uprisings of 1745, 1715 and earlier. The notable Jacobite, 'Bonnie Dundee' to his friends and 'Bloody Claverhouse' to his enemies, is buried in the chapel of the town's castle, and the current Duke of Atholl is the only person in Europe entitled to raise a private army, though it was not defending his hills as I set out for them.

As the mountains here protrude from flattish lands, the views are unusual: sharp ridges and well-rounded hills elbowing each other within a landscape of generally low-level hummockiness.

The route over the top of *Carn a' Chlamain* (hill of the buzzard) provides such views, though it starts at a lower level in Glen Tilt. This glen is a huge U-shaped valley, which for hundreds of years was a road for droving cattle, and a link across the Cairngorms to Aviemore and beyond.

I bike up the glen to reach Marble Lodge, named after the local prevalence of this rock. The area has drawn many geologists over the centuries, most notably James Hutton, in 1785. His interpretation of the evidence here, that veins of hot molten granite must have squeezed through cooler surrounding sedimentary rock, helped his emerging theory of Plutonism win the battle against the prevalent Neptunism (Plutonism held that hot magma wells up and forces land upwards from beneath the sea. The opposing Neptunism held that all rocks are deposited on top of each other, out of the sea). This in turn was an essential step in proving that the Earth was indeed older than the 6,000 years claimed in the Bible.

Having reached the top of the bike track, the summit is merely a few kilometres away. There, in dense mist, I come across a couple eating their sandwiches in the shelter of the cairn. In the next week they are to compleat their joint round of the Munros, at the grand ages of 75 and 77, having climbed 30 of those hills in the last two years.

This is inspiring, but on my way back down the hill, I have an encounter that is even more moving. I take a shortcut through rough scrub down the side of the mountain, and as I round a bluff a roe deer springs up out of the heather barely six feet in front of me. She must have been lying down, and I cannot understand why she has let me get so close, since deer normally run a mile if you get within a kilometre of them.

Then I see it... from the spot from which the deer has bolted, not six feet away from my feet, is a faltering fawn – caught between first breath and first step. Hind legs staggering, front legs not yet. Less than ten minutes old, a new life in an ancient landscape. I move quietly away, glad to note the mother's cautious return.

A twisting ridge

Beinn a Ghlo is a single winding range of hills that comprises 40 square kilometres of mountain protruding from a relatively level, if hummocky, plain.

To visualise the ridge atop Beinn a Ghlo, imagine a long block of ice cream with a Blancmange-like cross-section. Then take 19 differently-sized scoops (one for each corrie) and scoop out hollows, in contact with each other, all the way around. Down the spine of the block, where the hollows meet, the remnants of the slab would have a ridge similar in character to the twisting and rolling path that crosses Beinn a Ghlo. No wonder there is a rumour that a rifle fired in one corrie cannot be heard in the next one.

I traverse this range by the most popular route that first climbs *Carn Liath* (grey hill) to reach the ridge and its 19 corries. Next comes the Munro with the best-sounding name of all: *Braigh Coire Chruinn-bhal-gain*, pronounced 'bray correr croon-vaalakun' (brae above the corrie of the little blisters – i.e. hillocks), and then the third and final Munro of *Carn nan Gabhar* (hill of the goats). No goats there, but a few squawking ptarmigans instead, and a group of three solo walkers who have coincidentally congregated near the dishevelled cairn.

We break bread together, making us instant companions in the literal sense (from the French *com* + *pain* meaning with + bread). Mary looks to be in her 20s, lives in Perth, and is studying photography. Replete with long camera lenses, her pack appears to be the heaviest of the lot, and even viewed on the inadequate screen of her camera, her photos suggest she has talent. Gordon, probably in his 30s, has clearly taken a shine to Mary and as I arrive is talking loudly and attentively, making it hard for Dave from Penrith to get a look in. The dynamics evolve, with Mary apparently interested only in photography.

As we stand up to leave, Mary leads the duo a merry dance over a top that will take them to the steep path down the nose of a long ridge; I bid them farewell and instead take the low road, heading down to the path that descends via the final corrie and glen. Congruent with the principle of *wu wei*, this flowing path saves me from a knee-crunching descent – but then again, my boots become so water-logged down in the glen that they need three days to dry out fully.

A truly red hill

I have already climbed seven Munros named after the colour red and Atholl's *Beinn Dearg* (red mountain) becomes the eighth. In most cases, these hills are not red during the day and only acquire a fiery-orangey hue at dawn or dusk as they catch the early or final rays of the sun. Blair Atholl's Beinn Dearg is red all day, however, as it comprises large volumes of the hard-wearing red granite responsible for its protrusion from the nearby plain.

Once again I approach by bike to save walking 19 of this route's kilometres. I then take to a path that darts deep into a minor valley then zigzags helpfully to gain height. From the intermediate shoulder of the hill, the rolling countryside beneath resembles a mosaic of deep peaty muirburn, and in the distance the surprisingly wide Bruar Water sparkles with the intense white reflections of the sun.

The summit itself is non-descript and the view from it is non-existent as cloud lingers over the final hundred metres of ascent. But my Munro summits are still running cloud-free for two-thirds of the time, so I am not complaining.

* * *

Via Drumochter Pass, I now venture to Loch Ossian and Loch Ericht, which I have to approach by train, and which promise my first experience of a bothy night.

Corrour to Culra

The Tetrapak dynasty now owns the Corrour Estate, but it was an earlier Victorian owner who allowed the West Highland Railway Company to cross his land and had Corrour Station built so his family and guests could board and alight the train.

In a remote location on the banks of Loch Ossian, public access to Corrour is only by train or lengthy hike or bike ride. I am therefore as surprised as others have been to see cars and vans parked there (they belong to the estate). Nevertheless, the land here feels extremely remote. The great swathe of loch that extends before you to the Beallach Dubh (black col) is perfectly framed on its nearer shores by wee islands and promontories on which native-looking trees have established themselves. Ossian is a picture-postcard scene.

After arriving at the station in the early morning, I bike to the far end of the loch and survey the ridge that will lead me for 12 kilometres over four Munros and many intermediate bumps, beyond the distant black col, and onwards to Culra bothy – of which more in a moment. This is a slightly unconventional way to climb these hills, but on the laptop at home, it looked logical.

From the loch, I soon leave the lower path and take to grassy un-pathed slopes. Having recently read several scientific papers on the best way to walk up mountainsides, I aim for the optimum gradient and *wu wei* takes me to the first Munro: *Beinn Eibhinn* (delightful mountain).

My ridge path is then relatively straightforward until I arrive at the edge of a corrie set all about with sheer cliffs. Fortunately, a guidebook had provided the grid reference from which the only safe path of descent starts, and with the help of my Blackberry GPS I locate 47990 75069 to within a metre or two.

From this vantage point, huge sweeping valleys now come into view; sparkling rivers and streams issue from glinting lochs and lochans; and in the middle distance, the sharp scalpel of the Lancet Edge – a more exciting route of descent, but heading off in the wrong direction for my destination today.

With the previous two Munros passed – *Aonach Beag* (little ridge) and *Geal-charn* (white hill) – there is just the ascent of *Carn Dearg* (red hill) before dropping down to the bothy.

On the way I re-fill the water bladder. For five years I had thought the bladder to be too much hassle, and had instead relied on a collection of Evian water bottles. With convenient square cross sections, they fit neatly in the rucksack, and I typically carried the whole day's supply of water. The bladder is a large rubber bag with a tube you can suck through, and I had always assumed this system would be more complicated to clean.

My grandfather, a canny Scot, had once warned me against drinking from the streams since 'ye never know what's died upstream'. Climbing up beside a burn one day, I was tempted to fill an almost empty bottle, but at the last moment thought better of it. Twenty yards up the burn I did indeed come across the rotting carcass of an ex-sheep, and never again was I tempted to fill the bottle from the stream...

Yet with an imminent stay at the bothy overnight, and no potable running water there, I had succumbed and bought the bladder, chlorine dioxide tablets, and an inline filter. That system also seemed more *wu wei* than lugging ten kilograms of water over ben and glen.

I had chosen this route partly to experience Culra bothy – since without visiting a bothy, no tour of the Highlands could be complete.

For the uninitiated, a bothy is a shed with no running water or electricity, an earthen floor, and, if you are lucky, some raised planking on which to sleep. It serves both as an emergency shelter and as a staging point for longer routes. Optional extras include candles, firewood (which you should replace), a shovel (which you are expected to use; there will be no toilet), and a view through a window of plastic instead of glass. Some bothies are haunted, sometimes by the ghosts of stalkers who have hung themselves from beams stretched wide above the very spot on which you lie.

But Culra is a five-star bothy and though it is 15 kilometres by foot or bike from the nearest road, it attracts a crowd. Derek and James are English but volunteer a week a year to maintain the bothy, which they are doing with diligence as I arrive. Brian, Jim, and Dave are farmers from the Lake District who 'for a change from farming' go on annual hillwalking holidays together in Scotland. Hazel and Janine are getting in some practice for their Duke of Edinburgh Gold. And just when I think I am getting the smaller room to myself, two athletic Scots with chiselled features and a purposeful air arrive. The ten of us indulge in idle chat and re-live favourite hiking moments until the early evening. As we turn in we each prepare a slightly different sleeping system, and each begin a slightly different dream of our challenging plan for tomorrow.

A triple rainbow?

The bothy was warm, but with only a thin Thermarest between me and the plywood mattress, my slumber was not comfortable.

Next morning I click bones back into sockets, arise and dress, splash water on my face, and consume as many muesli-borne calories as possible. After bidding farewells, I set off along the river on a new route back to Corrour, having been reassured the previous evening that there was no need to go downstream to the bridge since there would be plenty of crossing points upstream.

After a very long walk, I eventually find a place to cross the river and head up to *Beinn Bheoil* (mountain of the mouth) via a combination of track, stalkers path, heathery slopes and animal tracks. The weather is all Scottish enigma: simultaneously brilliant sunshine and cold fine drizzle, the result of which is the most perfect double rainbow I have ever seen: two huge arcs with the second bow's colours reversed. Since the clouds behind me are inky black, I swivel around. Just sometimes you can catch a tertiary rainbow, but you have to look towards the sun (17 degrees from it, to be precise) and need a dark background of the clouds with the sun just peeping though a hole. No luck, as usual!

After the rainbows there is mist, cloud and rain for much of the day. The trusty GPS keeps me on the right path, and using precipitous cliffs as what walking books euphemistically call a 'handrail', I reach the summit trig point of *Ben Alder* (hill of rock and water). I force down half a sandwich, but cold air and damp drizzle are gnawing away at me, and I press on due west.

There is an elegant simplicity about my compass bearing: it is rare to travel precisely towards a cardinal point. But on this descent I keep precisely due west for over an hour as all sorts of terrain drift past me like a video montage, from avoided chasms to peat hags and streams. In due course, I reach the river, and after unshackling the bike, eventually reach the warmth of Corrour Station House Hostel.

Flanks of Loch Ossian

The Station House was a bunkhouse until the year 2000. Now it has a Swedish design that in my view is more hotel and less hostel – certainly if you have your own private room. After a night of deep sleep and an excellent breakfast with porridge offered both 'the English Way', with milk, or 'The Scottish Way', with water (I normally do half-and-half), I bike round the southern shores of Loch Ossian to start my route across two Munros.

The paths to *Carn Dearg* (red hill) and *Sgor Gaibhre* (goat's peak) are clear and require relatively little hacking over grass and heather. En route, I catch up a fellow walker and as we reach the summits the real prizes of the day become apparent: the sweeping braes eastward down to Loch Ericht; the tiny stream to the south-west that is the farthest headwater for the vast Blackwater reservoir. Then, glimpses to the north-east of Loch Ossian, and half-way to the loch, a herd of about 50 deer which suddenly catch our scent and scarper.

When passing tops that are fractionally lower than the magic 3,000 feet in elevation, Munro-baggers often wonder whether to scale them. The elevations of most trig points are accurate only to plus or minus 60 centimetres, and of spot heights from aerial charting to about 3.3 metres, so there is always the chance that a more accurate survey might one day promote a peak to Munro status, and thus require a return visit.

At the hotel, a fellow breakfaster had mentioned that Sgor Choinnich, now standing just to my right, was a promotion candidate, though not because of its height. At 929 metres, it is actually well above the 914.4 metres that equates to the required 3,000 feet. But is it a 'separate mountain' from the summit I am now standing on? To my mind, it is not, since it's only 900 metres away, and the rise from the intervening col is little more than 100 metres. I believe it should remain a non-Munro.

Instead of climbing the hill, I descend from the col into the vast but relatively shallow basin of a corrie. My line of descent follows the deer I had seen earlier, and now I stand where they had gathered with the tell-tale pockmarks made by hundreds of hoofs, each hoof trampling scores of times before their flight.

I reach the bike and circle the loch to the foot of *Beinn na Lap* (mottled mountain). Perhaps one of the easiest Munros to climb, Beinn na Lap nevertheless offers an excellent bird's eye perspective over Loch Ossian and its fractal shoreline, and on the horizon, every line of sight ends on a mountain. Indeed, it is on this hill that the following question first comes to me: from which Munro is the greatest number of other Munros visible? This has subsequently been the source of much banter in pubs, tents, and hotel bars. Answers on a postcard or via Facebook please...

Back at the station, it is a long wait for the 9:18pm train, and I eventually reach Tulloch station and my car, barely in time to reach my next destination by 11pm, when my accommodation would close.

▲▲▲

What is the ideal angle at which to zigzag uphill?

The hill-slope that rises in front of us often bears no path. In compleating my round of the Munros, I guess I was off-path about 40 per cent of the time (perhaps I was particularly inept at finding the hidden tracks!).

Yet I am surely not the first walker to ascend a virgin hillside to suddenly find a boot-mark or two previously impressed where I was treading, and then a path.

This led me to feel that in getting from A to B up a hill, some strategies must be more efficient than others. Too few zigzags require you to take uphill steps that are large and inefficient and leave your Achilles tendons strained; too many zigzags deliver too little ascent for every step, and so you have to walk farther. For help in understanding this aspect of *wu wei*, I turned to science for help.

Imagine my delight, then, at finding a whole eco-system of theoretical and practical research into this topic, buried within which was the answer I sought.

If the slope is inclined only slightly, then, not surprisingly, the answer is to go straight uphill – but at what gradient should you start to zigzag? It turns out that a gradient of about 25 per cent, or one in four, is best for most people (or slightly less than this if your metabolism is being strained – e.g. during exertion at high altitude).

If you are interested, consult the paper by AE Minetti, *Optimum gradient of mountain paths*, listed in the Suggested Reading section. This professor combined experimental results on the metabolic cost of walking uphill, with insights into the biomechanics of gait. Walking uphill essentially involves two types of movement: a slight pendulum sway (or 'waddle') at lower gradients and pure muscular flexing (think 'treadmill') at steeper gradients. Analysing the combined movements, he found that for most people, the most economical gradient of mountain paths is approximately 25 per cent.

Or consult the later paper *Zigzagging: theoretical insights on climbing strategies* by Llobera and Sluckin. These professors note that trails made on steep hillsides by both humans and animals often exhibit dramatic hairpin bends and shortcuts, and they developed a model of how we walk on a hilly terrain.

Technically, they find that

> the structure of the theory resembles the Landau Theory of Phase Transitions, much used in theoretical physics. We find that both switchbacks [hairpin bends] and shortcuts appear as efficient strategies for downhill walkers, while uphill walkers retain switchbacks. For weakly inclined slopes, the best strategy involves walking directly uphill or downhill. For sufficiently steep slopes, however, we find that the best strategy should undergo a transition to a broken symmetry solution corresponding to the switchback trail patterns typical of rugged environments.

On a separate note, however, whatever route takes you to the upper reaches, be prepared for unexpected insight – at least as suggested by another one of the many fascinating research papers on mountains: *Why revelations have occurred on mountains? [sic] Linking mystical experiences and cognitive neuroscience* in the Journal of Applied Physiology, by S Arzy and others.

In their words,

> the fundamental revelations to the founders of the three monotheistic religions, among many other revelation experiences, occurred on mountains. These three revelation experiences share many phenomenological components like feeling and hearing a presence, seeing a figure, seeing lights, and feeling of fear. Similar experiences have also been reported by non-mystic contemporary mountaineers. The similarities between these revelations on mountains and their appearance in contemporary mountaineers suggest that exposure

to altitude might affect functional and neural mechanisms, thus facilitating the experience of a revelation. ... Prolonged stays at high altitudes, especially in social deprivation, may also lead to prefrontal lobe dysfunctions such as low resistance to stress and loss of inhibition ... we suggest that exposure to altitudes might contribute to the induction of revelation experiences.

On a wet afternoon, you could do worse than to explore these and similar findings – such as *The optimal locomotion on gradients: walking, running or cycling?* cited in the recommended reading. On a sunny afternoon, you could be on the hills zigzagging up in whatever direction takes your gradient to 25 per cent.

▲▲▲

The shortest way to walk across Scotland traces the 40 kilometres from Glasgow to Grangemouth. But some of the best routes across the Highlands go with the grain of the glaciated glens that run from Inverness to Glen Shiel and on to Skye. With a north-east to south-west lie, these glens and lochs create a landscape that has mighty ripples, and through the glens of Affric, Mullardoch and Monar, the walker who wishes to scale the intervening ridges and peaks finds access on dramatic routes.

The Gate

Read any book on walking the Munros and you will come across the Impediment of the Locked Gate. The route around the four Munros accessible from Glen Strathfarrar makes for a six to seven hour outing, so you really don't want the additional effort of biking 30 kilometres up and down the length of the glen: driving in is far preferable.

By a compromise agreed in the mists of time, the owners of this estate allow vehicular access to the glen between certain times and on certain days of the week. For anyone planning a linked series of days on the hills, it is therefore important to avoid turning up when the gates are locked.

I arrive just after nine o'clock in the morning, expecting to be confronted by an officious gatekeeper, but am pleasantly surprised to find instead a helpful lady playing this role – much younger than I had presumed – who had moved with her husband to Scotland from Yorkshire for the love of the hills.

Access granted, I drive on, and hope I can eventually make it out of the glen before the gate is locked in the late afternoon. Depositing my bike where my day's walk will end, I drive on to the start. This makes me the only one of five parties that day to complete the circuit clockwise; perhaps they know something that I do not? As usual, I base the direction of my circuit on my preference for keeping boots dry and light for as long as possible, and for having the wind at my back rather than in my face when on the ridge.

The path up to *Sgurr Fuar-thuill* (peak of the cold hollow) has to be one of the most perfectly graded in all of Scotland. Specifically, the path from the upper loch rises 400 metres over a distance of just over 1,500 metres, making for a perfect gradient of 25 per cent. Amazingly, the path maintains this grade consistently for its full length to the top – sustained even as it rounds the face of a steep corrie.

The eponymous 'cold hollow' of the corrie is indeed cold as I traverse it, and though it is mid-June I still need most of my layers of clothing to stay warm. Alas, the weather deteriorates as I progress to *Sgurr a' Choire Ghlais* (peak of the green-grey corrie) which is indeed green, *Carn nan Gobhar* (hill of the goats) where the goats must have been in hiding, and *Sgurr na Ruaidhe* (peak of the redness), which is indeed red.

The descent from the final peak is extremely wet and boggy, and I am glad I did not start my route here. At the bottom another walker claims she had spent her childhood years holidaying in the glen and knew it sloped in such a way as to make the *anti*-clockwise route better for the return bike journey of six kilometres. I am not convinced but, regardless of the relative merits, we all make it out of the glen before it is locked for the night.

Tom and Toll

Glen Affric is considered by many to be the most beautiful valley in Britain. It comprises 30 kilometres of sparkling rivers and glinting lochs that are dotted with miniature island jewels, edged by slopes that support remnants of the ancient Caledonian Forest and overlooked by a complete ring of enticing peaks.

I had previously biked down the south side of the glen. But on the north side I am closer to the water, and the twinkle of the loch is more visible through the trees.

I am now making up for missing the last day of my previous trip with Steven Fallon, though I plan to circuit the five Munros on two separate days rather than Steven's one, to build greater flexibility into my schedule for the coming days.

Once away from the lochs, the route around *Tom a' Choinich* (hill of the moss) and *Toll Creagach* (rocky hollow) is not spectacular by Munro standards, apart from the view over the path twisting westward to the huge ridge to Carn Eighe and Mam Sodhail, which I would climb tomorrow.

Would you climb the same Munro twice?

A new dawn, and I head deeper into Glen Affric. You could be forgiven for thinking that the estate-keeper's house is the main lodge, so perfectly picturesque is its setting. Only on my return at the end of the day do I see the large true lodge, built in granite-grey and sited in a position that is simultaneously hidden yet all-seeing.

The day's route is one of many possible permutations over the peaks, and at the cost of having to climb one Munro twice, I choose the circuit that will both keep my boots dry for longest, whilst also including the non-Munro Sgurr na Lapaich. I include the latter as someone had tipped me off that it may be in line for promotion to Munro status – and I wanted to avoid the 1,000-mile round-trip that might be required to bag it!

So having passed Affric Lodge, I ascend the dry and easy path up the valley of Allt Corrie Leachavie to reach *Mam Sodhail* (hill of the barns). On its summit at 1,181 metres the mist is skimming the hilltop, but I can just make out two figures paused at the large cairn. They are an engaging couple with whom I walk and converse for much of the day.

Less than a kilometre away apparently stands *Carn Eighe* (file hill), higher than Mount Snowdon in Wales and the 14th highest mountain in the UK. It is a pity that it is invisible.

Yet a few seconds later the mists miraculously part, and through a gap that looks like a huge fluffy picture frame comes one of the loveliest sights. Vast flanks of mountainside in cadmium green, flecked and peppered with taupe rocks, sweeping hundreds of metres down to an azure blue lochan 600 feet below, and rising precipitously upwards to the cairn just visible from our elevation. A few seconds later it is gone. 'That's what makes it all worthwhile,' whispers one of my new companions in awe. While treasuring this unique moment, I personally hope that a 27-kilometre, ten-hour, hike will deliver more than just this!

I proceed over Carn Eighe and out to the remote *Beinn Fhionnlaidh* (Findlay's hill), for if you don't include it in the route, you'd probably have to spend another day climbing it separately, with Carl the boatman ferrying you in and somehow out too.

The clouds continue to kiss the tops for the rest of the day, breaking the views again as I return: seguing around Carn Eighe, re-ascending

Mam Sodhail, and taking in Sgurr na Lapaich's ridge. Returning then along the loch-side, the real Affric Lodge briefly shows itself in all its mysterious beauty, then disappears as I continue my return.

▲▲▲

The Highland Cross and other challenges

I had entered Glen Affric just in time, as wardens were about to 'close the glen' for an unusual event called the Highland Cross, which included guest star Pippa Middleton.

In 1982, serving Fire Officers Gerry Grant and Calum Munro dreamt up The Midsummer Madathon. It was a challenge that required typical Scottish grit, to race 75 kilometres across the Highlands from coast to coast.

From Morvich in Kintail you ran for 30 kilometres through the mountains into Glen Affric, then switched to the bike and cycled a further 45 kilometres to Inverness. Invitees were emergency service and military units in the Highlands; all proceeds to charity... the final total donation came to over £12,000 shared between five charities.

Re-named the **Highland Cross**, this event now attracts 700 participants and in 2010 raised over £200,000, with nearly £3 million donated to charity since its inception. If you prefer, you may walk the route instead of running it!

Other charity sporting challenges to consider include:

The Corrieyairack Challenge

The Glencalvie Challenge

The Great Wilderness Challenge

The Heartbeat Challenge

The Loch Ness Marathon

The Nairnshire Challenge

If you can field a team of three sailors and two fell-runners, then consider **The Scottish Islands Peaks Race**, held annually on and around the most stunning bays on the West Coast of Scotland. This race starts in Oban with a short hill run, then you sail to Salen on Mull, run over Ben More, sail to Craighouse on Jura, run the Paps, sail to Arran, run Goat Fell, and finally sail to Troon. The Race takes two to three days and caters for Multihulls, Racers and Cruisers. Its strapline: 'A Long Weekend with a Difference.'

What next?

With your round of the Munros nearing compleation, the question starts to bubble up: what next? This issue appears to trouble even those who neither tick lists nor collect manically. Perhaps the desire for another outdoor challenge is simply the siren song of the glen, the Pied Piper of the hill's breeze, or the call of the wild. Whatever the reason, here are some thought-starters, heart-stoppers, and leg-warmers. The more obvious options fall into six broad categories:

1. **More Munros**: more rounds on varied routes? In winter? At night? Fully self-propelled? In sequence (by height, alphabetically, north to south, east to west)? You would not be the first to attempt any of these rounds (except perhaps the nighttime one). Or perhaps the Ramsay Round of Ben Nevis and 22 other Munros within 24 hours (that's 93 kilometres horizontally and 8.7 kilometres of ascent)?

2. **More of Scotland's outdoors**: hills such as the Munro Tops, the Corbetts, Grahams, Donalds? Long-distance paths such as the Cape Wrath Trail, or walking The Watershed? What about a collection of glens (as an inverse of hills)? Lochs? Rivers?

3. **More British hills**: Marilyns? Wainwrights? Hewitts? HuMPs? The Bob Graham Round of 42 Lake District peaks and 72 miles in 24 hours? The Ten (or more) Tors of Dartmoor? Cumbria's County Tops?

4. **National Trails**: The Pennine Way? Hadrian's Wall? Offa's Dyke? The Long Distance Walkers Association's Hundred Miler?

5. **Europe**: The Camino de Santiago de Compostela, and on to Finisterre to cross Spain? The Alpine Pass Route across Switzerland? The GR20 across Corsica? Across Spain or France on the GR10, GR11, or Haute Route Pyrenees?

6. **Further afield**: the many trails across the USA such as The John Muir Trail? Or, for example, Taiwan has its own list of 164 mountains and 258 peaks that exceed 3,000 *metres* in altitude and which rival even the Munros for sheer spectacle.

For further inspiration, I recommend the photographically amazing *Top Treks of the World* edited by Steve Razzetti, which almost had me off to the base camp of K2. Or perhaps the smell of the heather can linger in the memory as you *cultivez votre jardin...*

The last three days have brought me deep into the glens that lie at the heart of Scotland, and I now move on to Strathcarron on the West Coast.

Gerry's Hostel

Between Achnasheen and Loch Carron 30 kilometres away, there are six Munros, and to visit them all you typically camp or stay for at least a night at Gerry's Hostel in the hamlet of Craig.

Gerry's is the Fawlty Towers of hostels. It is an institution well-known to those who have trodden this region. Many people report that Gerry himself is rude, though he was polite and well-mannered during my visit. However, I find the premises dank, damp and virtually uninhabitable; if I lift a floorboard I expect to find several dead bodies. To his credit, Gerry switches on the two industrial strength humidifiers when asked. One way or another, a visit will be memorable and I must admit that the three other guests are all returning guests – albeit they have not visited for the last 20 years! Surely there must be a better spot at which to stay in the area.

I survive the night and prepare for the bike ride of five kilometres that will take me up steep hills and deep into the Allt a Chonais glen. When the steep but bikeable track runs out, I cross the river and head up over *Sgurr Choinnich* (peak of moss) and along the fine buttressed ridge to *Sgurr a' Chaorachain* (peak of the little field of berries).

The Strathcarron area receives more than double the average UK rainfall, and this particular ridge must receive double that again. I feel that the day's trip has little to recommend it as I head on to the appropriately named *Maoile Lunndaidh* (hill of the wet place). This is not a standard extension to the route of the two prior Munros, and there is no path. Even with a compass and a GPS receiver loaded with maps, the navigation in low visibility is challenging.

I am glad to reach the reassuring safety of the glen, and wish I had known of the walkers' hut next to Glenuaig Lodge, kindly provided by the estate. Miles from anywhere, this warm garden shed sports a pair of bunk beds and electricity for heat and light spurred from the adjacent mini hydro-electric plant. It feels drier than Gerry's Hostel.

A badly-placed glen

It is raining and cloudy today, and I loiter in my car to see whether conditions will improve. Eventually I see someone else taking to a track and I decide to set off too, despite the fact that people have gone astray on today's long route, even in clear weather.

The path follows that of yesterday for the first few hours, but today is bound to be a bigger day, with 33 kilometres to travel horizontally, and more than two vertically, in an outing of nine and a half hours plus ten kilometres of biking.

Unfortunately, I spend much of the day in driech dampness and mist, and although we are only three days away from another Midsummer's Day, the mercury has fallen and neighbouring hills are even blasted with snow and hail!

I soldier on nevertheless over Beinn Tarsuinn (a Corbett) and on to *Bidein a' Choire Sheasgaich* (peak of the barren corrie) with the mists lifting for just long enough to show the horror of the required climb ahead, up through its serried ranks of vertical protective buttresses: 300 metres upwards in less than 200 horizontally. After the summit, I continue my roller-coaster route to a bealach and up to the top of *Lurg Mhor* (big shin) itself – a huge ridge that stretches out purposefully, in the manner of a leg.

The books talk of two options for the return: either back over all the hills of the outward journey, or back just to the bealach and then down into the corrie – contouring around so as not to lose too much height – and then re-joining the original path nearer its start. I choose the latter approach to avoid re-climbing the Corbett, and as I emerge from the clouds, I am rewarded with yet another one of those sights that makes even a wet and cloudy outing worthwhile.

For spread out behind my right shoulder is the spectacular corrie I have just descended, at once imposing yet welcoming. In front of me stretches Loch Monar, huge and arresting even when viewed through rain, and to my left are the wonderfully carved sinews of the glen up which I am to return.

I start contouring around the bowl of the corrie. I am doing well, hardly losing any height. Very well. In fact, am I not doing *too* well? Something must be wrong... Suddenly I realise with horror that the deep glen I am ascending is actually just in front of the even deeper glen that hosts the correct route. In retrospect I should have gone back to correct the error, but it looked like such a long way... Soon I do re-join the original path, but at the wrong point – meaning that I must re-climb Beinn Tarsuinn all over again before regaining bike and road. I'm not even bagging Corbetts, and now I've done the same one twice on a single, rainy day.

Most walkers have at some point descended into a wrong glen, but this is the first time I have *ascended* one. I am comforted only by the recollection that the famous mountaineer Chris Bonnington of Annapurna and Himalaya fame once admitted to having climbed the wrong mountain on a weekend outing in Cumbria.

No hanging about

Sometimes it just makes sense to nip up and down a hill, and with continuing cloud and rain in Strathcarron, and with Glen Shiel beckoning me southwards, I succumb to the temptation of the quick and easy route, knowing that the views from the flanks and top of *Moruisg* (big water) will today be limited at best.

* * *

I am now on the homeward stretch of this circuit of Scotland and snake down past the Kyle of Lochalsh to overnight in Glen Shiel before climbing one of its routes.

Glen Shiel

Glen Shiel's history rivals that of Glencoe, and is outlined in the next chapter. It also offers fine walking by any standards, and many walkers have created their own daily record by bagging all seven Munros of the South Glen Shiel ridge in a single day.

I am however merely 'passing through' and my aims are more limited, since once I have climbed today's hills I will be continuing southwards to the island of Mull.

Today's track could take you all the way through to Glen Affric, but I turn off before then to climb the nose of A Chralaig. I proceed with some trepidation, since a year earlier I had heard in a pub of a party that had turned back before the second Munro of this route, since the path is so exposed.

The initial route up to *A' Chralaig* (the creel – a small wicker basket used by anglers to catch lobsters or store fish) does not disappoint. As is so often overlooked in the guidebooks, the views from halfway up can be far better than those from the top, and here is no exception. Spread out below is Glen Shiel as it cradles Loch Cluanie, all curving road and meandering river, with the white spot of the Cluanie Inn where a toasty breakfast is doubtless being served. Above this rises the South Glen Shiel Ridge itself – its peaks 'written across the sky in a high, stiff hand' (to steal a line from WH Murray).

With clouds gathering, I pray merely that I shall reach the ridge before my boots attract a kilo of rain-watery weight. The elements oblige me, though the ridge itself peeps in and out of mist. When it is visible, the ridge ahead does indeed look as daunting as the story I had heard: *very* spiky pinnacles, for a *very* long way. I wonder how I shall negotiate it. As I approach, however, it becomes clear that a reasonable path skirts just

below the pinnacles themselves, and my confidence returns for the continuation to *Mullach Fraoch-choire* (peak of the heather-corrie).

As I start to descend, the mists clear fully and an unusual sight presents itself: an entire crinkly ridge concertina-ed out before me, with mist
appearing to boil off its windward edges and simultaneously billowing
up from its leeward corrie (to the extent that anything is leeward in the
Highlands) – yet all in perfect sunshine.

I take many photographs then head back along the ridge for as long
as feasible to avoid what the books describe as the very muddy start of
the track in the glen below, and end with a descent down steep flanks on
conveniently stepped and ridged grassy slopes.

Back in the car, I consume the sandwiches of cheddar cheese and raspberry jam that I would have eaten en route if I had taken longer, and
prepare to drive southwards.

Mull

Ben More (big hill) on the island of Mull is often the last Munro of a
walker's compleat round since it is more difficult to reach than most and
relatively solitary. The thought is perhaps, 'only climb it if you have to'.

I had wanted to visit the hill sooner than that – hoping to finish my
round on a hill that afforded easier access for unfortunate yet obliging
friends who might join me. Cairn Gorm perhaps, as the railway would
allow access for virtually any companions (although the attentive reader
will observe that I have already climbed that hill, and will perhaps here
question my balance of pure ethics versus consideration for others).

I reach Mull via the Lochaline to Fishnish ferry and next day head off
towards the start of the route. The chiselled features of Staffa that tower
on the horizon and the gaunt sheer cliffs of the middle distance all tell of
the island's volcanic origins.

I make progress on good paths to the top of Ben More, and with cloud
cover at less than 25 per cent, from the vantage point of the summit's
wind-screen, I take in the vast and ancient vista. Unusually, three distinct
ridges emanate tripod-like from the central summit below me. Three kilometres away, Beinn Fhada and the remains of immense volcanic earthworks are caught in mid-broil; in the distance are sprinkled across the
sparkling seas the island jewels of Iona and Staffa, Rum and Eig, Skye
and Jura. And beyond, Tiree – whose name always sounds to me like an
island breezing off into the Atlantic.

Bridge of Orchy revisited

Late that afternoon, I am back on the single-track road headed for the Fishnish ferry and for three Munros that are on my way home to London.

Having overnighted in Glencoe with Ivan and Thea (yet again), I head south down the A82, and turn off near Bridge of Orchy to the walker's car park that the farmer at Achaladair has kindly provided.

The day's route falls into four distinct parts: first, the walk-in to an initial col, which takes longer than expected because the path rises to 700 metres elevation. Then comes the side-route to and from *Beinn Mhanach* (mountain of the monks) where I am lucky enough to literally stumble onto a barely-visible but helpfully-graded path. Next comes the ridge route up to *Beinn a' Chreachain* (mountain of the clamshell) and along to *Beinn Achaladair* (mountain of the field of hard water) that alas is mist-bound. And, with the light fading, I finally descend via the corrie to a large lochan overlooked by heavy buttress guards.

Although the photograph I take there does not depict the most daring of exploits, it helps me to capture the ancient, unyielding, pervasive beauty of these hills – and to recognise that the best views are not necessarily in the sun, and not always from a summit.

I spend the night at the nearby Ewich House – more designer hotel than bed and breakfast establishment (though attractively priced as the latter). The next day sees cloud set in at 100 metres and with the promise of rain and thunder, I return home, thankful for 15 days on 35 amazing hills. Having now climbed 228 Munros, I start to marvel that each new hill can feel so wonderful in so unique a way.

But then, you have to drink a lot of wine before you can appreciate the subtleties!

The heart of the Cairngorms

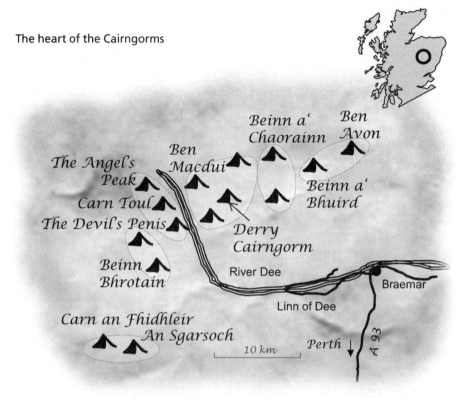

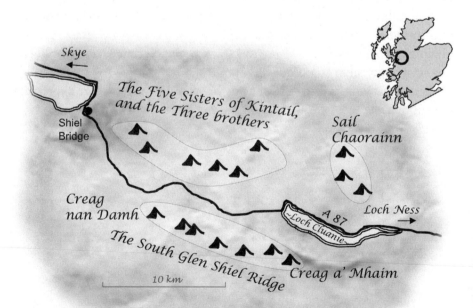

Glen Shiel North and South

CHAPTER 14

May the Road Rise Up to Meet You

Sure, by Tummel and Loch Rannoch and Lochaber I will go,
By heather tracks wi' heaven in their wiles;
If it's thinkin' in your inner heart braggart's in my step,
You've never smelt the tangle o' the Isles.

The Road To The Isles

THE GIANT PLUTON of the Cairngorms massif, of which I have so far only taken in the northern and western edges, is capped by hundreds of square kilometres of arctic tundra. Swelling from its plateau are five of the six highest mountains in Britain, and the area's combination of altitude and inland location generates extremes of cold and wet. The high plateau has seen winds of 274 kilometres per hour. Braemar has seen record-breaking lows of 27°C, and in the year of the Muckle Spate (the Great Flood of 1829), a two-day thunderstorm over the Cairngorms led to cataclysmic flooding of the Spey, Nairn and Findhorn to the North, and of the River Dee to the South, which rapidly rose by five metres in a single day. The arctic mountain landscape is also home to species that are found nowhere else – including extreme human ice-climbers who have endowed their routes with names like 'The Magic Crack', 'Damnation', 'Salvation', 'Cardiac Arête', and 'The Hurting'.

The natural base for any exploration of this plateau is Braemar. Indeed, Brae-mar means the 'braes or uplands of Mar'; the ancient earldom of Mar, home to the oldest peerage in the UK and perhaps Europe, having once extended across the plateau.

Though it is now August and I am tempting fate weather-wise, I set off in high spirits for a week to explore and 'compleat' the massif, after which I plan a few days in Glen Shiel.

Cataract

The Linn of Dee, a few kilometres from Braemar, is a magical twisting ravine, excavated as successive spates of the river have cut deeply into the bedrock. Many Cairngorm hikes start here, progressing then by bike up the idyllic Glen Lui to Derry Lodge.

Today is not going to be idyllic, however. Sometimes it just rains non-stop, and this is one of those days. I have left the picturesque lower paths of Derry Lodge behind me, and now it is the grim, knee-high heathery trudge uphill to reach *Beinn Bhreac* (speckled mountain), and then four kilometres of utter bogginess along the plateau to *Beinn a' Chaorainn* (mountain of the rowan).

I thought the return down Glen Derry would be more cheery, but a wet summer has engorged mountain burns to rivers, rivers to torrents, and torrents to churning, dirty-white cataracts tumbling haphazardly downhill, crashing over huge boulders which must surely surrender to the combined power of water and gravity. I have been provided with my own personal Muckle Spate, 'Big Flood', since one of these cataracts must now be crossed.

I make sorties uphill, downhill, and along tributaries, but there is no alternative. Since I don't want to re-climb 1,000 metres to skirt its source, the Glen Allt Mor will make me very wet. I consider stripping off for the crossing, but eventually just crab across, arms braced downwards and sideways to buttress myself against the downhill surge, boots still on to avoid battering my feet if I am swept away.

I survive, completely drenched, to squelch six kilometres back to the bike, and then home.

Fionn's Hound?

Some say Fionn mac Cumhaill, the Celtic hero, had a jet-black hound called Brotan who chased the white fairy deer, and that *Beinn Bhrotain* (hill of the mastiff Brotan) takes its name from him. Others say the name merely means mastiff. Whatever the truth, the mountain certainly makes a great grandstand from which to take in the view of many neighbouring peaks and the glens that thread between them.

It looked like rain again today, but the lady of Schiehallion House promised an immediate improvement, so I take to the bike and, past Derry Lodge, start along the delightful track of easy gradient for 30 minutes to White Bridge – where the Geldie Burn conflows with the youngster River Dee. I chance the further biking alongside the Dee to the foot of Beinn Bhrotain and luckily the terrain is good, though professionally sunk channels across the path have to be spotted and jumped.

In the company of a fellow walker, just met, the uphill work of the day begins. Paths are few, hidden, or lost and we largely tramp heather and granite boulders. The slight monotony of the day is relieved by views from *Monadh Mor* (big hill) – albeit through shifting veils of mist – to the icons beyond: Ben Macdui, and The Devil's Penis that lurks suspiciously close to the Angel's Peak.

The bike ride back from White Bridge surpasses even the ride in, as I speed alongside the galloping white horses of the River Dee that grow in confidence with every metre down which their racetrack drops.

The Devil's Penis

Within the gazette of mountain names, an award of some sort must surely go to two nearly neighbouring Munros that lie just north-east of Monadh Mor: The Devil's Penis, and the Angel's Peak. Their etymology illustrates the tectonics and metamorphosis of not only the land, but its naming too. The Devil's Penis is shown on later maps as The Devil's Point, the change from the former name apparently triggered by courtesy in light of a visit by Queen Victoria, and the original Gaelic name is Bod an Deamhain. Interestingly, when early maps were being drawn, the Glencoe peak of the same name – transcribed locally as Boddindeaun – suffered a similar fate and its name was changed to Bidean nam Bian, which conveniently meant 'the peak of the hides'. The name Angel's Peak has no link to mythology, but was invented by a Cairngorm enthusiast, the late Alexander Copland, as a counter-balance to the Devil's Point to its south.

It feels like a day of many kilometres: bike six, walk eight, climb ten, walk back eight, bike back six. *The Devil's Point*, *Cairn Toul* (hill of the barn), *Sgor an Lochain Uaine* (peak of the little green loch, called Angel's Peak): undoubtedly the highlight is the aspect across the little green loch to where a burn, having oozed from the ground at the Wells of Dee near Braeriach opposite now splashes, slithers, slides, not quite fully tumbles as the Falls of Dee to then become a river.

With my Munros 'running out' – only 22 to climb after this fortnight's trip – that view gives me an idea for the next project... would it not be fascinating to trace the Dee from source to sea? And how about a few more Highland rivers too? How about another List?

A'an

'Avon' is an ancient Celtic word, found across Britain, for river or water, but in the central Cairngorms the word has a different origin. It is an Anglicisation of *Athfhinn* (bright one), the wife of Fionn the legendary Celtic warrior. Fionn drowned while trying to cross the river now named

Avon in his honour. In this part of the world it is pronounced without the 'v', helping it reek of still greater age.

In search of Ben Avon, I first find the North Top of *Beinn a' Bhuird* (table mountain), after an intriguing bike ride up through the so-called Fairy Glen, alongside meanders, around an ancient ruin and then on well-trodden paths to the summit. There, great tors present themselves, sculpted by wind and wet, and across huge swooping corries I spy the knobbly summit of distant *Ben Avon – Leabaidh an Daimh Bhuidhe* (mountain of the bright one – bed of the yellow stag).

From The Sneck (notch) that divides the two hills, the great glaciated valley below is dappled with sunlight from some invisible source, painting it with impossible and irrepressible greens. I suppose all that Cairngorm rain is good for the grass at least.

Talking of rain: it now starts suddenly and violently. Icy whips lash; too late now to bother getting out the waterproofs, do it later if it gets really freezing; no visibility; struggle on; reach the summit. Well, sort of the summit, for there are three high tors and I had not checked which is the tallest. To be on the safe side, or in slippery conditions the *unsafe* side, I climb all three. Jung was right: whether invoked or not, the gods are watching...

Britain's second highest mountain

This is a day of reckoning. The plan for today always included Ben Macdui – a mere 40 metres lower than Ben Nevis – and two other peaks, to make for quite a long circuit. The question is whether to add the additional straggler, Beinn Mheadhoin. You may recall I had foreseen this dilemma from the summit of Bynack More last year. But if I don't include it, I'll have to stay in Braemar for another night, and I guess that everywhere is booked up because of the imminent Braemar Gathering – the Highland games for which local accommodation is often reserved a year or more in advance.

I start early and, via Derry Lodge again, head through the stand of ancient Caledonian Forest to climb and traverse *Derry Cairngorm* (blue hill of Derry; *doire* meaning thicket). To ensure I complete the route in daylight means using my *wu wei* learnings, though in the spirit of the teachings I aspire to do so intuitively, rather than with forced intent.

On the mountain's far side a blockfield presents challenging terrain over which to try to glide: irregular blocks, sometimes stable and sometimes not; steps downward that are inevitably too much of a stretch to accomplish smoothly – all the result of ice having gnawed away for thousands of years at weakened joints in the rock. But I press on and reach a lip in the landscape that overlooks the tongue-twisting Loch Etchachan, and beyond it the base of *Beinn Mheadhoin* (middle hill). I lighten my pack, record from my GPS the grid reference of the deposited items and continue to the visible slopes and farther summit. It really is a 'middle' hill, in the midst of not merely mountains, but of lochs and rivers too.

Returning to reclaim my deposited items, I strike uphill to reach the top of *Ben Macdui* (hill of the black pig, or hill of the sons of Duff) where on this Saturday a crowd is accumulating at the rate of four or five people per minute. I encounter a rocky blockfield, and remember my parents' story of their excursion from Aberdeen University to climb Ben Macdui. The best bit was always where my father recounted leaving the summit, in darkness, guided only by the spark of hob-nailed boots ahead to the periodic bellowing of a distant stag.

I cross a patch of scree that is covered with neat parallel ridges. They look hand-combed, but are in fact created by alternating heat and cold. Descending now, I must again traverse a third huge blockfield, but today the *wu wei* force is strong, and I soon reach the col below, *Carn a' Mhaim* (peak of the rounded hill) beyond, and the long walk out.

Three river crossings

You have to cross three rivers to reach *An Sgarsoch* (place of sharp rocks) and *Carn an Fhidhleir* (Fiddler's hill) if you are setting off from the Linn of Dee. With rain coming and going and having seen babbling brook mutate to raging monster in the course of a single hour, I wanted to time this trip carefully. People who study rivers have something called an instantaneous unit hydrograph: it gives a picture of how much water will flow past a given point at a certain time if you have an 'instantaneous' thunderstorm upstream. I don't have the data, so I take pot luck.

I start on the long trip of 42 kilometres and am lucky with the rivers, so reach Geldie Lodge with dry-ish boots. An initial path helps and then disappears, and as I make a direct assault charging up the eastern flank of An Sgarsoch I gradually forget my *wu wei*. This is the painful way up and I regret it, so after reaching the summit and taking the subsequent col, I regain my composure to ascend Carn an Fhidhleir. I focus on gliding along, using efficient walking technique, calm breathing and a smooth line of ascent. Immediately my progress is easier, and whenever the path is lost, inexplicably it reappears beneath my feet a few minutes later. My notes from that day include, '... magic mountain: paths keep re-appearing.' But I now realise it is not the mountain that is magic, but the mind-set, body-set, and spirit-set of the *wu wei* with which it is approached.

Ruins of Altanour

John, who with Kathleen owns Schiehallion Guest House, is the keenest of keen golfers and knows Braemar's weather intimately. He assures me it would rain by half past noon today, so I pack quickly and dash for *Carn Bhac* (peak of peat), my last Cairngorm.

I reach a lodge bristling with 4x4s, detour around it, and start the grind by bike up a neighbouring hill-track. Then from across the valley there is much bellowing at me and beckoning. I return to the lodge with its gesticulating figure, to find that I should have biked through the crowd of vehicles whose owners were gathering to shoot grouse. I am assured by the head gamekeeper that I shall be safe: 'Dinna ye worry; the shot only carries a hundred yards...'

After an initial uphill pull, yet another enchanting glen opens up, this time following the Ey Burn to its source above Altanour Lodge through dappled braes of peaty hue. This glen demands to be re-visited; you would expect it to be much frequented, yet I see not a soul.

The great advantage of having biked uphill is, of course, the freewheel back down. I get back to my starting point at half past noon. The heavens open, as predicted, and I depart for three days on the other side of Scotland, which promises fairer skies.

Glen Shiel, again

Bonnie Prince Charlie: few revolutionaries have inspired such passionate support, for so many centuries, from a nation's sons and daughters both at home and abroad. Though they may not realise it, even non-Scots will be honouring his memory when they sing 'will ye' no come back again' after *Auld Lang Syne* this New Year's Eve.

Landing near Loch Morar with just seven men and no money, he so nearly succeeded: striking to within 200 kilometres of London before his retreat to defeat at Culloden. But here at Glen Shiel, 50 kilometres to the North, is the site of a Jacobite foray and Spanish invasion that was a precursor to Charlie's arrival.

The Jacobite cause had been born in 1688 with the arrival of the son of James II of England and VII of Scotland. Now that a male heir was apparent, the threat of the next King being Catholic sent shudders up Protestant spines and sent peers to summon William of Orange. In exile, the heir became the 'Old Pretender', and in due course his own son,

Bonnie Prince Charlie, assumed the mantle of 'Young Pretender'. 1715 and 1745 saw the two main Jacobite Uprisings, and in between them was the invasion of 1719. From two frigates, 300 Spaniards under Jacobite command landed on the mainland near Skye. With the support of 1,500 Highlanders, they set out to take Britain – starting with Inverness.

The militia first claimed Eilean Donan Castle (of postcard fame), then advanced along Glen Shiel, but was halted and soon routed by English forces at the Battle of Glen Shiel. The few remaining Spaniards retreated to a mountaintop where their fate was immortalised in its name: Sgurr nan Spainteach (peak of the Spaniards). This is one of the Five Sisters of Kintail: a British hillwalking classic, not just a Munro-bagger's dream.

As this is my first day in Glen Shiel on this trip, I warm up with a relatively easy route that takes in *Carn Ghluasaid* (hill of movement), *Sgurr nan Conbhairean* (peak of the hound keepers) and *Sail Chaorainn* (heel of the rowan trees), and delight in peering down the precipice beneath Conbhairean to the stunning emerald folds of the corrie surrounding Lochan Uaine.

Along the ridge is a farther summit that the map says is only one metre lower that Sail Chaorainn. What if a more accurate survey deems that top to be higher and therefore the true Munro? With two hard days ahead to complete this trip, I decide against incurring the extra kilometre and a half of ridge-walking to claim the insurance policy of that peak.

The South Glen Shiel Ridge

The Cluanie Inn stands like a lonely strayed beast at the head of Loch Cluanie, where the loch meets Glen Shiel. Here in the remote 75-kilometre furrow that separates the hamlet of Glen Shiel from the village of Invermoriston, I sit at the bar and put finishing touches to the plan for tomorrow's lengthy seven-Munro route. '... and don't descend that way,' says the owner-publican, tapping the map, 'someone died there last month. And someone else the month before'.

The next day is overcast, the clouds mothballing the summits for now. Again I wonder which came first: a 3,000 foot cloud base that erodes the mountains down to that height,, or the 3,000 foot mountains that push the cloud base up to that level?

The weather says dry and this airy marathon traverse starts well, except for the irritation of having to re-ascend *Druim Shionnach* (ridge of the fox): *Creag a' Mhaim* (crag of the large rounded hill) is stuck out on the end of the ridge and requires an out-and-back foray. The next four peaks come with metronomic regularity: *Aonach air Chrith* (trembling ridge), *Maol Chinn-dearg* (red-capped hill), *Sgurr an Doire Leathain* (peak of the broad thicket), *Sgurr an Lochain* (peak of the wee lochan). But when they are visible between the clouds, the stunning aspects down to the River Shiel to the north and Loch Quoich to the south sustain the excitement for the 12-kilometre promenade. Finally I reach *Creag nan Damh* (crag of the stags), and the clouds have now lifted enough to display tomorrow's challenging agenda – my North Glen Shiel Ridge.

But I am focused now on that fatal descent route which will take me to the spot that the map labels with two crossed swords, commemorating the Battle of Glenshiel. Well... it is steep, it is wet and slippery, and the ground is so saturated that the vegetation just skids off the rock wherever you put a heel to it. And then comes the hard bit. Perhaps there is a path, but I can't find it and the flank of the hill is near vertical. I grab a sturdy branch, test its strength and anchoring, then swing down a few feet. I grab and test a sturdy tree-root protruding at chest level and swing down a few more feet. Five minutes of similar monkey-like manoeuvring take me to flat ground and then the road.

I am therefore surprised when a passing motorist stops to give a lift back to the Cluanie Inn to a figure so sweaty and dishevelled as myself; so covered in soil, bark, midges and worse, and so foolish as to have forgone the longer but easier descent. Luckily, the salesman who picks me up is himself planning a similar hike next week and believes in karma.

The Five Sisters of Kintail, the Three Brothers, and a baby

After today, my journey across the Munros will have only ten more days to run, so I seek to experience today as fully as possible. I can always climb more hills later, but they will be hills of a different journey, so these last ones are special.

When my Munro journey ends, body will have had a treat: cigarettes successfully banished, heart rate lowered, muscles toned. And mind, too, will have improved: a deeper understanding of how a landscape was fashioned, of how a language grew and of how a nation has been formed. But spirit: how will spirit have been nurtured?

Today I shall be a traveller, not a tourist. To misquote Paul Theroux's distinction, 'tourists know where they are going; travellers know where they have been'. I will travel a path and see how far I get. I will have escape routes, but will not pace myself.

I set off for *Ciste Dhubh* (black chest), which stands as a sentinel, even before the start of the northern ridge of Glen Shiel. There is only cloud, nothing to see, so I listen to my boots. With each step I try to quieten my boots, treading more gently until they fall silent, and soon I am on the first summit of the journey.

Aonach Mheadhoin (middle ridge) comes next, the first of three Munros sometimes called the Three Brothers. There is path, then there is no path. I find an easy line, and then am on the ridge. *Sgurr a' Bhealaich Dheirg* (peak of the red pass) comes next. There is still no view, so I listen to my breathing until it is peaceful, then *Saileag* (little heel) is reached. The cloud still clings, though there is no rain yet. I am hungry so I eat, but not much, then go on. Sgurr nan Spainteach: a 'top' but not a Munro. And then the two of the Five Sisters that are also Munros: first *Sgurr na Ciste Duibhe* (peak of the black chest), then *Sgurr na Carnach* (stony peak). There is still no view and the rain has already turned from drizzle to large but slow-moving drops. I know this route should have stupendous views, but their invisibility does not bother me greatly. I have banked 260 Munros in my memories. I can summon them at will as I have done for the last six years. I have had more sun than rain. What do I care about more rain than sun today?

Then I start to climb *Sgurr Fhuaran* (the meaning of which is apparently uncertain)...

▲▲▲

Does the road rise up to meet you?

It is while climbing Sgurr Fhuaran that I have a mind-body-spirit experience of the deepest impact.

I have been trying as far as possible to *wu wei* myself up the perfect cone of this hill, the last Munro of the Five Sisters of Kintail. *Wu wei* requires making subtle changes to my walking technique so as to be as energy-efficient as possible, and more importantly to be at one with the hill and the path. The efficiency with which we hillwalk is certainly important: to climb all the Munros requires expending approximately half a million calories more than in normal living, so any saving is worth it. More importantly, this mind-set of least effort helps you emerge more completely into the zone of *wu wei* and its principle of intimate engagement with your surroundings and environment.

I am using techniques I had learned in the Himalaya – perhaps the best place in the world to find insights into techniques for walking mountains. Porters there often carry loads of twice their own body weight, do so consuming relatively little energy and routinely achieve speeds that can be 60 per cent faster than an untrained walker. After my return from Nepal, I tried consciously to emulate their walking style – both as I had observed it, and as I had read about it. There have been relatively few rigorous studies of Nepali porters, but Professor Alberto Minetti of Milan University did conduct one – the results of which were published in the Proceedings of the Royal Society in 2006.

Combining the findings of Minetti and others with my own observations, I aim consciously to *glide* up the hill: to walk silently and smoothly; specifically, to walk so that I make no sound of footfall, and so that my centre of gravity moves as smoothly and consistently in a straight line as possible. Moving your centre of gravity smoothly is more difficult than it sounds. It requires some practice, since for each step it means: a) not wobbling side-to-side, b) not surging forwards-and-backwards, c) not bouncing upwards-and-downwards, d) not detouring your path sideways from as smooth a line as possible, e) avoiding large steps upwards or downwards by taking a line that has half-steps if needed, f) not wasting energy in stumbling or misplacing your feet, while g) not slumping your posture. These instructions are phrased as negatives – the positive is: just *glide*.

Having practiced these techniques, they have gradually become more automatic in recent months. But it is on Sgurr Fhuaran that I am able to forget the techniques completely; my body has become tuned and entrained. And then, as if by magic, I start to feel the walking is easier. After a further ten minutes, the walking feels completely effortless – even though I am going uphill! Ten minutes after that, I feel the path rising up to meet my boot, and lift me... Words flit in and out of my consciousness, eventually forming a type of mantra:

When the path springs up to meet your boot
The hill will lift you on your route.

The path really is lifting me, rather than I climbing it.

Imagine my surprise, therefore, when at breakfast the next morning, in my next accommodation, I happen to notice the bread basket on the table – inside which is a tea towel with the words GAELIC BLESSING writ across its top. I part the rolls and read the expression – which I have never heard before, and which completely reflects and encapsulates yesterday's experience:

May the road rise up to meet you.

It is a complete reflection and encapsulation in words of yesterday's experience. Later checks reveal this blessing to be a free translation of the Irish Gaelic: *go n-éirí an bóthar leat*. More accurately, though less engagingly, this translates as 'may you have a successful journey (through life)'. Congratulations to whomever came up with the intriguing mistranslation, and I trust it will help other walkers to summon support from the path.

Phase 5 – Broader Horizons

IT IS NEARLY seven years since I embarked on the adventure of The Munros. I had at first been gripped by the endless parade of stupendous sights and other sensory pleasures, by the satisfaction of exploring the defined agenda of The List and by the captivating spirit and language of the Gael.

After several years, I had started to shift my focus, avidly and unashamedly, to the blatant bagging of peaks – to satisfy my hunger for visible progress on map, land, List; and to test my physical limits. A thousand kilometres later, eventually disengaging from the totals and sub-totals, I began to seek Quality over Quantity: still purposeful, I became more Trophy-hunter than Munro-bagger.

But is the Quality of a Trophy more important than the Quality of experiencing the Trophy intimately, and of being at one with the Trophy's world? I came to understand in subtle ways that the latter must surely be the goal, and that – for me at least – the way of *wu wei* is an entrance to that world and to its entrancing features.

But is this the ultimate goal? My journey so far has been quite solitary. For reasons mainly logistic, I have too infrequently been accompanied by friends, or even by strangers. It seems I have now reached another turning point, into a new phase...

At this juncture, I again reflect on the meaning of Munro's List. My determination to complete The List amused my friends back home, and then my obsession started to concern them. Ultimately, I too start to wonder why The List has assumed such importance in my life: why not just go out for a gentle stroll?

While descending Sgurr Fhuaran the clouds parted briefly, and as I surveyed the panorama, my every line of sight seemed to end on a peak. If you landed here with no List, I realised, you would not know where to start; there would be just too many options. Things then seemed to click into place and – for me at least – the great contribution of Sir Hugh Munro and his List became clear.

1. The List provides focus; it saves you from a near-infinity of choices that is so daunting you might never make a start.

2. Once you have started, it's not just the person with the psychology of die-hard 'completer-finisher' who wants to compleat The List. Something in all of us just requires that things get finished, resolved.

Imagine Beethoven's 5th Symphony starting with dah-dah-dah and omitting the following DAAH! Or, when confronted with a near-complete sentence, most people want to... finish it. In music, there is the 'final cadence'; without this final chord a song or other musical work feels incomplete, and without it, we have no post-climactic repose. Then there is the Japanese Daruma doll: sold with white eyes devoid of pupils, you ink in one pupil when you start a task and then the doll sits there nagging at you, until you have completed the task.

And if you accept this premise that completion is necessary, then you are bound to set off climbing hills even on days when rain is probable – because as the previously-quoted adage says, 'if you insist on seeing all the Munros only in sun you will require more than one lifetime'.

3. The List also provides a step-wise and feasible journey for anyone to find an engrossing and rewarding passion. As my friend Michael Worrall helpfully pointed out, as I was trying to make sense of my increasingly time-consuming pastime: 'it's your rapture'. He was right, and he was alluding to the observation of the unique Joseph Campbell (world expert on myths and their meanings) that:

> People say we seek the meaning of life.
> What we're really seeking is an experience of the rapture of being alive.

4. Finally, The List creates a vocabulary: a defined lexicon with which you can communicate with other fanatics. The 283 designated mountains are specific nodes, linked to which are journeys that can be compared and shared. There is even a group of walkers who meet in a pub once a week; one of them calls out a number between 1 and 283, and they all sit there in silence with misty eyes recalling their journey up that particular hill, then in due course someone else calls out another number...

So while compleating The List will inevitably involve ticking and bagging, there are psychological and indeed social reasons for the journey.

Now, however, I am in the final phase of my development as a hillwalker. For while collecting the Munros has indeed brought me to destinations that hold the potential to be art gallery, gymnasium and sacred sanctuary all in one, I now see the true pleasure is in finding a broader horizon: a human landscape, a sense of community linked to those hills. More specifically, this next phase reflects enjoying the hills with friends and family; introducing the hills to new recruits, and portraying the mountains in words or images so that others can be encouraged to visit them, or enabled to experience them; art and literature as a vehicle for communicating in a way that goes beyond geography and geology.

* * *

We eventually reach a stage where our mission is neither about our Destination, nor even about our Journey, but is about inspiring others to make *their* Journeys.

Knoydart and nearby

CHAPTER 15

Going out to go in,
and vice versa

Farewell to the mountains, high-cover'd with snow,
Farewell to the straths and green vallies below;
Farewell to the forests and wild-hanging woods,
Farewell to the torrents and loud-pouring floods.

ROBERT BURNS *Farewell to the Highlands*

'WHAT'S THIS FOR, Uncle Max?' demands ten-year old Scarlett as she dangles a gaiter one inch from my face and wiggles it around so as to *almost* touch my nose. Though Scarlett is not really my niece, she and her parents Mike and Zoe have come to climb with me in the Loch Quoich and Glen Shiel areas, since they cannot join me later for the ascent of my last Munro.

We have started our hillwalking year in mid-April, and this means we may bask under clear, sunny skies – or equally likely, may have to draw our jackets in close as we strain into arctic winds. But at least this early start provides time for a further visit if needed, to ensure I have only one more Munro to climb when the chosen date of June 10 comes around and a large group of friends join me in a final celebratory hike up Beinn Dubhchraig.

Perhaps I have become greedy, but these days the views by themselves are not enough. After years of relatively solo walking, I now feel that a view, however grand, can be at least equalled by a more modest vista seen in the company of family, of close friends, or even of fellow walkers recently met. Earlier in my Munroing days, I could walk solo for weeks, but for whatever reasons good company has now become a crucial dimension. Fortunately, I am about to enjoy some. Today we are a group of three and a half adults, and our strength in numbers will allow us to share burdens and to lug up the hills a few luxuries.

Yet while the week as a whole promises more companionship than I have typically had, I know there will be a sting in its tail: the route up Sgurr nan Gillean, which can be Skye's most challenging peak. I remember the observation of my guide, Tony, on my first visit to Skye:

in bad weather some routes up Sgurr nan Gillean make the In Pinn look easy. Unfortunately, there was to be uncertainty about both the weather there and the choice of route, until the very last moment. Perhaps the experience of the magical Knoydart peninsula will compensate.

Loch Quoich

Loch Quoich (the loch of the cup) lies just west of Loch Ness. There, four shapely Munros dominate the northern and southern rims of the loch and sweep down to the water's edge. At first it seems unfortunate that access by car is solely via a rough, single-track, dead-end road. But what a road it is!

As sun bloodies the cloudy tail end of a weather system, Scarlett, Mike, Zoe and I skirt the loch and agree this must be one of the finest lochside drives in Britain. The road starts through the vast conifer forests that surround Loch Garry, and once past a higher dam small islands appear. The valley, initially open, becomes more enveloping. Verdant colours are the legacy of much rainfall, except where altitude or gradient render the vegetation scarce and the land a browny-grey.

We spy a likely camping spot, close to the shoreline, and soon have our tents up and water boiling. Over a basic dinner, we confirm our plans that will take in Scarlett's first four Munros over the next two days, and perhaps a few more thereafter. But though the ridges still sport snowy caps and summer is a month away, the midges are undaunted and we eventually declare defeat, giving up on the Saint Vitus Dance and the self-slapping, instead taking shelter in our tents for the night.

Light clouds overhead keep the next day's heat at bay as we start steeply at first up the shoulder of *Gleouraich* (uproar), and then along the ridge to *Spidean Mialach* (peak of the deer, or wild animals, or louse). This name – pronounced 'Spid-jun Mee-luch' – is one I always want literally to spit out and it certainly sounds like a mucky hill on which the louse would want to live. Yet the views from the top and the shoulders are far from lousy: to the south across wee Loch Fearna and then across the great slash of Loch Quoich to rows and rows of mountains, many of which I have now climbed and which I now feel, with a smug smile, are somehow 'mine'. To the west, Loch Quoich stretches right out to the sea, and to the north last year's Glen Shiel ridge trips merrily along in and out of the clouds. Having skirted or traversed with crunchy tread the snowy hollows, we are soon back at the roadside for a quick lunch. We also make a quick decision that Mike and I will travel light and nip up *Sgurr a' Mhaoraich* (peak of the shellfish) in the afternoon

For the rest of the day, Mike and I cast nervous glances south to *Gairich* (roaring). With its pointed top, Gairich stands proud and picture-postcard beautiful across the loch. Yet it seems to be creating its own permanent summit-shroud of dark cloud: one that it threatens to cast in our direction at any moment.

We approach Gairich the next day, having struck camp, and find – as with the quest for many objects of extreme desire – that there is a toll to be paid along the way. In this case, the toll is the three kilometres of boggy approach – allegedly a permanent feature of the hill.

'We'll never get up *that*,' says Scarlett as we view the final ascent to the summit from a halfway point. It looks vertical; it seems impassable; it feels impossible. But with enough zigzagging, even the steepest of inclines can be conquered, and Gairich is no exception. The summit's cloud endures, however, and the mountain has to be added to the list of 'mountains to be climbed again in better weather'.

As we leave the mountain and the loch, we peek over our shoulders at the dam: apparently, the water level in the upper reaches of Loch Quoich is ten metres below normal, not because of a lack of rain, but for reasons of safety after a crack appeared in the retaining wall!

Glen Shiel

We spend the night at Inverinate, a charming hamlet a few glens north of Loch Quoich, and familiar from its proximity both to the endpoint of last year's long traverse that took in the Five Sisters of Kintail, and also to the starting point for the demanding Highland Cross challenge. By a stroke of good fortune, we avoid staying at the guesthouse where the body of Fiona Graham (whose surname is given to Scotland's hills between 2,000 and 2,500 feet in altitude) was discovered after her tragic murder several decades earlier.

Like giant bulldogs with creased and folded skin, *Beinn Fhada* (long hill) and *A' Ghlas-bheinn* (the grey-green hill) lay stretched out to greet us the next morning, as they guard the pass to secret glens that lurk beyond. The dogs may be slumbering – but if they awake, will they bite?

As we approach, the dogs cooperate, and we are lifted by easy paths – well-maintained by the owner of the Inverinate Estate, allegedly the ruler of Dubai. At last we reach the complex summits of the long hill itself and witness the spectacle of the range's serried corries, fractal and self-similar: corrie within corrie, within corrie. In the middle distance we are confronted by the vast and unfamiliar backsides of the Sisters of Kintail.

We re-trace our steps and take in the day's next Munro, and while Mike and his family wisely take the correct route down, I unwisely seek extra adventure by taking a more direct line: one that will lead through almost impenetrable forest, almost uncrossable gullies and almost unfordable rivers. It is only by employing a fallen tree as a vast, moveable ladder that I manage to cross a ravine: lodging the straight 20-foot trunk into successive notches down the ravine's side, and using the stumps of snapped-off branches as convenient handholds and footholds for the descent. Do not try this at home.

The next day is a day of rain: monotonous, sullen, grey rain with no life in it. Mike and family decide to head home, but from the hotel I rustle up some company: two women heading, like me, up the fabled *Saddle* (meaning obvious) and *Sgurr na Sgine* (peak of the knife). The Saddle is 'fabled' because one line of ascent tiptoes along the Forcan Ridge, which is so sharp and exposed that photos of it are used as a front cover or a core illustration of many a walking guidebook.

It continues to be a day of monotonous, sullen rain, and I am tempted to spend it on a Munro that is less exciting; but since I have now climbed most of the Munros, access to my nearest unclimbed one would require a road journey of more than 60 kilometres.

It drizzles. We press on, and in the slippery wet we decide against the Forcan route to The Saddle's summit, and opt for an easier though still steep path. But the company of good conversationalists brightens the day. As we eventually descend, we pause to compare The Saddle's summit with that of the nearby trig point. Debate rages as to which top is the higher and even the Ordnance Survey map appears to hedge its bets by designating the altitude of the trig point as '1,010 (1,011)': perhaps the only instance of such uncertainty expressed by the Ordnance Survey. Just to be sure, we had of course touched both tops.

Skye: the South End

The Black Cuillin of Skye rise as dark, Tolkienesque battlements in a horseshoe that crowds and nearly encloses Loch Coruisk. In a very real sense, those peaks hurl thunderbolts down at the loch, and do so with such severity that after a visit in 1831, JMW Turner was inspired to try and capture the wildness of the scene in watercolour.

I had climbed the central section of this range five years earlier and now look forward to tackling the so-called South End. If the weather holds up, I will take in the North End too, including the ominous Sgurr nan Gillean that serves as an exclamation mark to end the ridge. Even if the weather turns icy, as it threatens to, I will still be very keen to climb the Sgurr, since the day of my final Munro party beckons. Many friends will be joining me, and so I am locked into climbing my remaining Munros before the appointed date.

My good friend Neels accompanies me this week, and we share Loch View cottage for five days of varied hiking. For several of the days I will again join Steven Fallon's Mountain Guides – this time in the guise of Bruce Poll. As this extended group gathers for a preparatory pint or two at the Old Inn, I can see that my fellow clients are both fit and august. Stewart has been a Scottish hill-running champion many times over; Harriet has competed at the highest levels in equestrian events and is also an accomplished climber; Chris has spent much of his career with outdoor pursuits. And Bruce himself is no ordinary mountain leader: he guides regularly in the Alps and beyond and has run the 11 Munros and 12 kilometres of the entire Cuillin ridge in just 10 minutes outside the record time of 3hrs 17min 28sec. My only credential is that I have now climbed 269 Munros, which is apparently enough to gain me access to the party.

The next morning we set off for the South End. Seen from a distance, the southern end of the Cuillin ridge appears to bulldoze its way straight into the Sound of Soay below. This makes for a steep climb through the initial corrie, and we are glad of Bruce's lead since passing feet have left little sign of transit or pathway on the Cuillin's hard, steep slopes.

Up past Loch Coir' a' Ghrunnda with its lagoon-like feel, we zigzag on paths less travelled, sometimes roped together for safety and some-times not, to reach the ridge. We dump packs to lighten loads, scale a further 150 vertical metres and claim the top of *Sgurr nan Eag* (peak of the notches).

For most of us, this peak is a merely a prelude to the real work of the day, but it holds a special appeal for me. It affords an excellent view over the Isle of Soay – uninhabited since 1953, but of note in my family's legends as the place where my mother spent a school holiday one long hot summer and gained a grounding in ecology, in the shadows of Gavin Maxwell's shark factory. Half a century later, I email a photo to her iPad, and call her from my Blackberry.

Snow and ice is intermittent on the ridges and as we press on, we are again glad of Bruce's intimate knowledge of hidden paths and correct turnings. At last we reach first *Sgurr Dubh Mor* (big black peak), and then *Sgurr Alasdair* (Alexander's peak), the highest point on Skye, by a route that skirts the climber's route of the 'TD Gap'. As with all climbs, getting to the top is of course only half way, and the return down the Great Stone Chute holds its own challenges, especially as its top half is plastered with melting snow that somehow clings to the 45-degree slopes. At the foot of the chute, we strain our gaze up to the north, where the Inaccessible Pinnacle is just visible looking like an ant rearing up on the ridge. And with the help of the camera's 50-times zoom, the rocky ant is seen to be infested with even tinier human ants climbing up its back.

Skye: a non-Munro

If proof were needed that the charms of Scottish hillwalking extend beyond the Munros, Sgurr na Stri provides it.

Only 497 metres high, this hill appears on few lists defined by height criteria – yet regularly tops polls for the place in Britain that has the Best View. Neels and I set out to reach it and explore it, and are not disappointed. For despite the gale force gusts, the panorama makes it all worthwhile, embracing sea, isle, river, estuary, beach, track and an eagle's eye view deep into the gash of Loch Coruisk.

I am not joining Bruce and his other clients today, as I have already climbed the hills they are tackling. On their return, I find that the plan is to take in the North End in two days' time rather than tomorrow.

So the next day Neels and I head off for Neist Point. This is the most westerly point in Great Britain that you can drive to (as opposed to the most westerly point on the mainland, which is Corrachadh Mor, just south of Ardnamurchan Point); there is scope to win many bets in pubs with this knowledge. Given its location, it is no surprise that Neist Point offers not only superb birdlife, but also an unparalleled view out over the Sea of the Hebrides. To the south, the sun glistens with uncompromised dazzle off the cold, dark waters, yet far off to the west a dark band of cloud lurks and loiters. The Munro mission must be resumed before Skye's notoriously unpredictable weather changes for the worse...

Blaven

So that afternoon I make the short climb up the Munro of *Bla Bheinn* (*Blaven;* blue hill). Once up through the woods and alongside the waterfalls, the slog is rewarded with now-familiar but still-exceptional views of Rum, Eigg and Muck; the Rough Bounds of Knoydart still unexplored to the south-east, and 75 kilometres north-west the thin line of mascara that is the Outer Hebrides. And of course the sheer rock-faces of the mighty Cuillin ramparts are almost within touching distance of the summit.

Skye: the North End

The next morning is bitterly cold. No-one is out except Bruce and our gang of four. In the car park, Bruce suggests we wear extra layers under our trousers and I duck into my car to slip on thermal leggings.

Soon we are off, with the broken teeth of the Cuillin's North End periodically bared to reveal a fang or two. Sharpest of the fangs is Sgurr nan Gillean which seems to mock, 'come on then, if you dare.'

After ten minutes, I glance at Stewart's pack and wonder how it can be so small if he has remembered to pack his climbing harness. (A harness is a crucial piece of equipment by means of which a climber attaches himself to a rope.) And then I realise with horror that my own pack feels a fraction lighter than it should. I stop, rip the pack open – and realise that in taking my thermals out of my pack I have forgotten to re-pack my harness. I shout to Bruce up ahead, and before he can return to me I am running back to the car and figuring out the basic arithmetic: it will be another 15 minutes at least before I get back to this spot from the car, by which time the team will have moved a further 15 minutes on. I am in danger of being caught in a Zeno's paradox of my own making unless the team slows down or stops, and no-one likes standing around in freezing conditions.

I eventually make it back to the group, with sweat pouring off me. Bruce looks at me nonchalantly, 'I bet you're glad you put on those thermals,' he grins. 'If you hadn't dashed off so quickly I was going to say that I could have made a harness out of rope when we get to the top...'

We press on, with the route still not guaranteed because of unknown snow and ice that may lie ahead. We, the guided, ask about the route and wonder why people had been either confused or impressed yesterday when they had heard that we were climbing all three Munros today in icy conditions.

To cut a long story short: one way to climb all the North End Munros in a single day is by using the Tourist Route, the other way is to take a short cut via the Chimney. 'Chimney' is a climbing term for a long, narrow, vertical slot in a rock-face, up which you shimmy through contacts with the two opposite sides of the slot. Many routes call for abseiling down Nicholson's Chimney, but we are about to ascend it too.

Bruce sets up our ropes: we will ascend as two pairs. The temperature is dropping quickly now and as we stand around we are starting to freeze, our fingers starting to solidify, even in professional gloves. Bruce has disappeared up the towering slot that is the chimney. He is now invisible because of overhang or mist: we know not which. We hear his call and I start to climb, but there seems no purchase for boot or gloved hand. And in the bitter cold, with fingers that have a fraction of their normal strength, using handholds that seem to slope downwards, and grasping at rock that is covered in rimy ice, my progress is slow and my stomach queasy. It is like climbing an icicle with a 3,000 foot drop behind you.

Patiently, Bruce gets us up the chimney, then along a line which threads under a suspended rock and at last to the summit of *Sgurr nan Gillean* (peak of the young men).

Thanks to Bruce's experience, we do eventually complete our outing without accident, including *Am Basteir* (the baptiser) and *Bruach na Frithe* (heather slope of the deer forest). There was no doubt, however, that in those conditions, the traverse did make the climbing of the supposedly Inaccessible Pinnacle five years earlier seem like a walk in the park.

I am glad we are descending quickly now, because even greater pleasures await in Knoydart, and the ferry sets sail soon.

Knoydart

Knoydart is one of the most remote places on mainland Britain. Its single hamlet of Inverie is accessible only by boat or eight-hour trek, and during the Second World War it was isolated enough that the Special Operations Executive, forerunner of the SAS, based a training centre there. Its wild scenery is so stunning that the MOD's attempt to buy it in 1983 triggered uproar and the establishment of the John Muir Trust to prevent that purchase and to sustain public access. (Please give generously: the Trust aims to protect wild land and now manages over 60,000 acres across Scotland, including parts of Ben Nevis, Schiehallion and Skye.)

I have described the landscape of the Rough Bounds of Knoydart earlier. Suffice to say here that this remote land comprises all imaginable types of knobble piled on top of all the unimaginable types of knobble. This whole morass of knobbles is also riven by deep sea lochs and scarred with spatey streams and burns. Navigation is awkward and challenging even with good visibility. Nevertheless, this stunning location has attracted me ever since I saw the view from one of its mountains, spread across the cover of an old edition of Cameron McNeish's *The Munros*.

I am back in solo mode for a few days, but on the boat from Mallaig where I had spent the previous night, I strike up conversation with Drew.

Drew is the cruiser's captain, proud to mention that he was a professional deer stalker in the area for 15 years, and is a mine of helpful advice on shortcuts and scenic spots.

We land at the pier close to the Old Forge Inn, and I gaze back out to seaward and sniff the breeze. I guess that today's clouds may be gone by tomorrow, so I set off to climb *Meall Buidhe* (yellow hill) and *Luinne Bheinn* (hill of anger, mirth, or melody) – affectionately known as Loony-Bin – reserving tomorrow for Ladhar Bheinn and its captivating view. As Drew had suggested, I bike up to the top of Loch an Dubh-Lochain, which stretches out at the feet of the Munros and their ridges. Continuing on foot, I take to the shoulder of Meall Buidhe and am soon on the long, high ridge on which its summit is perched.

The clouds are closing in and rain or worse threatens. Over the years, I have learnt that, in the fleeting gaps between swirling mists, the absolute priority is to snatch confirmation of the location of markers, waypoints, destinations and paths. Even with a GPS, navigating these knobbles in mist can be treacherous.

There is no extensive view from the top so I delay lunch and press on towards the surprisingly distant ridge on which my next summit lurks. In time I reach it, but Drew was right: even with his shortcut, this is going to be a long walk – and the occasional glimpses of the snowy ridge ahead warn of unexpected challenges.

The shortcut involves descending a corrie wall that is very steep, but, Drew promised, 'just make sure ye don't cut down it too early, and ye'll be fine'. The corrie bears the unusual name of Torc-choire – unusual in that the normal Gaelic word order would be Choire Torc, whereas the reversed order of Torc-choire suggests Norse origins. The name means corrie of the wild boar and is pronounced Torkerry. But with visibility down to ten metres and a blanketing of snow obscuring the slightest bump underfoot, I am soon blundering around, even with the GPS and the detailed OS map embedded within it. I search first in frustration and then in gathering panic for the right point of descent off what I assume is the high corrie rock-face. Words that rhyme with Torkerry come to mind: lottery, mockery, contrary, buggery.

Eventually I take the plunge and turn off the ridge, only to be confronted by what – I assume – is a parallel furrow and then a further ridge. I press on anyway and am soon going downhill steeply, but too steeply. I stop on the slushy grass and slippery rock and take stock. Only five more Munros to go: it would be a pity to fall off a cliff when a few more days' climbing will see my mission complete. The mists lift their skirts for a second, and I can instantly see a smoother line of descent to my left. It will mean climbing a hundred near-vertical metres back up the slope, but it will be worth it.

I descend the safer way, still having to take care on the wet grass and down the twisting gorge to reclaim my bike and the track to The Gathering.

The Gathering in Inverie calls itself a bed-and-breakfast yet is a cut above many a hotel. After a long day, I forgo the outdoor jacuzzi, and after a pint and noisy dinner in the Old Forge, head for recuperative slumber.

Ladhar Bheinn

The eastern shoulder of *Ladhar Bheinn* (*Larven*, hill of the hoof or claw) is peeping out early the next morning from behind intervening bluffs, but the vast immensity of its massif becomes apparent only as I round a final corner of forest, just past the broken ruins of a croft called Folach.

I press on up the eastern ridge of the cloven-hoof hill, following a flirtatious path that endears, then disappears, then re-emerges unexpectedly and with undue familiarity. As I ease my way to the top, I am greeted by a wondrous sight and a terrible memory. The horrifying reminder is the sight of Beinn Sgritheall over the loch, to the North – the Munro on which I had become completely lost and mildly hypothermic six years ago.

The wondrous view – best of the many in the panorama – has the hulking north-east limb of the Ladhar Bheinn in the foreground, the dark ink of Loch Hourn (Loch of Heaven) in the middle distance, and the vast expanse of the Rough Bounds beyond that. I have made it: it is the picture from the book cover that I had desperately wanted to see in real life, the view even copies from the book cover the late-lying snow that highlights the ridges. As if to add further magic, tiny snowflakes start to flutter inexplicably from a cold but completely cloudless sky.

In high spirits, but with cloud racing in with alarming speed from Loch Nevis ('Loch of Hell') in the west, I skip back along the ridge. It's getting colder now, with drizzle just starting to wet the rocks. I grab gloves and jacket from the pack and speed down to the bike, the track, and Drew's boat which will soon depart to take me back to Mallaig.

* * *

The last ten days have taken me to the wilds and delights of Skye and of neighbouring Quoich, Shiel and Knoydart. But they have also brought me closer to old friends and into contact with new ones .

The big party, of course, will be on my last Munro. The appointed date looms a few weeks away, and my support group has swelled to number 14 people – ten of whom have not yet climbed a big hill. So now I must journey southwards to climb my penultimate Munros, and in doing so survey the safety of the route of ascent that these Munros share in part with my final one.

Thus I stop near Tyndrum to take in *Ben Oss* (hill of the loch outlet), *Ben Lui* (hill of young deer) and *Beinn a' Chleibh* (hill of the creel). These are fine hills, and I describe below the wooded route up towards Ben Oss, most of which I will re-tread on my day of compleation.

An ending and an insight into the beginning

To the skirl of the pipes and the sway of the kilt, we follow piper Ian Macintyre along the track that leads towards *Beinn Dubhchraig* (hill of the black crag).

My clan had gathered near Tyndrum, just north of Glasgow: kith and kin, friends and family. It had taken some organising, but kindly the gang has convened to 'cheer me up' my last Munro. After some thought and consultation, I had chosen Beinn Dubhchraig to be my final Munro. My friends could climb this hill without needing military fitness; it is accessible, since anyone could literally step off a train at Tyndrum, just 60 kilometres north of Glasgow to start the walk. There is also plenty of accommodation nearby, and the stunning views would make the climb worthwhile, even for non-baggers of Munros. I had not anticipated, however, that so many relative novices would join the group and my sense of responsibility for their welfare had grown during recent weeks. But I feel we are prepared, as I am armed with nitro-glycerine pills (in case anyone has a heart attack), a mouldable aluminium splint and other safety items.

We had stayed yet again at the delightful Ewich House, where owners Ian and Deb generously had sent us on our way with a luxury breakfast, cake (already consumed) and whisky (retained for later). So it is in good form that we set off behind our piper along the track that lies south of the Cononish goldmine and crosses river, railway, and burn to reach the Caledonian pines that are a remnant of the post-Ice Age forest that once blanketed much of Scotland.

It is early June and the warming weather is already drawing out the conifers' sap and scent. Our 9am start means we have time to amble quite slowly to appreciate the bounce of last year's pine needles underfoot and the bob and chuckle of the darting jackdaw. Less easy to appreciate is the bogginess that we then encounter, but this is soon left behind as we snake our way up the hill towards Beinn Dubhchraig's summit.

To squeals of delight from the youngsters, we reach a small flat plateau with wee lochans and pause for half a sandwich. 'Are we going all the way to the top?' asks young Robbie, 'will it be like Mount Everest?'

We continue the uphill slog, alas, now in mist and cloud. Foot by foot we continue upwards and, sensing the importance of the occasion, those in front slow down and pull back as we near the top. A silence descends on the clan, and as we ascend step by step so, stone by stone from its top down, a rather bedraggled cairn is revealed. My 283rd Munro: I kiss the cairn despite its misshapen appearance.

It is the end of a journey that I had not originally set out to complete. Strange, then, that it should rank as one of the best journeys I have ever made. All my other journeys had started with clear goals: win a scholarship to Cambridge, get a first class degree, become a Partner in a multinational firm, gain the affection of a beautiful yet well-balanced girlfriend... But for many years this Munro journey had no goal beyond pure enjoyment – the goal of compleating the round had been a relatively late addition. The arrival therefore comes as an enigma: the intense enjoyment of the journey that is now over means its conclusion is tinged with a hint of sorrow.

My brother draws a bottle of whisky from his backpack, 'a drink the Highland way, anyone?' He pulls out the cork and hurls it so far away that it disappears: we'll just have to drink the whole bottle!

It is too cold for a long speech, but I mumble a few words: 'The immortal John Muir said, "we go out to go in." I agree with him. Going outwards has helped me go inwards: to understand better my passions and motivations, limits and limitations. But looking inwards has helped me look outwards too: to reach out, have fun with friends and family, and perhaps to share a passion with others who might make the journey too:

We go out to go in; but we go in to go out.

Thank you all for sharing with me one of the best days of my life.'

The patter of applause is polite, brief and barely audible over the splatter of rain: we are all getting cold and chase off downhill, urgently seeking the hemline of the mists, and warmth.

That night we limp on aching limbs to a celebratory dinner at the Crianlarich Hotel. Over sticky toffee desert, my brother stands up and delivers a very witty speech, ably followed by my good friend Neels and then by my sister. My sister concludes by reading a few words that my mother had sent along, which ends in a way that provides the answer to a big question:

> ... I have never really understood the depth of your passion for Scotland and for her mountains. Yes, you were born in Scotland – yet you left when you were barely three years old. Yes, your grandparents were Scottish – yet they passed away while you were still quite young. On the other hand... it was in the summer before the spring of your birth that I climbed my first and only Munro: Ben Macdui. And I suppose it could be... that as I struggled up the slopes and felt the exhilaration of that climb... perhaps you had already been conceived, and so were relishing the ascent of your first Munro before you were even born!

Dinner concluded, we eventually stagger out of the hotel, and as I turn to peer through the summer gloaming back up towards the summits, a warm midnight zephyr ripples down the glen, parting the grass with a slow sweeping flow. And on the breeze I surely catch a whisper: 'will ye no come back again?'

Acknowledgements

It often seemed harder work to write this book than to walk the thousand and more miles on which it is based, and this account could not have been published without the support of many friends and family members.

Some of my literary guides were also travelling companions, whom you have already met in the preceding pages. Others have played a less visible but very valuable role. All have been both generous and gracious in offering their time and their expertise to help in some way to bring this book to life.

First and foremost, I thank Sylvia Landsberg for her huge contributions to reading and improving the manuscript, proving an unending source of quotations and applying her expert understanding of the ecology of Scotland.

My thanks also go to fellow Munro-baggers Ryan Bishop, Daniel Cebenko, Jocelyn and Rob Dehnert, Hille, Lara and Neels Kriek, Ken and Olivia Landsberg, Andrey Litvinov, Andrei Stepanov, Jessica and Simon Swales, and Michael Worrall.

The extreme value of guidance and of shelter are much more tangible when one is in the wild, than when the comforts of town or home are at hand. In this context, I offer many thanks to Steven Fallon and his Mountain Guides, to Bed and Breakfast hosts (and now close friends) Deb and Ian Richards of Ewich House in Crianlarich and Ivan and Thea Smith formerly of Heatherlea in Glencoe. And walking can be enjoyed only with good footwear: I thank Danny Fox of Snow & Rock for helping to keep me well shod over the years.

On the literary and scientific sides, Fay Ballard, Julia and Richard Barkley, Anna Baverstock, Kwanruthai Daduon, Penny Daniel, Saeid Dehdashti, Dr Graeme Delort-McNaught, Andrew Franklin, Ann Gales, Emeritus Professor Charles Gimingham, Sandra Lawson, Shih-Ping Lin, Professor Norman Maclean, Dr Elisabeth Marx, Lucinda McNeile, Professor Paul O'Prey, Greg Rice, Professor Tim Sluckin, Regis Soublin, Dr Jon Stokes and Jessica Swales each contributed in his or her own special way; thank you all.

Finally I thank Gavin MacDougall and his team including Louise Hutcheson and Kirsten Graham at Luath Press, and my agent Francesca White, who all worked their magic to help shape a dream into a tangible reality.

Suggested Reading

I have grouped the suggested resources below into four areas: Routes, guidebooks and safety; Geology; Place-names; and Other works cited. Online sources are listed before printed books, with my personal favourites near the top of each list.

If you only view one source, this DVD is it: *Mountains of Scotland – Binnein nam Beann*, from Enlightenment Media Ltd.

Routes, guidebooks and safety

Best overall site for routes across hills in Scotland (though you might not be as fast as indicated!):

- www.stevenfallon.co.uk

Other good forum-based sites for Munros:

- www.walkhighlands.co.uk/munros
- www.munro-madness.com

Useful mapping app: WheresThePath

- wtp2.appspot.com/

All those lochs and hamlets: Gazetteer for Scotland

- www.scottish-places.info/

Mountain Rescue Committee of Scotland – please give generously:

- www.mrcofs.org/

Safety list at Registers of Scotland:

- www.ros.gov.uk/pdfs/hillwalking_safety.pdf

Books

McNeish, Cameron. *The Munros* Edinburgh: Lomond, 2006. *A fantastic starter, great maps though they lack detail*

Kew, Steve. *Walking the Munros. Vol 1: Central & Western Highlands.* Milnthorpe, Cumbria: Cicerone, 2004.

—. *Walking the Munros. Vol 2: Northern Highlands & Cairngorms.* Milnthorpe, Cumbria: Cicerone, 2006. *Excellent detail to follow when walking – I tear out the pages and take them with me*

Scottish Mountaineering Club. *The Munros*. Scottish Mountaineering Trust, 2006. *Definitive*

Murray, W. H. *Mountaineering in Scotland*. London: Baton Wicks, 1997. *Written in Colditz on lavatory paper. Stunning*

Butterfield, Irvine. *The Magic of the Munros*. David & Charles, 2005. *Some ultimate photos; one of the first comprehensive walking guides to the Munros*

Razzetti, Steve, ed. *Top Treks of the World*. London: New Holland Publishers, 2008. *Will tempt you*

Roberts, John, L. *The Highland Geology Trail*. Edinburgh, Scotland: Luath Press, 2013

Storer, Ralph. *The Ultimate Guide to the Munros. Volume One: The Southern Highlands*. Edinburgh, Scotland: Luath Press, 2008

— *The Ultimate Guide to the Munros. Volume Two: Central Highlands South*. Edinburgh, Scotland. Luath Press, 2009

— *The Ultimate Guide to the Munros. Volume Three: Central Highlands*. Edinburgh, Scotland. Luath Press, 2010

— *The Ultimate Guide to the Munros. Volume Four: Cairngorms South*. Edinburgh, Scotland. Luath Press, 2012

Geology

The Geology of the Scottish mountains from a climbing point of view, with a table giving the principal hills, arranged according to the nature of the rocks of which they are composed

by Lionel W. Hinxman *Scottish Mountaineering Club Journal Volume 5 Number 6* Available at:

- gdl.cdlr.strath.ac.uk/smcj/smcj030/smcj03001.htm

Fascinating custom animations: ODSN Plate Tectonic Reconstruction Service:

- www.odsn.de/odsn/services/paleomap/paleomap.html

Best source for north-west Scotland and Moine Thrust Zone:

- www.see.leeds.ac.uk/structure/assyntgeology/geology/thrusts/introduction.htm

Great online geology:

- www.discoveringfossils.co.uk/how_britain_formed.htm
- www.scottishgeology.com

The ultimate graphic on fold structures right across the Grampians:

- openlearn.open.ac.uk/file.php/3480/!via/oucontent/course/439/ sxr339_chap5.pdf page 54 (from Stephenson and Gould (1995) The Grampian Highlands, HMSO)

Joint Nature Conservation Committee has detailed reports on individual sites: JNCC DEFRA blocks

- *jncc.defra.gov.uk/page-4171*

E.g., JNCC re Lochnagar:

- jncc.defra.gov.uk/pdf/gcrdb/GCRsiteaccount369.pdf

Books

McKirdy, Alan and Crofts, Roger. *Scotland: a landscape fashioned by geology*. Battleby, Scotland: Scottish Natural Heritage, 1999.

Stephenson, David and Goodenough, Kathryn. *Ben Nevis and Glencoe: a landscape fashioned by geology*. Battleby, Scotland: Scottish Natural Heritage, 2007. *A brilliant series; succinct, with great diagrams*

Turnbull, Robert. *Granite and Grit: A Walker's Guide to the Geology of British Mountains*. Francis Lincoln, 2011. *Accessible and engaging*

Danson, Edwin. Weighing the World. New York: Oxford University Press, 2006. *Engaging account of the Schiehallion experiment and context*

Maskelyne, Nevil. 'An Account of Observations Made on the Mountain Schehallien for Finding Its Attraction.' Philosophical Transactions (1683–1775) 65 (1775): 500–542. *Schiehallion – from the man himself*

Rider, M.H. *Hutton's Arse: 3 Billion Years of Extraordinary Geology in Scotland's Northern Highlands*. Rider-French Consulting Ltd, 2005. *A great page-turner*

Trewin, N.H. *The Geology of Scotland*. Geological Society, 2003. *Expensive but authoritative*

Ballantyne, Colin K. *The Periglaciation of Great Britain*. Cambridge: Cambridge University Press, 1994. *Authoritative and not quite so expensive as Trewin*

Gordon, John E. et al. *Natural Heritage Zones: Earth Sciences*. Inverness: Scottish Natural Heritage, 2002. *Outstanding (and free) resource covering all eco- aspects of Scotland*

Place-names

Ordnance Survey guide:

- www.ordnancesurvey.co.uk/oswebsite/freefun/didyouknow/ placenames/gaelic.html

Scottish name resources:

- medievalscotland.org/scotnames/#pictish

Scottish Place-Name Society:

- www.spns.org.uk/

The Influence of Latin and Norse on the Goidelic Languages; Jan 28, 2003 – © Morag Gladstone from

- www.suite101.com/article.cfm/celtic_internet_resources/98104/1 retrieved 13 July 2011

MacBain, Alex Place Names: Highlands & Islands Of Scotland; Stirling: Eneas Mackay, 1922 Accessible at:

- www.archive.org/stream/cu31924028080533/ cu31924028080533_djvu.txt

Books

Drummond, Peter. *Scottish Hill Names: Their Origin and Meaning.* Scottish Mountaineering Trust, 2007.

— 'The Hill-names They Are A-changing....' n.d. *Scottish Corpus of Speech and Text.* 25 July 2011 < www.scottishcorpus.ac.uk/corpus/ search/document.php?documentid=1410>.

Other works cited

Anderson, George and Anderson, Peter. *Guide to the Highlands and Islands of Scotland.* Edinburgh: Adam and Charles Black, 1850.

Burke, Edmund. *A Philosophical Enquiry into the Origin of Our Ideas of the Sublime and the Beautiful.* London: J. Dodsley, 1757.

Campbell, Joseph. *The Hero with a Thousand Faces.* New World Library, 2012.

Dempster, Andrew. *The Munro Phenomenon.* Edinburgh: Mainstream, 1995.

Groeppel-Klein, A & Bartmann, B. 'Anti-Clockwise or Clockwise? The

Impact of Store Layout on the Process of Orientation in a Discount Store.' *European Advances in Consumer Research* 8 (2008): 415.

Fletcher, C. and Rawlins, C. *The Complete Walker IV*. New York: Knopf, 2002.

Kempe, Nick & Wrightham, Mark (eds). *Hostile Habitats: Scotland's Mountain Environment*. Scottish Mountaineering Trust, 2006

Kaplan, R & Kalpan, S & Ryan, Robert L. *With people in mind: design and management of everyday nature*. Island Press, 1998.

Linklater, Eric. *The Prince in the Heather*. London and Edinburgh: Hodder and Stoughton Ltd., 1965.

Llobera, M. & Sluckin, T.J. 'Zigzagging: theoretical insights on climbing strategies.' *Journal of Theoretical Biology* (2007): 249 (2007) 206–217.

Macfarlane, Robert. *Mountains of the Mind*. London: Granta Books, 2003.

Miller, Jim. *The Dam Builders: Power from the Glens*. Edinburgh: Birlinn Limited, 2007.

Minetti, A E, Formenti F & Ardigò L P. 'Himalayan porter's specialization: metabolic power, economy, efficiency and skill.' *Proc. R. Soc. B* (2006): 273, 2791–2797.

Morton, H. V. *In Search of Scotland*. London: Methuen, 1929.

Payne, Peter L. 2. *The Hydro: Study of the Development of the Major Hydroelectric Schemes Undertaken by the North of Scotland Hydroelectric Board*. Aberdeen: Pergamon, 1988.

Prebble, John. *The Highland Clearances*. London: Penguin, 1969.

Theroux, Paul. *Fresh Air Fiend: Travel Writings, 1985–2000*. London: Penguin, 2001.

Townsend, Chris. *The Advanced Backpacker: A Handbook of Year Round, Long-Distance Hiking*. International Marine/Ragged Mountain Press, 2000.

Schama, Simon. *Landscape and Memory*. New York: A.A. Knopf, 1995.

Zimmerberg, B., Glick, S., & Jerussi, T. 'Neurochemical Correlate of a Spatial Preference in Rats.' *Science* (1974): 623–625.

Appendices

1. Alphabetical List of Munros, including name, translation, pronunciation, height, region, grid reference, indexing to page number
2. Gaelic – further notes on place names
3. Selected scenic chronology

APPENDIX I

Index of Munros

(m)	Height in metres
A	SMC area, 1–17 as indicated below
P	page number
Name	including pronunciation ['ch' is per 'loch']

01	Loch Lomond to Loch Tay (20 Munros)
02	Loch Tay to Rannoch Moor (26 Munros)
03	Strath Orchy to Loch Leven (26 Munros)
04	Loch Linnhe to Loch Ericht (34 Munros)
05	Loch Rannoch to Drumochter (7 Munros)
06	Glen Garry to Braemar (15 Munros)
07	Glen Shee to Mount Keen (14 Munros)
08	The Cairngorms (18 Munros)
09	Glen Roy to The Monadh Liath (9 Munros)
10	Loch Eil to Glen Shiel (26 Munros)
11	Glen Affric and Kintail (22 Munros)
12	Glen Cannich to Glen Carron (14 Munros)
13	Coulin and Torridon (9 Munros)
14	Loch Maree to Loch Broom (19 Munros)
15	Loch Broom to Easter Ross (7 Munros)
16	Coigach to Cape Wrath (4 Munros)
17	The Islands (13 Munros)

(m)	A	P	Name	Pronunciation
936	5	134	A' Bhuidheanach Bheag	'a voo-an-ach vek'
997	14	74	A' Chailleach (Fannaichs)	'a chal-yach'
930	9	137	A' Chailleach (Monadh Liath)	'a chal-yach'
1,120	11	189	A' Chralaig	'a chraa-lik'
918	11	211	A' Ghlas-bheinn	'a glash vin'
967	14	104	A' Mhaighdean	'ah vay-tyin'
975	5	134	A' Mharconaich	'a var-kan-eech'
934	17	216	Am Basteir	'am bas-tar'
1,032	4	155	Am Bodach	'am pod-ach'
953	15	72	Am Faochagach	'am foe-cha-kach'
995	1	56	An Caisteal	'an kash-tyal'
923	14	71	An Coileachan	'an kil-yach-an'
982	4	17	An Gearanach	'an gyer-an-ach'
1,129	12	168	An Riabhachan	'an ree-av-achan'
1,006	6	197	An Sgarsoch	'an skaar-soch'
921	11	169	An Socach (Glen Affric)	'an soch-kach'
944	6	90	An Socach (Glen Ey)	'an soch-kach'
1,069	12	168	An Socach (Mullardoch)	'an soch-kach'
1,118	2	61	An Stuc	'an stoo-chk'
1,021	10	199	Aonach air Chrith	'oen-ach ayr chree'
1,116	4	177	Aonach Beag (Badenoch)	'oen-ach bayk'
1,234	4	154	Aonach Beag (Lochaber)	'oen-ach bayk'
1,001	11	201	Aonach Mheadhoin	'oen-ach vain'
1,221	4	154	Aonach Mor	'oen-ach more'
1,197	8	196	Beinn a' Bhuird	'bine a voord'
1,083	8	194	Beinn a' Chaorainn (Cairngorms)	'bine a choe-ran'
1,049	9	138	Beinn a' Chaorainn (Monadh Liath)	'bine a choe-rin'
1,087	4	165	Beinn a' Chlachair	'bine a' claa-char'
916	14	77	Beinn a' Chlaidheimh	'bine a' shleev'

(m)	A	P	Name	Pronunciation
916	1	219	Beinn a' Chleibh	'bine a chlayv'
980	3	35	Beinn a' Chochuill	'bine a' cho-chil'
1,081	2	191	Beinn a' Chreachain	'bine a chrech-yin'
940	1	57	Beinn a' Chroin	'bine a ch-roan'
1,038	2	191	Beinn Achaladair	'bine ach-a-la-tu'
1,004	2	97	Beinn an Dothaidh	'bine daw-re'
1,019	4	178	Beinn Bheoil	'bine vy-awl'
931	8	194	Beinn Bhreac	'bine vrechk'
1,157	8	194	Beinn Bhrotain	'bine vro-tan'
948	1	145	Beinn Bhuidhe	'bine voo-ee'
933	1	31	Beinn Chabhair	'bine chav-aar'
1,008	6	175	Beinn Dearg (Atholl)	'bine jer-rack'
1,084	15	99	Beinn Dearg (Ullapool)	'bine jer-rack'
1,076	2	97	Beinn Dorain	'bine doo-ran'
978	1	219	Beinn Dubhchraig	'bine doo-kraik'
1,102	4	177	Beinn Eibhinn	'bine ay-veen'
989	3	35	Beinn Eunaich	'bine ay-neech'
1,032	11	211	Beinn Fhada	'bine at-a'
1,005	11	184	Beinn Fhionnlaidh (Affric)	'bine yoon-ly'
959	3	111	Beinn Fhionnlaidh (Appin)	'bine yoon-ly'
1,103	2	61	Beinn Ghlas	'ben glas'
1,078	2	84	Beinn Heasgarnich	'bine hes-kar-neech'
1,045	6	93	Beinn Iutharn Mhor	'bine yoo-arn voar'
926	13	70	Beinn Liath Mhor	'bine lee-a voar'
954	14	70	Beinn Liath Mhor Fannaich	'bine lee-a voar fan-nich'
953	2	191	Beinn Mhanach	'bine van-ach'
1,182	8	197	Beinn Mheadhoin	'bine vee-an'
935	4	180	Beinn na Lap	'bine na lap'
960	3	151	Beinn nan Aighenan	'bine yan yan-an'

(m)	A	P	Name	Pronunciation
926	1	26	Beinn Narnain	'bine nar-nain'
974	10	38	Beinn Sgritheall	'bine skree-hal'
937	3	111	Beinn Sgulaird	'bine skoo-lard'
937	14	104	Beinn Tarsuinn	'bine tar-shin'
915	9	138	Beinn Teallach	'bine tyel-lach'
946	1	56	Beinn Tulaichean	'bine too-lach-an'
1,011	5	134	Beinn Udlamain	'bine oot-lam-an'
1,148	4	178	Ben Alder	'ben awl-der'
1,171	8	196	Ben Avon	'ben aan
1,025	2	87	Ben Challum	'ben cha-lam'
931	1	37	Ben Chonzie	'ben hon-zee'
1,126	3	32	Ben Cruachan	'ben kroo-achan'
927	16	102	Ben Hope	'ben hope'
1,011	1	26	Beinn Ime	'ben eem'
962	16	100	Ben Klibreck	'ben klee-breck'
1,214	2	61	Ben Lawers	'ben lors'
974	1	28	Ben Lomond	'ben low-mond'
1,130	1	219	Ben Lui (Beinn Laoigh)	'ben loo-ee'
1,309	8	197	Ben Macdui	'ben mac-doo-ee'
1,174	1	55	Ben More (Crianlarich)	'ben more'
966	17	190	Ben More (Mull)	'ben more'
998	16	103	Ben More Assynt	'ben more ass-int'
1,344	4	153	Ben Nevis	'ben nev-is'
1,029	1	219	Ben Oss	'ben oss'
1,078	3	151	Ben Starav	'ben sta-rav'
915	1	26	Ben Vane	'ben vane'
943	1	25	Ben Vorlich (Arrochar)	'ben vor-lich'
985	1	53	Ben Vorlich (Loch Earn)	'ben vor-lich'
1,046	15	98	Ben Wyvis	'ben wivis'

(m)	A	P	Name	Pronunciation
945	12	188	Bidean a' Choire Sheasgaich	'bee-tyan a chora hays-geech'
1,062	14	74	Bidean a' Ghlas Thuill	'beet-yan a ghlas-hool'
1,150	3	147	Bidean nam Bian	'beet-yan nam bee-oan'
943	4	153	Binnean Beag	'been-yan bayk'
1,130	4	153	Binnein Mor	'been-yan more'
928	17	214	Bla Bheinn (Blaven)	'blaa-vin'
1,296	8	134	Braeriach	'brae-ree-ach'
1,070	6	175	Braigh Coire Chruinn-bhalgain	'bray corrie kroon vaa-lak-an'
998	7	91	Broad Cairn	'broad cairn'
958	17	216	Bruach na Frithe	'broo-ach na free-a'
1,090	8	136	Bynack More	'bie-nack more'
1,155	7	90	Cac Carn Beag	'kak karn bayk'
1,012	7	91	Cairn Bannoch	'karn ban-noch'
1,244	8	136	Cairn Gorm	'karn gor-om'
1,064	7	92	Cairn of Claise	'karn of clace'
1,291	8	195	Cairn Toul	'karn tow-al'
963	6	174	Carn a' Chlamain	'karn a klaa-van'
1,110	7	91	Carn a' Choire Boidheach	'karn a corrie vaw-yach'
975	6	90	Carn a' Gheoidh	'karn a yow-ee'
1,037	8	197	Carn a' Mhaim	'karn a vame'
994	6	197	Carn an Fhidhleir	'karn an yee-lar'
1,029	6	92	Carn an Righ	'karn an ree'
1,047	7	91	Carn an t-Sagairt Mor	'karn an tak-ar-sht more'
1,019	7	92	Carn an Tuirc	'karn an toork'
917	6	90	Carn Aosda	'karn oesh'
946	6	198	Carn Bhac	'karn vachk'
941	4	179	Carn Dearg (Loch Ossian)	'karn jer-rack'

(m)	A	P	Name	Pronunciation
1,034	4	177	Carn Dearg (Loch Pattack)	'caarn jer-rack'
945	9	138	Carn Dearg (Monadh Liath)	'karn jer-rack'
1,183	11	184	Carn Eighe	'karn ay-ya'
957	11	199	Carn Ghluasaid	'karn ghloo-a-sat'
1,029	2	60	Carn Gorm	'karn gor-om'
975	6	175	Carn Liath (Beinn a' Ghlo)	'karn lee-a'
1,006	9	139	Carn Liath (Monadh Liath)	'karn lee-a'
1,041	2	60	Carn Mairg	'karn mairg'
1,220	4	152	Carn Mor Dearg	'karn more jer-rack'
941	5	134	Carn na Caim	'karn a kym'
1,121	6	175	Carn nan Gabhar	'karn nan gow-er'
992	12	168	Carn nan Gobhar (Mullardoch)	'karn nan gow-er'
992	12	183	Carn nan Gobhar (Strathfarrar)	'karn nan gow-er'
920	9	138	Carn Sgulain	'karn skoo-lin'
1,046	4	150	Chno Dearg	'knaw jer-rack'
979	11	200	Ciste Dhubh	'kees-ta doo'
978	15	99	Cona' Mheall	'kon-i-val'
987	16	103	Conival	'kon-i-vaal'
947	10	199	Creag a' Mhaim	'kraik a vaim'
987	7	92	Creag Leachach	'kraik lye-chach'
1,128	9	139	Creag Meagaidh	'kraik meg-gie'
1,047	2	84	Creag Mhor	'kraik voar'
918	10	200	Creag nan Damh	'kraik nam dav'
924	4	165	Creag Pitridh	'kraik peet-rie'
1,100	3	146	Creise	'ky-aysh'
1,046	1	56	Cruach Ardrain	'kroo-ach ar-dran'
1,155	8	196	Derry Cairngorm	'Derry Cairngorm'
947	7	89	Driesh	'dree-sh'
987	10	199	Druim Shionnach	'drim hee-a-nach'

(m)	A	P	Name	Pronunciation
927	15	76	Eididh nan Clach Geala	'ayd-yee nan klach gy-ala'
933	14	127	Fionn Bheinn	'fy-oon vine'
919	10	211	Gairich	'gaa-reech'
1,013	10	166	Garbh Chioch Mhor	'garv kee-ach voar'
1,049	4	165	Geal Charn (Loch Laggan)	'gyul karn'
926	9	136	Geal Charn (Monadh Liath)	'gyul karn'
917	5	134	Geal-charn (Drumochter)	'gyul karn'
1,132	4	177	Geal-Charn (Loch Pattack)	'gyul karn'
997	3	152	Glas Bheinn Mhor	'glas vine voar'
1,068	7	92	Glas Maol	'glas moel'
1,051	6	92	Glas Tulaichean	'glas too-leech-an'
1,035	10	210	Gleouraich	'gly-aw-reech'
987	10	165	Gulvain	'gool-van'
1,020	10	218	Ladhar Bheinn (Larven)	'laar-ven'
939	10	217	Luinne Bheinne	'loon-ya vine'
986	12	188	Lurg Mhor	'loor-ak voar'
1,181	11	184	Mam Sodhail	'mam sool'
1,007	12	187	Maoile Lunndaidh	'moel-a loon-dy'
933	13	126	Maol Chean-dearg	'moel chan jer-rack'
981	10	200	Maol Chinn-dearg	'meeowl chan jer-rack'
928	7	89	Mayar	'may-yer'
1,108	3	147	Meall a' Bhuiridh	'meeowl a voo-ree'
926	2	63	Meall a' Choire Leith	'meeowl kora lay'
934	14	74	Meall a' Chrasgaidh	'meeowl a chras-kee'
932	2	60	Meall Buidhe (Glen Lyon)	'meeowl boo-ee'
946	10	217	Meall Buidhe (Knoydart)	'meeowl boo-ee'
951	5	134	Meall Chuaich	'meeowl choo-eech'
1,069	2	62	Meall Corranaich	'meeowl kora-neech'

(m)	A	P	Name	Pronunciation
953	3	149	Meall Dearg	'meeowl jer-rack'
968	2	61	Meall Garbh (Glen Lyon)	'meeowl garv'
1,118	2	60	Meall Garbh (Lawers)	'meeowl garv'
1,039	2	84	Meall Ghaordaidh	'meeowl gir-day'
959	2	86	Meall Glas	'meeowl glas'
949	14	71	Meall Gorm	'meeowl gor-ram'
1,001	2	61	Meall Greigh	'meeowl gray'
918	10	154	Meall na Teanga	'meeowl na ty-eng-a'
981	2	60	Meall nan Aighean	'meeowl nan yaan'
977	15	99	Meall nan Ceapraichean	'meeowl nan kya-pree-chan'
928	3	149	Meall nan Eun	'meeowl nan ayn'
1,044	2	64	Meall nan Tarmachan	'meeowl nan tar-mach-an'
1,113	8	195	Monadh Mor	'mon-agh more'
928	12	189	Moruisg	'more-oosh'
939	7	91	Mount Keen	'mount keen'
1,023	13	124	Mullach an Rathain	'moo-lach an raa-han'
1,019	8	137	Mullach Clach a' Bhlair	'mool-ach clach a vaar'
1,018	14	104	Mullach Coire Mhic Fhearchair	'mool-ach cora veechk er-ach-ar'
1,102	11	190	Mullach Fraoch-choire	'moo-lach froech corrie'
982	11	169	Mullach na Dheiragain	'mool-lach na yer-ak-an'
939	4	155	Mullach nan Coirean	'mull-ach nan koor-an'
1,056	4	153	Na Gruagaichean	'na groo-a-keech-an'
918	14	122	Ruadh Stac Mor	'roo-a stak more'
1,010	13	105	Ruadh-stac Mor	'roo-a stak more'
1,002	11	199	Sail Chaorainn	'sal choe-ran'
956	11	201	Saileag	'saal-ak'
1,083	2	63	Schiehallion	'shee-haal-yan'

(m)	A	P	Name	Pronunciation
926	15	75	Seana Bhraigh	'shenna vry'
991	5	134	Sgairneach Mhor	'skarn-yatch voar'
921	2	86	Sgiath Chuil	'skeea-chool'
1,258	8	195	Sgor an Lochan Uaine	'sgoor an lock-yn oo-anya'
955	4	179	Sgor Gaibhre	'sgor gy-ra'
1,118	8	137	Sgor Gaoith	'sgor goo-ee'
994	3	148	Sgor na h-Ulaidh	'sgor na hool-ya'
1,024	3	112	Sgorr Dhearg	'sgor jer-rack'
1,001	3	112	Sgorr Dhonuill	'sgor ghaw-wil'
967	3	149	Sgorr nam Fiannaidh	'sgor nam fee-a-nee'
962	13	126	Sgorr Ruadh	'sgoor roo-a'
1,036	11	201	Sgurr a' Bhealaich Dheirg	'sgoor a vy-al-eech jer-rack'
1,053	12	187	Sgurr a' Chaorachain	'sgoor a choe-rach-an'
1,083	12	183	Sgurr a' Choire Ghlais	'sgoor a corrie a ghlash'
973	17	44	Sgurr a' Ghreadaidh	'sgoor a ghray-tee'
918	17	44	Sgurr a' Mhadaidh	'sgoor a vaa-dy'
1,099	4	19	Sgurr a' Mhaim	'sgoor a vaim'
1,027	10	210	Sgurr a' Mhaoraich	'sgoor a voo-reach'
992	17	214	Sgurr Alasdair	'sgoor al-as-tar'
1,010	10	200	Sgurr an Doire Leathain	'sgoor an dir-a le-han'
1,004	10	200	Sgurr an Lochain	'sgoor an loch-an'
989	14	77	Sgurr Ban	'sgoor bawn'
999	14	74	Sgurr Breac	'sgoor brechk'
999	12	156	Sgurr Choinnich	'sgoor cho-an-yeech'
1,094	4	156	Sgurr Choinnich Mor	'sgoor cho-an-yeech more'
944	17	214	Sgurr Dubh Mor	'sgoor doo more'

(m)	A	P	Name	Pronunciation
1,010	4	153	Sgurr Eilde Mor	'sgoor ail-ta more'
1,067	11	201	Sgurr Fhuaran	'sgoor oo-aran'
1,060	14	74	Sgurr Fiona	'sgoor fee-ana'
1,049	12	183	Sgurr Fuar-thuill	'sgoor oo-ar hil'
948	17	43	Sgurr Mhic Choinnich	'sgoor vic chun-yeech'
986	13	125	Sgurr Mhor	'sgoor more'
1,110	14	70	Sgurr Mor (Fannaichs)	'sgoor more'
1,003	10	167	Sgurr Mor (Loch Quoich)	'sgoor more'
965	17	44	Sgurr na Banachdich	'sgoor na ban-ach-teech'
1,002	11	201	Sgurr na Carnach	'sgoor na karn-ach'
1,040	10	166	Sgurr na Ciche	'sgoor na keesh'
1,027	11	201	Sgurr na Ciste Duibhe	'sgoor na kees-ta ghoo'
1,150	12	168	Sgurr na Lapaich	'sgoor na lah-peech'
993	12	183	Sgurr na Ruaidhe	'sgoor na rooy'
946	10	212	Sgurr na Sgine	'sgoor na skee-na'
1,151	11	169	Sgurr nan Ceathreamhnan	'sgoor nan ker-o-anan'
1,093	14	74	Sgurr nan Clach Geala	'sgoor nan klach gee-ala'
953	10	166	Sgurr nan Coireachan (Glen Dessary)	'sgoor nan kor-ach-an'
956	10	164	Sgurr nan Coireachan (Glenfinnan)	'sgoor nam kor-ach-an'
1,109	11	199	Sgurr nan Conbhairean	'sgoor nan kon-a-var-an'
923	14	74	Sgurr nan Each	'sgoor nan yaach'
924	17	213	Sgurr nan Eag	'sgoor nan ayg'
964	17	216	Sgurr nan Gillean	'sgoor nan geel-yan'
963	10	164	Sgurr Thuilm	'sgoor hoo-lim'
981	14	123	Slioch	'slee-och'
1,055	13	124	Spidean a Choire Leith	'spee-tyan a corrie lay'
993	13	122	Spidean Coire nan Clach	'speet-yan corrie nan klach'

(m)	A	P	Name	Pronunciation
996	10	210	Spidean Mialach	'speet-yan mee-al-ach'
937	10	154	Sron a' Choire Ghairbh	'srawn a corrie garv'
1,105	4	140	Stob a' Choire Mheadhoin	'stob corrie vane'
945	3	146	Stob a' Choire Odhair	'stob a corrie oo-er'
977	4	155	Stob Ban (Grey Corries)	'stob baan'
999	4	155	Stob Ban (Mamores)	'stob baan'
1,165	1	55	Stob Binnein	'stob bin-yan'
1,177	4	156	Stob Choire Claurigh	'stob corrie clow-ree'
1,044	3	149	Stob Coir' an Albannaich	'stob kor an a-lap-a-neech'
981	4	18	Stob Coire a' Chairn	'stob corrie a cairn'
1,116	4	156	Stob Coire an Laoigh	'stob corrie an loo-ee'
1,115	4	140	Stob Coire Easain	'stob corrie e-san'
925	3	113	Stob Coire Raineach	'stob corrie ran-noch'
1,072	3	148	Stob Coire Sgreamach	'stob corrie skree-ya'
979	4	151	Stob Coire Sgriodain	'stob corrie sgree-a-dan'
1,021	3	112	Stob Dearg	'stob jer-rack'
998	3	34	Stob Diamh	'stob dyv'
958	3	113	Stob Dubh	'stob doo'
1,090	3	146	Stob Ghabhar	'stob gow-er'
956	3	113	Stob na Broige	'stob na broo-ker'
1,054	9	139	Stob Poite Coire Ardair	'stob pot-ya kor aar-dar'
975	1	54	Stuc a' Chroin	'stook a kro-in'
960	2	60	Stuchd an Lochain	'stook an loch-an'
933	6	90	The Cairnwell	'hill of bags'
1,004	8	195	The Devil's Point	'the Devil's point'
986	17	42	The Inaccessible Pinnacle	'the inaccessible pinnacle'
1,010	10	212	The Saddle	'the saddle'
1,054	11	184	Toll Creagach	'tow kraik-ach'
958	7	92	Tolmount	'tol-mount'
1,112	11	183	Tom a' Choinich	'towm a choan-yeech'
957	7	92	Tom Buidhe	'towm boo-ee'
922	13	124	Tom na Gruagaich	'towm na groo-ag-eech'

APPENDIX 2

Gaelic – further notes on place names

The Ordnance Survey provides a very comprehensive *Guide to Gaelic origins of place names in Britain*. Below I offer translations of Gaelic words often used in place names, together with a few of my own favourites, preceded by a brief guide to pronunciation.

Pronunciation

The os Guide also indicates pronunciation, of which a simple summary is:
bh or *mh* = v at beginning of word; w at end of word. *Bhac* 'vac' (peat)
dh = y when next to *e* or *i*; otherwise gh (as in French *rire*); silent at end. *Buidhe* 'boo-ie' (yellow)
th = h; but silent at end. *Thuill* 'hoo-ie' (hollow)
fh = always silent. *Fhada* 'atta' (long)

Colours

An important identifier of all aspects of landscape:

Gaelic	English	#	Example
Bla	Blue	1	Bla Bheinn (Blaven) – Blue hill
Buidhe	Yellow	3	Meall Buidhe – Rounded yellow hill
Dearg	Red	12	Stob Dearg – Red peak
Dhearg	Red	1	Sgorr Dhearg – Red peak
Dhubh	Black	1	Ciste Dhubh – Black Chest
Dubh	Black	2	Beinn Dubhchraig – Black creag hill
Fionn	Bright	1	Fionn Bheinn – Light (colour) hill
Geal	White	4	Geal-charn – White hill
Geala	White	2	Sgurr nan Clach Geala – Peak of the white stones
Ghlas	Green	2	Beinn Ghlas – Green hill
Glas	Green	5	Meall Glas – Green rounded hill
Gorm	Blue	3	Carn Gorm – Blue hill
Leith	Grey	2	Meall a' Choire Leith – Rounded hill of the grey corrie

Gaelic	English	#	Example
Liath	Grey	4	Carn Liath – Grey Hill
Liathach	Grey	2	Liathach – Spidean a' Choire Leith – Pinnacle of the grey corrie
Ruadh	Red	3	Sgorr Ruadh – Red peak
Gillean	Grey	1	Sgurr nan Gillean – Grey hill

= occurrences in names of the Munros

Other name-words

Topic	English	Gaelic	Example
People			
	Baptiser	Basteir	Am Basteir – The baptiser
	Complainer	Gearanach	An Gearanach – The complainer
	Maiden	Gruagaich	Na Gruagaichean – The maidens
	Malcolm	Challum	Ben Challum – Malcolm's hill
	Merchants	Ceannaichean	Sgurr nan Ceannaichean – Hill of the merchants
	Old woman	Chailleach	A' Chailleach (Monadh Liath) – The old woman
	Shepherd or Herdsman	Buachaille	Buachaille Etive Mor – big shepherd of Etive
	Stonemason	Chlachair	Beinn a' Chlachair – Hill of the stonemason
Adjectives			
	Broad	Leathain	Sgurr an Doire Leathain – Peak of the broad thicket
	High	Ardair	Stob Poite Coire Ardair – Peak of the pot of the high corrie
	High	Ardrain	Cruach Ardrain – High heap
	Long	Fhada	Beinn Fhada – Long hill
	Notched	Narnain	Beinn Narnain – Hill of notches
	Old	Seana	Seana Bhraigh – Old brae
	Pale	Ban	Sgurr Ban – Pale peak
	Transverse	Tarsuinn	Beinn Tarsuinn – Transverse hill
	Speckled	Breac	Sgurr Breac – Speckled peak

Topic	English	Gaelic	Example
Fauna			
	Boar	Tuirc	Carn an Tuirc – Hill of the boar
	Buzzard	Chlamain	Carn a Chlamain – Buzzard hill
	Cock	Coileachan	An Coileachan – The little cock
	Fowl	Eun	Beinn Eunaich – Fowling hill
	Goat	Gabhar	Carn nan Gabhar – Hill of the goats
	Goose	Gheoidh	Carn a' Gheoidh – Hill of the Goose
	Hawk	Chabhair	Beinn Chabhair – Hill of the hawk
	Hinds	Aighenan	Beinn nan Aighenan – Hill of the hinds
	Horse	Con	A Mharconaich – Place of horses
	Sparrowhawk	Dheiragain	Mullach na Dheiragain – Summit of the sparrowhawk
	Stag	Damh	Creag nan Damh – Creag of the stags
Flora			
	Bracken	Raineach	Stob Coire Raineach – Bracken corrie peak
	Heather	Fraoch	Mullach Fraoch-choire – Summit of the heather corrie
	Moss	Choinich	Tom a' Choinich – Pointed hill of the moss
	Rowan	Chaorainn	Beinn a' Chaorainn (Cairngorms) – Hill of the rowan tree
	Peat	Bhac	Carn Bhac – Cairn of the peat banks
Water features			
	River	Abhainn	
	Stream	Alt	
	Waterfall	Easain	Stob Coire Easain – Peak of the corrie of the wee waterfall
Body parts			
	Heal	Saileag	Saileag – Little heel
	Hoof	Ladhar	Ladhar Bheinn – Hill of the hoof or claw
	Shin	Lurg	Lurg Mhor – Big ridge stretching into the plain
	Shoulder	Ghaordie	Meall Ghaordie – Rounded hill of the shoulder

Topic	English	Gaelic	Example
Body parts			
	Snout	Socach	An Socach (Glen Ey) – West Summit – The snout
	Tongue	Teanga	Meall na Teanga – Rounded hill of the tongue
	Wind	Gaoith	Sgor Gaoith – Peak of the wind
	Back	Chuil	Sgiath Chuil – Back of the wing
	Mouth	Bheoil	Beinn Bheoil – Mouth hill
	Head	Chinn	Maol Chinn-dearg – Bald red head

A caveat

The name of a place may change from time to time – perhaps as a peak is renamed to honour an individual. For example, Sgurr Biorach became Sgurr Alasdair, after Sheriff Alexander Nicholson first climbed it in 1873.

Sometimes changes are made for reasons of decorum. As Peter Drummond comments in The Scottish Corpus of Texts and Speech, 'English speakers could probably be blamed for [the names] *Ben Chichnes* or *Beinn nan cìochan* (mountain of breasts, from its nipple-like tors) becoming Lochnagar (especially with royalty moving in below it).'

APPENDIX 3

Selected Events Affecting Landscape and Culture

500 Mya	Britain created from collision of three continental plates
11,000 BC	Mesolithic starts
10,000	Last Ice Age ends
6,500	Doggerland breached – Britain separated from Europe
5,000	Neolithic starts
2,500–500BC	Bronze Age
500BC–AD200	Iron Age; Brochs and Duns built from ~400BC
AD140	Romans build Antonine Wall
500–600	Celtic tribes (Scotii) arrive from Ireland
600–700	Anglo-Saxons colonise south-east Scotland
790	Vikings raid west coast
1057	Malcolm III kills Macbeth
1295	'Auld Alliance' with France
1297	Wallace defeats English, starting war of independence
1306	Robert the Bruce crowned King of Scotland
1314	English routed at Bannockburn
1542	Mary Queen of Scots crowned
1560	Protestant Church established by Scots Parliament
1583	Timothy Pont's Maps of Scotland
1590	1st documented ascent of a to-be Munro – Stuch an Lochain
1603	James IV of Scotland and I of England unites crowns
1610	William Camden: Britannia
1689	James II and VII deposed
1692	Massacre of Glencoe
1715/45	Jacobite Risings
1724–27	Defoe: *A tour thro' the whole island of Great Britain*
1747–53	William Roy's Military Survey of Scotland
1769	Thomas Pennant: *A Tour in Scotland*
1773	James Boswell: *The Journal of a Tour to the Hebrides*
1774	Schiehallion used to 'weigh' the Earth
1785	James Hutton: *Theory of the Earth*
1807–21	Highland Clearances peak in Sutherland
1846	Thomas Cook launches steamer and rail tours
1891	Munro's *Tables* published
1931	The National Trust for Scotland founded

1940s	Development of larger hydroelectric schemes
1949	Many conservation Sites of Special Scientific Interest (SSSI) originally notified
1951	First grid-connected wind turbine: Orkney Islands
1951	Beinn Eighe set up as UK's first national nature reserve (NNR)
1970	The 100th Munroist
1983	John Muir Trust founded
1986	Creag Meagaidh as NNR
1995	The film *Braveheart* released
1998	Munroist number 2000
1999	Devolved Scottish parliament first meets
2003	Cairngorms becomes a National Park
2010	Tiree community wind-farm established
2011	James Hutton Institute established in Dundee

Index

See Appendix 1 for details of each Munro and relevant page references.

The following index includes people; places; selected mountains that are not Munros; selected lochs, glens and isles; and the geological terms listed below.

Munro ranges indexed below:

Aonach Eagach, Cairngorms, Clachlet Traverse, Cuillin, Fannichs, Five Sisters of Kintail, Forcan Ridge, Grey Corries, Lochnagar, Ring of Steall, South Glen Shiel Ridge

Geological terms and geologists indexed below:

Acadian, Alps, Archean, Armorica, Avalonia, Baltica, basalt, Caledonian Mountains, Cretaceous, Devonian, diorite, drumlin, erratic, esker, felsic, gabbro, glacier, gneiss, Gondwana, granite, Highland Boundary Fault, Hutton (Charles), Hutton (James), Jurassic, kame, kettle, Laurentia, Lewisian, mafic, magma, Maskelyne (Rev. Dr Nevil), Mason (Charles), metamorphic, Moine Thrust Zone, Neogene, Neptunism, nunatak, Ordovician, orogeny, Palaeogene, Palaeozoic, periglaciation, Permian, plate tectonics, Plutonism, Pre-Cambrian, pre-glacial, pro-talus, quartzite, roches moutonée, sandstone, Scandian, Schiehallion Experiment, schist, sedimentary, Silurian, solifluction, stadial, terrane (geological plate), trimline, ultramafic, Volcanic Explosivity Index

Main Index

Some other books published by **LUATH** PRESS

The Ultimate Guide to the Munros

Ralph Storer
Volume 1: Southern Highlands
ISBN 978-1906307-57-8 PBK £14.99
Volume 2: Central Highlands South
ISBN 978-1-906817-20-6 PBK £14.99
Volume 3: Central Highlands North
ISBN 978-1-906817-56-5 PBK £14.99
Volume 4: Cairngorms South
ISBN 978-1-908373-51-9 PBK £9.99

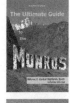

From the pen of a dedicated Munros bagger comes *The Ultimate Guide* to everything you've wished the other books had told you before you set off. The lowdown on the state of the path, advice on avoiding bogs and tricky situations, tips on how to determine which bump is actually the summit in misty weather... this series forms the only guide to the Munros you'll ever need.

Winner of the highly commended Award for Excellence (for Vol. 1) by the Outdoor Writers and Photographers Guild

His books are exceptional... Storer subverts the guidebook genre completely.
THE ANGRY CORRIE

Irresistibly funny and useful... makes an appetising broth of its wit, experience and visual and literary tools. Brilliant.
OUTDOOR WRITERS AND PHOTOGRAPHERS GUILD

Baffies' Easy Munro Guide

Ralph Storer
Volume 1: Southern Highlands
ISBN 978-1-908373-08-3 PBK £7.99
Volume 2: Central Highlands
ISBN 978-1-908373-20-5 PBK £7.99

Meet Baffies – the Entertainments Convenor of the Go-Take-A-Hike Mountaineering Club. Named after his footwear of choice ['Baffies' is a Scottish word for slippers], he's allergic to exertion, prone to lassitude, suffers from altitude sickness above 600m, blisters easily and bleeds readily. Show him a mountain and he'll find the easiest way up it. It's a gift of which he is justifiably proud and one whose fruits he has now been persuaded to share with like-minded souls. You'll find no easier way to climb Munros than to follow in his footsteps.

These rucksack guides feature:
- Detailed descriptions of easy walking routes to the summits of 25 Southern Highlands Munros
- Annotated colour photographs and OS maps
- Fascinating facts on landscape, history, Gaelic pronunciation and much more

The perfect guidebooks to Scottish mountains for the hillwalker who wishes to avoid rock climbing, scrambling and vertigo.

Caleb's List: Climbing the Scottish Mountains Visible from Arthur's Seat

Kellan McInnes

ISBN 978-1-908373-53-3 HBK £18.99

Edinburgh. 1898. On the cusp of the modern age. Caleb George Cash, mountaineer, geographer, antiquarian and teacher stands at the rocky summit of Arthur's Seat.

His reason for standing there was to chart which mountains were visible from his point on the summit – The Arthurs. He came up with a list of 20 mountains (all over 100ft/300m high), including Schiehallion and Ben Lomond. Caleb's list was first published in 1899, eight years after Munro published his list of mountains over 3,000ft, and since then it has been all but forgotten.

This book tells the story of how Caleb's list came about and provides directions and route descriptions for those wishing to climb the mountains on the list. More than just a climbing book, this is also the story of a survivor. The author was diagnosed with AIDS at the age of 33, and becoming an 'Arthurist' has helped him carry on with life.

Scotland's Mountains before the Mountaineers

Ian R. Mitchell

ISBN 978-1-908373-29-8 PBK £9.99

Winner of the Outdoor Writers' Guild Prize for Best Outdoor Book

The true story of explorations and ascents in the Scottish Highlands before mountaineering became a popular sport. Among early climbers were bandits, poachers and illicit distillers who used the mountains as sanctuary – not a Munro-bagger in sight. On the right side of the law were the mapmakers, road builders, geologists, astronomers and naturalists, many of whom ascended hitherto untrodden summits.

An intriguing read for the mountain amateur and the seasoned mountaineer, with controversial and passionately held views on the current state of the Scottish hills and mountains, issues of public access and conservation.

This is a book which every hill-goer, whatever their interests, should own, one of a rare breed offering new delights from hard worn research.

Hamish Brown, TGO MAGAZINE

Ribbon of Wildness

Peter Wright
ISBN 978-1-906817-45-9 PBK £14.99

The next big wild walk...

If you've bagged the Munros, done the Caledonian Challenge and walked the West Highland Way, this is your next conquest.

Ribbon of Wildness provides a vivid introduction to the Watershed of Scotland, which has hitherto been largely unknown. The rock, bog, forest, moor and mountain are all testament o the Watershed's richly varied natural state. The evolving kaleidoscope of changing vistas, wide panoramas, ever-present wildlife, and the vagaries of the weather, are delightfully described on this great journey of discovery.

Peter Wright has done lovers of wild places a great service and providing the first comprehensive description of the Watershed.
THE GREAT OUTDOORS

No other journey can give so sublime a sense of unity – a feeling of how the nation's various different landscapes link together to form a coherent whole.
THE SCOTSMAN

Walking with Wildness: Experiencing the Watershed of Scotland

Peter Wright
ISBN 978-1-908373-44-1 PBK £.7.99

A detailed guide to 26 selected day or weekend walks along Scotland's Watershed. Experience the magnificent scenery of Scotland's Watershed – the line that determines whether a raindrop falling on Scotland ends up in the Atlantic or the North Sea.

The first and only guide to cover this little-known Scottish treasure, with a selection of 26 routes to walk in a day or two over the major parts of the 745 mile Watershed.

The perfect Christmas gift for walkers and nature lovers who are looking for fresh ideas and a new challenge in Scotland's stunning countryside.

Black and white images throughout, with maps.

Arthur's Seat: Journeys and Evocations

Stuart McHardy and Donald Smith
ISBN 978-1-908373-46-5 PBK £7.99

Arthur's Seat, rising high above the Edinburgh skyline, is the city's most awe-inspiring landmark. Although thousands climb to the summit every year, its history remains a mystery, shrouded in myth and legend.

The first book of its kind, *Arthur's Seat: Journeys and Evocations* is a salute to the ancient tradition of storytelling, guiding the reader around Edinburgh's famous 'Resting Giant' with an exploration of the local folklore and customs associated with the mountain-within-a-city.

Inspired by NVA's Speed of Light, a major event in Edinburgh's International Festival and the country-wide Cultural Olympiad, *Journeys and Evocations* brings together past and future in a perspective of the Edinburgh landscape like no other.

Explores the facts and the fascinating fictions [of Arthur's Seat] ... to create a unique walkers' guide.
EVENING NEWS

The Joy of Hillwalking

Ralph Storer
ISBN 978-1-842820-69-8 PBK £7.50

Hillwalking is only one of the passions in my life. In my experience, those who love the mountains are passionate people who are passionate about many things. That said, there are times, as I describe herein, when I simply have to go to the hills.
RALPH STORER

Ralph Storer's highly entertaining exploration of the lure of the hills is underpinned by hard-won experience – he has climbed extensively in the British Isles, Europe and the American West, though his abiding love is the Scottish Highlands. His breezy anecdotes of walking and climbing around the world in all sorts of conditions are gripping and full of fun. His sense of humour is as irrepressible as his relish for adventurous ascents, but he doesn't have his head in the clouds when it comes to serious issues such as public access and conservation.

Alps, America, Scandinavia, you name it – Storer's been there, so why the hell shouldn't he bring all these various and varied places into his observations ... [He] even admits to losing his virginity after a day on the Aggy Ridge... Well worth its place alongside Storer's earlier works.
TAC

Details of these and other books published by Luath Press can be found at:
www.luath.co.uk

Luath Press Limited

committed to publishing well written books worth reading

LUATH PRESS takes its name from Robert Burns, whose little collie Luath (*Gael.*, swift or nimble) tripped up Jean Armour at a wedding and gave him the chance to speak to the woman who was to be his wife and the abiding love of his life. Burns called one of 'The Twa Dogs' Luath after Cuchullin's hunting dog in Ossian's *Fingal*. Luath Press was established in 1981 in the heart of Burns country, and now resides a few steps up the road from Burns' first lodgings on Edinburgh's Royal Mile.
Luath offers you distinctive writing with a hint of unexpected pleasures.

Most bookshops in the UK, the US, Canada, Australia, New Zealand and parts of Europe either carry our books in stock or can order them for you. To order direct from us, please send a £sterling cheque, postal order, international money order or your credit card details (number, address of cardholder and expiry date) to us at the address below. Please add post and packing as follows: UK – £1.00 per delivery address; overseas surface mail – £2.50 per delivery address; overseas airmail – £3.50 for the first book to each delivery address, plus £1.00 for each additional book by airmail to the same address. If your order is a gift, we will happily enclose your card or message at no extra charge.

Luath Press Limited
543/2 Castlehill
The Royal Mile
Edinburgh EH1 2ND
Scotland
Telephone: 0131 225 4326 (24 hours)
Fax: 0131 225 4324
email: sales@luath.co.uk
Website: www.luath.co.uk